MACRO PERSPECTIVE ON YOUTHS AGING OUT OF FOSTER CARE

MARY E. COLLINS

NASW PRESS

National Association of Social Workers
Washington, DC

Darrell P. Wheeler, PhD, MPH, ACSW
President

Angelo McClain, PhD, LICSW
Chief Executive Officer

Cheryl Y. Bradley, *Publisher*
Stella Donovan, *Acquisitions Editor*
Julie Gutin, *Managing Editor*
Sharon Fletcher, *Marketing Manager*
Sarah Lowman, *Project Manager*
Amanda Morgan, *Copyeditor*
Wayson R. Jones, *Proofreader*
Bernice Eisen, *Indexer*

Cover by Eye to Eye Design Studio
Interior design and composition by Rick Soldin
Printed and bound by Sheridan Books, Inc.

First impression: October 2015

© 2015 by the NASW Press

Library of Congress Cataloging-in-Publication Data

Collins, Mary E. (Mary Elizabeth), 1960–
  Macro perspectives on youths aging out of foster care / Mary E. Collins.
     pages cm
  Includes bibliographical references and index.
   ISBN 978-0-87101-488-7 (pbk) — ISBN 0-87101-488-2 (pbk) ISBN 978-0-
87101-489-4 (e-book) 1. Foster home care—United States. 2. Ex-foster children—
United States—Social conditions. 3. Ex-foster children—Services for—United
States. 4. Child welfare—United States. I. Title.
  HV881.C63 2015
  362.73'30973--dc23

                                                            2015023927

Printed in the United States of America

Contents

About the Author

Mary Elizabeth Collins, PhD, is associate dean for academic affairs, chair of social welfare policy, and professor at the Boston University School of Social Work.

Acknowledgments

Many thanks to Michelle Banks, who read a full draft of this book and provided terrific feedback and insight. I have benefited greatly from our conversations over many years and am continually impressed by her commitment to youths in foster care. Writing this book allowed me to reconnect with several people who have influenced my work. I particularly thank Jamie Lee Evans and Anthony Barrows for sharing their thoughts, which were influential in this book project. I also appreciate the research assistance of Emilie Swenson.

One cannot do this work without constant reflection on the importance of family in all phases of life. I am grateful to the support of my sisters in this endeavor and all others.

CHAPTER 1

Key Issues Confronting Youths Transitioning Out of Foster Care

In the last two decades, there has been increased attention to the circumstances under which young adults leave the foster care system when they achieve age-defined adulthood. In the United States, this is often referred to as "aging out" of care. Typically, this means these young people did not benefit from reunification with their family or a permanent family situation with kin or through adoption. Often exiting after relatively long stays in the care system, they tend to lack the support, skills, and resources required for a healthy, productive, independent adulthood. Some particularly resilient youths make a successful transition to independent adulthood. But for a significant proportion of youths in foster care, the basic goals of a higher education, employment, and stable housing remain elusive. Sustained attention in practice, policy, and research is needed to increase the likelihood that such young people will be able to achieve and maintain a healthy and productive adulthood.

An increasing number of studies, articles, books, Web sites, and conferences have been devoted to understanding of the needs of these vulnerable youths. This body of work has documented the comparatively poor outcomes of youths aging out of care and has aimed to identify policy and program supports that can help them achieve better outcomes. Although we now know far more than we did 20 years ago, and this knowledge has improved policy and practice, much more remains to be done.

On September 30, 2013, there were 402,378 children in foster care in the United States; 16 percent were between the ages of 16 and 18 and another 2 percent were 19 or older (U.S. Department of Health and Human Services [HHS], 2014). Of those who exited foster care during FY 2013 (N = 238,280), approximately 10 percent (23,090) exited through emancipation. Children and youths of color have been overrepresented in child welfare systems: According to federal data, 42 percent of the children and youths in foster care were white, 24 percent were African American, 22 percent were Hispanic (of any race), and 2 percent were American Indian or Alaskan Native. Thus, issues facing children and youths in child welfare systems, such as the challenges of transitioning from care, have disproportionately affected children and youths who are African American, Hispanic, or American Indian or Alaskan Native.

Primary attention until now has focused on youths as the unit of analysis—understanding their backgrounds, needs, and outcomes. For example, the early (and still often dominant) approach to assisting youths has focused on the development of independent living skills, including preparing a resume, opening a bank account, and getting a driver's license. Although important, this approach focuses on the individual level and ignores potential interventions in larger systems.

Ecological models (Garbarino, 1982; Germain & Gitterman, 1996) are central to social work analysis and practice and may be used to reorient analyses to some of the larger systems that affect human behavior and outcomes, including society, policy, institutions, organizations, and community. Of course, the microsystem (the environment in which a young person directly participates, such as school and family) exerts a critical effect on individual development (Garbarino, 1982). Recently, W. B. Smith (2011) provided a comprehensive treatment of youth transitioning out of foster care through a developmental lens, primarily focused on microsystems. Attachment theory (Bowlby, 1983) has been particularly valuable in understanding the impact on the development of youths in foster care when early family experiences lead to inconsistent and insecure attachments.

In regard to independent living policy, programming, and evaluation, Collins (2001) noted the limited theoretical basis of this work and suggested greater use of the sociological literature on life transition and the multidisciplinary literature on resilience, coping, and social support. M. Stein (2006) also identified a lack of theory in research on youths aging out of care and offered attachment theory, focal theory, and resilience as critical theoretical perspectives to inform research on this topic. More recently, Collins and Pinkerton (2008) brought attention to the need for more policy-oriented theoretical frameworks to guide planning of interventions.

Consistent with a social work perspective, this book emphasizes the larger macro systems of society, policy, organization, and community, in an attempt to balance microsystem-focused contributions. Outcomes of the transition from foster care depend heavily on the processes and structures that make up the external environment. Youths exiting from foster care may be especially influenced by the larger social context because they often lack the mediating advantages of a strong familial connection, which for other young people may buffer negative environmental effects and facilitate engagement with positive ones.

Theoretical frameworks that focus on larger systems must become a part of our thinking about young people's transition from state care. This could inform questions such as: What are the barriers to developing and implementing effective approaches? How can we bring more social attention to these youths? How might communities better support them? To what extent should policy and program supports be designed specifically for this population, as opposed to a broader population of vulnerable youths (such as youths receiving child welfare services in their homes and youths involved in more than one service system), or more general supports for all youths? This chapter reviews the core issues, which are addressed in greater depth in later chapters.

The term "macro," used to identify the focus of this book, includes various perspectives at the larger systems level, focusing on policy, community, and organizations as well as the larger society and culture. Scholars have defined "macro" in various ways, which may or may not include all of these settings. Commonly, macro practice has meant "professionally directed intervention designed to bring planned change in organizations and communities" (Netting, Kettner, & McMurtry, 1993, p. 3). The locus of activity is usually the community or organization, although "macro-level activities engage the practitioner in organizational, community, and policy arenas" (p. 3). These arenas are highly interrelated.

Articulating the Problem

Youths aging out of foster care are of compelling interest to the general public—and consequently, practitioners, researchers, and policymakers—for a number of reasons. Some adults, remembering themselves at the age of 18, may be horrified at the prospect of having to navigate the complexities of young adulthood without a family's financial, instrumental, emotional, and social support. Others, who experienced challenges themselves during their early-adult years and remember the anxieties, elements of both hard work and luck that helped them get through, and long struggle to attain stability, may want to support young people experiencing similar circumstances. This generosity of spirit may be heightened toward young people who have spent long periods in foster care and who typically have fewer internal and external resources. The widespread belief that "18 is too young to be on your own" and a sense (sometimes stereotypical and erroneous) of the hazards of childhood in foster care make the general public fairly sympathetic to this population.

Yet until relatively recently, attention to the needs of this population was limited. Although they have now attained some attention in the policy and practice environments, levels of assistance generally are not of sufficient amount or duration to have strong impacts. Moreover, there are gaps in coverage; many eligible youths may not receive assistance due to limited resources at the local level.

There are several potential explanations as to why the needs of these young people have historically been ignored and are still minimally addressed. First, the foster care system, along with child welfare more generally, is chronically underfunded and overstressed. For the most part, a strong social commitment to put resources into systems serving vulnerable populations is lacking. A recent study (Leber & LeCroy, 2012) found that although there was some support for federal spending on the foster care system, a majority of respondents rated foster care as a less serious problem and less deserving of federal funds than education or health care. In addition to lukewarm public support, common characteristics of the public child welfare bureaucracy (for example, large caseloads and inflexible rules) can negatively affect agency workers' ability to use best practices (B. D. Smith & Donovan, 2003). Such agencies also operate within an often harsh media environment that can negatively affect practice (Gainsborough, 2010).

Second, policies have emphasized prevention, family interventions, and children more than adolescents. Preventive interventions are generally geared toward infants and children more than adolescents or young adults and are intended in part to divert families from the child welfare system. In-home, family-based, preventive interventions are considered the best way to prevent maltreatment and its damage and to avoid entry into foster care, which can result in further trauma. Community-based practice, in a more familiar and culturally appropriate setting, is presumed to be better at engaging families and consequently achieving positive outcomes.

Rather than reducing expenditures, attention to older adolescents and young adults in the child welfare system may suggest the need for continued or transitional services. Thus, rather than diverting families from the system, extending services could increase short-term costs. Enhanced intervention during transition might reduce long-term costs in other state government services (for example, mental health, welfare, and corrections). But even if this is the case (an empirical question that needs to be addressed), many states have agency-specific funding streams and thus may not be able to take such savings into account.

An additional issue is social ambivalence toward adolescents, in contrast to more positive attitudes toward young children. In the public mind, adolescents are often linked with problems, and prevention is targeted primarily toward preventing these problems. For example, an entire federal office, the Office of Juvenile Justice and Delinquency Prevention, aims to prevent delinquency. Efforts to promote a more proactive, developmental approach under the label "positive youth development" have become part of the policy response. As will be shown, however, these efforts are not always well integrated into practice.

This conundrum—a highly compelling problem facing a sometimes stigmatized population generating a minimalist policy response—is of central interest to understanding the policy status and prospects for youths aging out of care. Theories of social construction lend considerable insight on the policy treatment of vulnerable youths.

Arnett (2000, 2004) articulated the concept of "emerging adulthood," a period between adolescence and adulthood, which may bode well for a long-term strategy lodged within a developmental perspective. This period, lasting from the late teens through the 20s, is a time of slow progress to adulthood. It is exploratory, unstable, with intermittent progress and occasional regression, and fluid in regard to relationships, living situations, and employment. This perspective provides a more contemporary understanding of the process of attaining adult stability in industrialized nations, which can inform a more realistic policy response than the historic presumption of a sudden onset of adulthood at age 18.

Social problems are also constructions; the objective conditions that cause distress may or may not be identified as social problems requiring intervention. Issues of rhetoric are central; child advocates deliberately frame issues to achieve political traction (Gormley, 2012). Specific population groups can be socially constructed (Schneider & Ingram, 1993); these constructions and their implications for policy will be discussed later in this book. Social construction of problems and populations is a highly political process that frames them in ways that are most advantageous to the framer's policy goals. Numerous issues compete for attention on the policy agenda, and "the victors in this competition typically benefit from persuasive and compelling problem definition" (Portz, 1996, p. 371). Problem definition, therefore, is central to the political process.

Data are also important in providing the evidence that a problem exists or that a specific intervention is effective. At least two major areas of research have been central to providing the evidence to help establish aging out of foster care as a problem requiring policy attention. One identifies the poor outcomes experienced by youths after leaving care. Courtney and Heuring (2005) reported that research conducted as far back as 1924 demonstrated this concern. Most such studies, however, have been conducted since the 1980s. Initially, they were small in scale and local in scope (for example, Barth, 1990; Mallon, 1998), but larger statewide and multistate studies (Courtney, Dworsky, Lee, & Raap, 2009; Pecora et al., 2006) using rigorous research designs have been instrumental in providing the type of data needed to understand youth circumstances and inform policy and program development. The threat of homelessness for youths leaving foster care has been identified both in follow-up studies with foster care alumni (for example, Festinger, 1983) and in studies focusing on the larger homeless population (for example, Burt, Aron, & Lee, 2001).

Social thinking about youths leaving foster care has consistently focused on the individual level; there has been little recognition of the role of the social networks (or lack thereof) and neighborhood settings in which they begin their independent adult lives. When young people's physical environment is healthy, safe, and dynamic, with opportunities for employment and socialization, their ability to attain a solid level of well-being is much enhanced. But the reality is that, given the limited economic resources at their disposal, their neighborhood settings often lack these advantages.

A new national data collection system, the National Youth in Transition Database (NYTD) (2012), authorized by federal legislation, has been developed to track the independent living services provided by states to youths and the outcomes attained by youths. States were required to begin collecting data in October 2010; the initial data from this effort have only recently become available. States identified 28,318 youths who turned age 17 during federal fiscal year (FFY) 2011 and were eligible to take the NYTD survey; of these, 60 percent completed the survey. Of these respondents, 28 percent reported at least one employment experience (full- or part-time job or paid or unpaid apprenticeship, internship, or other on-the-job training), 93 percent were currently enrolled in and attending some type of education programming, 93 percent reported having a positive connection to an adult, 16 percent reported having been homeless at some point, 27 percent reported having been referred for substance abuse assessment or counseling at some point, 35 percent reported being incarcerated at some point, 7 percent reported having given birth or fathered a child, 81 percent reported having Medicaid coverage, and 16 percent reported having some other type of medical insurance (NYTD, 2012).

These baseline data tell a limited story. Given the poor response rates in some jurisdictions, increased efforts will be required to reach youths in subsequent data collections. The establishment of a database is, however, a testament to the increased importance of this population on the national stage, and in years to come these data may prove vital to understanding and improving state efforts and the resulting outcomes.

Sociological and demographic research has also identified some of the larger social trends in the life circumstances and prospects of adolescents and young adults. Such research provides important comparative information about levels of support for adolescents and young adults, as well as a critical understanding of emerging adulthood in contemporary life. Intergenerational support can significantly influence life chances for the younger generation (Schoeni & Ross, 2005; Swartz, 2008). Furthermore, demographic data have identified trends that show that young people are leaving the family home at later ages and, after leaving, are returning to live with parents more frequently (Goldscheider & Goldscheider, 1999). The option to return home gives many young people a built-in safety net.

Youths transitioning from foster care usually lack access to such resources, and this exacerbates their risks and challenges. Many of them have experienced sustained trauma. Furthermore, given the known race and class issues associated with foster care (McRoy, 2014; Roberts, 2002), there are social justice issues related to the permanence of social stratification and the social and policy mechanisms that institutionalize this stratification.

Justification for increasing support for youths transitioning out of foster care comes from several of these sources. In removing a child from the home, the state is obligated to operate in loco parentis and thus mirror the parenting practices of the larger sociocultural environment. The term "corporate parent" is used in the United Kingdom (Bullock, Courtney, Parker, Sinclair, & Thoburn, 2006) to reflect this and thereby formulate strategies of local authorities in serving the needs of children in care, including during the process of leaving care. Situated within the emerging-adulthood framework, this provides normative guidance for policy perspectives. One example of system adaptation to the emerging-adulthood framework is the greater flexibility allowed for youths to return to care after leaving at age 18. Serving these youths is now an option left to states within provisions of the Fostering Connections to Success and Increasing Adoptions Act of 2008 (P.L. 110-351) (hereinafter, Fostering Connections Act), discussed further in the next section.

Federal Policy Framework

Federal funding for child welfare services was first authorized under the Social Security Act in 1935, and Title IV of that act provides the overarching federal policy framework for foster care and subsequent transition services. A series of amendments expanded what child welfare services could be paid for by federal funds and instituted requirements that states provide matching funds to their share of federal child welfare funds.

Before 1985, there was no specific policy on transition-related services. As part of the Consolidated Ominibus Budget Reconciliation Act of 1985 (P.L. 99-272), funding for Independent Living Initiatives was authorized as part of Title IV-E of the Social Security Act to provide federal funds to states to help youths in foster care develop independent living skills. Services that could be funded included assistance in obtaining a high school diploma or GED, training in daily life skills, and individual and group counseling. At that time, use of federal funding for housing was not allowed.

A more expansive policy response was embodied in the Foster Care Independence Act (FCIA) of 1999 (P.L. 106-169), which established the Chafee Foster

Care Independence Program (CFCIP). This legislation provided more funding, allowed the funding to be used for a wider variety of services, and expanded eligibility for receiving assistance. In 2001, the Chafee Education and Training Voucher Program was established to help states financially support postsecondary training and education for youths aging out of the foster care system and youths adopted from public foster care after age 16.

The most recent legislation relevant to the aging-out population is the Fostering Connections Act (P.L. 110-351). This federal legislation gives states the option of extending Title IV-E foster care to the age of 21. Before its passage, states bore the full cost of any foster care extension. It also amends the CFCIP to add the purpose of providing services to youths who leave foster care after age 16 for kinship guardianship or adoption, and it amends the Education and Training Voucher Program to permit vouchers for youths who, after reaching age 16, enter into kinship guardianship or are adopted from care. In addition, the law creates a new requirement that during the 90-day period prior to the youth's emancipation, the caseworker must develop a personalized transition plan as directed by the youth.

Since passage of the Fostering Connections Act, 15 states and Washington, DC, have opted to extend foster care past age 18 with federal support (Fostering-Connections.org Project, 2013). The Fostering Connections Act is at the critical stage of policy implementation by the states, and consequently, its full impact is not yet known. The Commission on Youth at Risk (2010) identified some of the challenges to implementation of this legislation for state policymakers and other community leaders. These include (1) identifying which sections of the law are mandatory and which are optional, (2) deciding whether to fund optional provisions, and (3) managing potential unintended consequences (for example, does extending foster care to age 21 create potential disincentives to permanency?).

Public child welfare agencies are complex organizations. In the implementation of policies, numerous issues arise related to collaboration with community agencies, contracting and monitoring procedures, workforce issues related to hiring and skill development, and use of evaluation and other information for program planning. The effective delivery of transition-related services will rely on skillful administration.

The Fostering Connections Act has provided considerable policy momentum toward expanded supports, but continued progress is not a certainty. State-level implementation has been uneven. In difficult fiscal times, some states do cut back on services for transition-age youths. Alternatively, they may support transition services for youths aging out of foster care but reduce spending for other populations of vulnerable youths. It is not clear to what extent crossover youths (those in more than one state service system) may be affected by the Fostering Connections Act. A critical question to be addressed in coming years will be how to respond to young people who terminate from care at a later age (such as 21) but still face numerous challenges.

The policies identified earlier are specific to youths leaving care. These youths might also benefit from a variety of other federal policies, particularly in the areas of public assistance, housing, employment and training, education, and health care. The Patient Protection and Affordable Care Act of 2010 (ACA) (P.L. 111-148) expands Medicaid coverage to former foster children up to age 26 as long as they were in foster care at age 18 (or older if the state's federal foster care assistance under Title IV-E continued beyond 18) and receiving Medicaid at that time. The Workforce Innovation and Opportunity Act (P.L. 113-128) authorizes job training programs for unemployed and underemployed individuals through the Department of Labor and includes specific programs for vulnerable youths. Low-income youths formerly in foster care may also apply for housing assistance (public housing units or rental vouchers), but the demand for such assistance is far greater than the supply.

In summary, federal legislation since 1985 has incrementally provided more resources for youths aging out of foster care. Coverage remains incomplete, and funding limitations ensure that not all youths who need services receive them. There is also significant variation between states in the assistance available; states must pass legislation consistent with federal legislation but have significant flexibility in designing their own support services. Finally, although youths are potentially eligible for a range of federal and state supports, few of these programs are entitlements. States are not required to offer all services to all eligible youths who are aging out of care. Consequently, access is limited, potential recipients may be unaware of their eligibility, and application procedures are often cumbersome. Equity among vulnerable youth populations may also need consideration. Providing more resources to one category of vulnerable youths (for example, youths aging out of foster care) at the expense of another category (for example, delinquent youths) is not a solution youth advocates envision.

Youths as an Interest Group

In other policy sectors, powerful interest groups influence the agenda and policy choices. Research has long been conducted on this, but little of it has focused on youths. It is often acknowledged that young people, especially vulnerable young people, lack political power. Children and adolescents cannot vote, rarely lobby, and do not have money to influence public and private authorities; their interests are articulated by others, who may have their own agendas (Minow & Weissbourd, 1993).

Historically, children were often analytically grouped with the elderly as dependent and deserving of assistance. In the United States, however, the political status of these two groups has clearly diverged (Grason & Guyer, 1995). The elderly have become a powerful political force in their own right, whereas children and youths must rely on others to advocate for them (Grason & Guyer, 1995; Minow & Weissbourd, 1993).

Schneider and Ingram (1993) articulated the "social construction of target populations" as "the cultural characterizations or popular images of the persons or groups whose behavior and well-being are affected by public policy" (p. 334). The social construction of a population is substantially linked with the types of policies enacted for it. Discussing social constructions of youths leaving care, Collins and Clay (2009) wrote, "Claims about these youths' vulnerabilities in childhood (for example, victims of abuse), data regarding poor outcomes after transition from care, and ideological perspectives that these are 'our children' and are owed something by the state attempt to portray this population as 'worthy' of intervention" (p. 750). Sometimes youths leaving care are also portrayed as at risk of becoming homeless, welfare-dependent, and criminal. While such portrayals are meant to support arguments for providing assistance, they may burden youths in foster care with a negative social construction that risks compounding their disadvantage in the policy process. At what point within their child-welfare history do "deserving vulnerable children" transform into "difficult, troubled, undeserving adolescents" in the public eye? What can youths themselves and their advocates and partners do to influence this construction?

Theoretical perspectives on the empowerment of youths have articulated the means to include them in service delivery and organizational decision making. There has recently been increased attention to youth participation in research and evaluation, public policy, and community development (Checkoway, Allison & Montoya, 2005; Christens & Dolan, 2011). The literature on consumer involvement and positive youth development approaches is broader than this and will be discussed further in later chapters. These are separate issues but have similar conceptual elements and could be fused in ways that may be useful to advancing young people's political interests.

Undoubtedly, organized youth initiatives have succeeded in focusing policy-makers' attention on the issues facing youths formerly in foster care and developing youth-driven policy solutions. The potential for further developing these networks for policy impact is substantial. Particularly as youths aging out of care gain the right to vote, this may strengthen their political voice. But compared with other well-established, powerful, financially strong interest groups, vulnerable youths remain at a disadvantage in the political process. Further, different categories of vulnerable youths (such as aging-out youths, crossover youths, and youths in the juvenile justice system) may have to compete for resources. The prospects for unifying youths (and emerging adults) for political purposes require further exploration.

Agency– and Community–Based Macro Practice

Macro-focused social work practitioners have a significant role to play in creating the institutions, organizations, agencies, programs, and community collaborations that are needed to support youths with the transition from care. Three critical areas are workforce development, program planning and evaluation, and developing community supports.

Workforce Development

Child welfare systems engage in extensive efforts to recruit and train professionals to meet the needs of children, youths, and families. Enhancing training, in response to new policy and practice initiatives, is a major mechanism for improving intervention. Although commonly conceptualized as a human resource issue, training in public agencies is also a key variable in policy implementation; agencies are expected to translate general policy guidelines into specific procedures, and line staff members are expected to translate specific procedures into interventions with clients. Thus, through mechanisms of training and workforce development, social workers are heavily involved in implementing policy through human services programming.

Effectively addressing issues of transitioning from care requires specialized training. A recent study evaluated nine federally funded projects focused on training workers to assist youths transitioning from foster care (Collins, Amodeo, & Clay, 2007). These training projects were funded through the Child Welfare Training Program (Section 426 of Title IV-B, of the Social Security Act) and focused on developing curricula and delivering training to public child welfare workers to strengthen their capacity to work with youths transitioning from care.

The training projects focused on improving services to youths aging out of foster care and were designed to emphasize a youth development philosophy, which supports active participation by youths in their case planning, a strengths-oriented focus, empowerment strategies, and attainment of positive outcomes (for example, education, employment, and healthy relationships) rather than the avoidance of negative outcomes (for example, drug use and pregnancy).

Evaluation of these efforts (Amodeo, Collins, & Clay, 2009; Clay, Amodeo, & Collins, 2010; Collins et al., 2007) identified numerous strengths and ongoing challenges to workforce development efforts in this area. Numerous lessons were identified related to collaboration, engaging youths as partners, linking training to related organizational change efforts, and agency leadership, among other processes. These were also linked with important lessons related to sustainability of training initiatives (beyond the initial funding period), the required administrative supports for training, and the mechanisms of dissemination and institutionalization that build systems of workforce development. These lessons are not specific to the field of youths leaving care but are perennial challenges to large human services bureaucracies and the community-based partners with which they work. Greater understanding of the potential and limitations of workforce development initiatives, and their linkage with the implementation of new policies and practices, requires considerable attention to effective organizational change.

Program Planning and Evaluation

The increase in policy attention to youths leaving care has led to numerous programmatic strategies and initiatives targeting many different domains. Services listed by the FCIA as possibly being provided by states with federal funding included assistance in obtaining a high school diploma; career exploration, vocational training, and job placement and retention; training in daily living skills, budgeting, and financial management; substance abuse prevention; preventive health activities; education; preparation for postsecondary training and education; mentoring and other interactions with adults; and financial, housing, counseling, employment, and education support.

The state child welfare agency that administers the Title IV-E Foster Care Program engages in a planning process to determine specific needs and resources within the state, and then develops an application to HHS for independent living funds for a period of five years. The plan must detail the planned implementation of the program and certify that the application was developed in a collaborative process that included the input of youths in foster care and other key stakeholder groups such as relevant state agencies (for example, mental health and juvenile justice agencies) and service providers.

The NYTD provided the first national snapshot of service delivery efforts by state CFCIP agencies aimed at helping youths transition to adulthood. In FFY 2011, states reported that 98,561 youths and young adults received at least one independent living service (NYTD, 2012). The field is currently undergoing extensive program development, some of which is likely to be innovative and creative. There is, however, no catalog of the range of available program models.

Typically, evaluation of programming efforts is minimal, and thus no compelling body of research exists to identify programs that should be replicated on a larger scale. Neither research evidence nor institutionalized support exists for many transition-focused programs. Many are locally developed and implemented with little opportunity for knowledge sharing. Although funders typically require evaluation of programs, many agencies lack the capacity to conduct evaluations on an ongoing basis and apply the results to program planning.

Developing Community Supports

Although federal and state legislation provides the policy parameters and some funding for a program response, much of the work takes place at the community level, some of it on an informal basis. The same community networks (neighborhoods, schools, religious congregations, athletic teams, and cultural institutions) that have always had a role in young people's socialization are needed to help youths transition from foster care. How might communities support these young people?

Many community-based efforts can be broadly grouped under the term "positive youth development." This incorporates several beliefs about the inherent strengths of youths and their need to engage in a variety of opportunities and supports to successfully move into adulthood. Existing within a range of settings and portrayed in various forms, these opportunities for youth development have long been part of the social fabric. In this conceptualization, youths are not problems to be managed or controlled but have a variety of skills, strengths, talents, and assets that they can contribute to the community. Through an interdependent and reciprocal relationship with the community, youths gradually and naturally move into adult roles.

Positive youth development is based on research suggesting that certain protective factors can help young people succeed. The Family and Youth Services Bureau (HHS, Administration for Children and Families [ACF], Family and Youth Services Bureau, 2015) noted that research has indicated that young people may have fewer behavioral problems and may be better prepared for a successful transition to adulthood if they have a variety of opportunities to learn and participate at home, at school, in community-based programs, and in their neighborhoods. Key elements that can protect young people and put them on the path to success include family support, caring adults, positive peer groups, a strong sense of self and self-esteem, and involvement at school and in the community. Leadership- and skill-building opportunities under the guidance of caring adults are critical.

Positive youth development has several similarities to the strengths perspective well known to social work. These include viewing individuals as having untapped abilities and as doing the best that they can even when struggling, partnering with individuals to foster self-efficacy, and focusing on empowerment and self-advocacy for individuals and groups who are often marginalized (Amodeo & Collins, 2007).

Community-based in origin, positive youth development approaches have been recognized in federal policy. As part of its mission to provide leadership on youth and family issues, the Family and Youth Services Bureau (part of HHS, ACF) promotes positive youth development among the federal agencies, within state and local governments, and with youth workers and the general public (HHS, Family and Youth Services Bureau, ACF, 2015).

Both supports and opportunities are essential to the practice of positive youth development. The literature on the importance of social support to various populations is extensive. Aging-out youths are often thought to be alone and isolated, but studies have shown they do have connections, including with family (Collins, Paris, & Ward, 2008). One study found that among youths formerly in foster care, those with the best outcomes had substantive relationships with birth parents and other parental figures (Cushing, Samuels, & Kerman, 2014); the authors suggested that these youths potentially had greater capacity to develop relationships than other youths, or that relating to multiple sources of support was a more comfortable way of managing relational needs within complicated family structures.

In the last few years, mentoring has received considerable attention as a potential mechanism to help transitioning youths in community settings. Various mentoring models exist, and others are being developed. These include special attention to youths in foster care through existing mentoring organizations, mentoring organizations designed specifically for youths in foster care, online mentoring, and peer mentoring, either in an independent living program or elsewhere (Spencer, Collins, Ward, & Smashnaya, 2010).

There is a minimal but growing amount of research on mentoring programs for youths in foster care. One study found a positive association between formal mentoring and good outcomes (Rhodes, Haight, & Briggs, 1999). Another study did not find positive effects, but did find an increase in delinquent behavior among those youths whose mentor matches terminated early (Britner & Kraimer-Rickaby, 2005). Given the vulnerability of youths in foster care, there is reason to proceed cautiously when developing mentoring relationships (Spencer et al., 2010).

Research has also examined the mentoring relationships that emerge informally from youths' existing social networks and identified some positive outcomes for youths (Ahrens, DuBois, Richardson, Fan, & Lozano, 2008; Collins, Spencer, & Ward, 2010; Munson & McMillen, 2009). Through qualitative interviews, Ahrens et al. (2011) identified factors that helped and hindered relationships between youths in foster care and nonparental adults and suggested potential ways to use mentoring to support youths in foster care, such as incorporating these natural mentors more formally into planning for youth transition.

Although relationships of many types are critical in helping young people transition to independence, they also need concrete opportunities to gain experience in a variety of domains. Jobs, internships, training, and leadership opportunities help youths develop adult skills. Involvement in a wide range of cultural, educational, athletic, and social groups contributes to youths' interpersonal and emotional development. Social-capital concepts have been used to study these issues, particularly in Europe (for example, Holland, Reynolds, & Weller, 2007), where issues of social inclusion have been central to the discussion of youth transition.

Role of Social Work

For a number of reasons, social work is particularly well suited to influencing policy and other aspects of the social environment to enhance the life prospects of youths transitioning out of foster care. From its earliest days, social work has been involved in addressing the needs of vulnerable children and families, and it remains fundamentally committed to good practice in child welfare (National Association of Social Workers, 2013). Within child welfare systems, social workers are engaged at all levels—clinical practice, program development, administration, and policy—in both public agencies and community-based organizations. Long before policies existed to support youths transitioning out of care, social workers in the field would have noticed the limitations of the policy response and acted to link youths with whatever resources were available. Social work researchers were also instrumental in providing the evidence base to advance the interests of aging-out youths on state and national policy agendas.

Effective practice with youths leaving care will require additional attention to community-based youth work. This is an area in which social work has historic expertise (beginning with the settlements of the Progressive Era) but which is shared with various other professional groups, paraprofessionals, and community volunteers. Transition-oriented services are inherently community based and require the development, maintenance, and negotiation of community-based services, resources, and networks. Further tapping and expanding the community orientation of social work would be particularly applicable to serving young people leaving foster care.

Social work's ecological orientation includes a macro approach to intervention. There is a substantial amount of research and theory, in social work and related fields, that may be applied to better understanding the impact of larger systems on prospects for youths leaving care. Overall, our models of policy, program, and practice for this population are born of institutional mechanisms. For example, our approach to adolescents is often constrained by child welfare systems more accustomed to working with children, and efforts to use youth development models conflict with norms of child protection. Better understanding of these contextual elements may facilitate development of more powerful interventions.

Social work is also committed to both empirical evidence and value-based perspectives in regard to social justice. Social workers have been instrumental in providing the evidence base to guide policy and practice regarding youths aging out of care. They continue to have this role. In addition, they are educated in and practice by an ethical code in which social justice is central. The difficult prospects of these youths have been so well documented that their moral claim to further resources fits squarely within a social justice framework.

How This Book Is Structured

The chapters that follow explore the issues raised in this introductory chapter in greater depth. Part I examines some foundational issues in research and theory. It reviews the research on youths aging out of foster care (chapter 2) and theoretical perspectives on the sociology and politics of youths and young adults, with attention to normative comparisons of youths leaving care with the larger population of youths (chapters 3 and 4).

Part II focuses on policy. Chapter 5 reviews the federal policy framework, early origins, related legislation, and the recent Fostering Connections Act, which has several provisions related to youths transitioning from care. The implementation of this legislation is still unfolding. Stages of the policy process are examined in chapters examining agenda-setting (chapter 6) and implementation (chapter 7). There are rich theoretical perspectives on these processes that are rarely applied to child welfare. These chapters are intended to further understanding of the best ways to use policy to promote success for youths.

Part III examines several core areas of macro practice relevant to youths leaving care: workforce development (chapter 8), building community supports (chapter 9), and programming and evaluation (chapter 10). These components are also central to the implementation of policy and often provide the context in which social workers practice. The final chapter synthesizes these policy and macro perspectives and proposes next steps for developing policy, programs, and practices to help youths leaving foster care enter adulthood with safety and well-being.

PART I

Foundations in Research and Theory

Young People Leaving Foster Care: Common Traits and Outcomes

The number of youths aging out of care each year is documented in the national Adoption and Foster Care Analysis and Reporting System (AFCARS) (HHS, 2014), operated by the Children's Bureau of HHS. AFCARS collects data from state child welfare systems on the number of children in care, the number entering and exiting foster care, some demographic data on the children in care (such as age, race, ethnicity, and gender), and other characteristics of the care experience such as length of time in care, placement type, and the number of children who were adopted.

AFCARS data indicate that 23,396 young people aged out of foster care in FY 2012. The total number of children in foster care on September 30, 2012, was 397,122, of whom 29 percent were adolescents (ages 13 to 17). Although they make up a significant percentage of the foster care population, adolescents have received little research attention compared with infants and toddlers (Simmel, 2012). Young adults (ages 18 to 20) account for another 5 percent. Until recent policy changes allowed some young people in some states to remain in foster care after age 18, there would have been no young adults reported among the foster care population. Table 2.1 identifies some trends related to exiting foster care over time. Since 1998, the number of young people leaving foster care has declined (reflecting reductions in the foster care population), whereas the number leaving foster care as a result of emancipation has increased. Examining these trends together indicates that the percentage of those leaving foster care because of emancipation has increased slightly, from 7 percent to 10 percent.

The Fostering Connections Act allows federal reimbursement for state extension of foster care to youths over age 18. According to a recent report (U.S. Government Accountability Office [GAO], 2014), the numbers of youths age 18 and older receiving a monthly Title IV-E foster care maintenance payment increased from 3,292 in 2008 to 4,997 in 2012. But this was considered to be an underestimate, because states had not fully updated their reporting systems.

Table 2.1: Trends in Emancipation as the Reason for Leaving Foster Care

Fiscal Year	A. Total Leaving Foster Care	B. Total Leaving due to Emancipation	Column B % of Column A
2012	240,923	23,396	10
2011	245,260	26,286	11
2010	254,114	27,854	11
2009	276,266	29,471	11
2008	285,000	29,516	10
2007	293,000	29,730	10
2006	289,000	26,517	9
2005	287,000	24,407	9
2004	283,000	23,121	8
2003	282,000	22,432	8
2002	282,000	20,358	7
2001	269,000	19,039	7
2000	272,000	20,172	7
1999	250,000	18,964	8
1998	257,000	17,310	7

Source: U.S. Department of Health and Human Services. (2014). *AFCARS report: Preliminary FY 2013 estimates.* Retrieved from http://www.acf.hhs.gov/sites/default/files/cb/afcarsreport21.pdf

How does a young person come to the point of transitioning out of care? Child welfare policy clearly emphasizes family preservation, reunification, and permanency through adoption. Yet many youths, as identified in the AFCARS data (see Table 2.1), are still transitioning directly from foster care to life on their own and facing daunting challenges. Many have been in the system a long time. Therefore, more than the general foster care population, the aging-out group is particularly disadvantaged.

Research has identified some characteristics of youths who are most likely to remain in the foster care system until they age out, including entry into the child welfare system after age 12 (Bass, Shields, & Behrman, 2004). Wertheimer (2002) noted that those who enter foster care as teenagers have the highest risk of aging out of care; those age 16 or older were less likely than younger children to enter foster care but accounted for nearly all those aging out of care. Older youths in foster care are less likely to be living with a foster family, more likely to be living in group care or an institutional setting, and less likely to be adopted (Wertheimer, 2002). Of 15 studies of the foster care experiences of youths leaving care, all but one reported the mean age of entry into care as 10 years or older (Havlicek, 2011).

The number of placement changes while in foster care is also problematic. Havlicek's (2011) review of 15 studies found that the mean number of placements ranged from 2.4 to 9.5. Changes in foster home settings occur for a variety of reasons, and some are necessary, but numerous moves can have negative consequences, including disruption of interpersonal attachments and social networks as well as effects on schooling (W. B. Smith, 2011). Frequent moves between relatives, foster homes, and group care settings may be part of the problem, as this instability can disrupt attachments needed for healthy development. One study (Hyde & Kammerer, 2009) found that adolescents' perspectives on the reasons for placement moves included behavioral problems, a mismatch between the youth and the foster parent, and a planned "step down" to a less restrictive environment. Youths in foster care are greatly affected by these moves (Unrau, Seita, & Putney, 2008); the changes in homes, families, and parents create challenges to developing relationships that can continue to have adverse effects.

Studies have found a greater use of group care among those aging out (Simmel, 2012; Stott, 2013). Havlicek's (2011) review found that the proportion living in a group care placement at discharge ranged from 15 percent to 42 percent. Placement in a group home (rather than a foster home) has been related to serious negative outcomes such as delinquency (Ryan, Marshall, Herz, & Hernandez, 2008) and imprisonment as adults (Collins, Schwartz, & Epstein, 2001). Adolescents' reports of congregate settings voice serious concerns including perceptions of the environment as chaotic and unsafe and of rules as unclear and inconsistent (Hyde & Kammerer, 2009). Aside from related poor outcomes, the transition to independence is likely to be even more challenging from group care than from a foster home, because of the change from a highly structured setting to one with little or no structure. Youths in residential settings often have few opportunities for a gradual transition involving the practice of living skills and development of community-based networks.

Youths aging out of care have been identified as having more challenges and service needs than the general population of youths in foster care. A disproportionate percentage of youths in foster care have serious mental health and behavioral problems (Szilagyi, 1998) that are likely to require some level of ongoing care. Havlicek's (2011) review found high rates of psychiatric hospitalization within the past year (7 percent to 14 percent) and high frequencies of running away while in foster care (19 percent to 56 percent).

Racial disproportionality has been documented at several junctures of child welfare decision making—for example, removal from the home, receipt of services, and placement for adoption (McRoy, 2014; Roberts, 2002). As a consequence, racial disproportionality is particularly visible at the end of system involvement.

Lesbian, gay, bisexual, transgender, and queer (LGBTQ) youths are also dispro-portionately represented among those transitioning from care (Stott, 2013).

Although efforts must focus on supporting families and avoiding placement in foster care, removal from the home remains necessary in some cases. There are positive aspects to the foster care experience. In comparison to remaining in an abusive setting, adequate foster care, and certainly excellent foster care, is likely to have a positive effect on well-being. Small, qualitative studies often show the impact of caring foster parents or other child welfare professionals in helping young people (Collins, Spencer, & Ward, 2010) and the ways in which the foster care systems saves youths by providing new opportunities for educa-tion and positive relationships (Hines, Merdinger, & Wyatt, 2005).

Some studies have identified these positive effects more systematically. Jonson-Reid (2004), drawing on theory and existing research, suggested sev-eral potential benefits of foster care placement, including a healthier family and community environment, positive adult relationships, and greater access to services. Snyder and Medeiros (2013), using data from the National Longitudi-nal Study of Adolescent to Adult Health (Add Health), compared young adults with and without histories in foster care and found few differences in rates of substance abuse and other illegal behavior; they found the general population had a higher probability of buying, selling, and holding stolen goods; injuring someone in a fight; or having sold drugs. They suggested that this might reflect that young adults from the general population have greater difficulty adjusting to the lack of parental monitoring during the young adult years than foster care alumni with otherwise similar patterns of behavior.

Individual Development

Although the focus of this book is on the systems level, these systems must have a thorough understanding of some of the developmental and clinical char-acteristics of the population. How do young people function when they have severely compromised relationships with their parents? This experience informs future relationships, and these relationships have a potentially strong impact on outcomes.

W. B. Smith (2011) provided an in-depth treatment of the developmental and relationship-based aspects that influence the experience of youths leaving foster care. A developmental perspective allows us "to consider the young person in terms of what has occurred (or failed to occur) up to the point of transition" (p. 37). Such a perspective is necessary to more fully understand the transition expe-rience. The frequently poor outcomes for aging-out youths may have only limited relation to the specific aging-out experience and may be more the result of a host of adversities throughout childhood, adolescence, and young adult development.

W. B. Smith (2011) began exploring the developmental trajectory by applying brain science to infancy and childhood, noting how maltreatment and trauma affect the ability to manage stress as well as cognitive and emotional self-regulation. Severe stress and posttraumatic stress disorder as a result of dysfunctional parent–child relationships are associated with alterations in biological stress-symptom response and brain function, with numerous adverse effects on brain, cognitive, and psychological development (DeBellis, 2001).

Attachment theory is central to understanding the challenges of youths in foster care over the course of their development; the attachment relationship is the critical context within which an infant develops and optimally provides three protective factors: the learning of empathy, the control and balance of feelings, and the development of cognitive capacities (W. B. Smith, 2011). Attachments remain important in all stages of child, adolescent, and young adult development; disruptions in key attachments can have numerous negative effects, particularly if they are not addressed (Bowlby, 1983). Attachment theory has been used to better understand the experiences of foster children, who by definition are separated from their parents (Mennen & O'Keefe, 2005). Trauma, maltreatment, and disruption of attachments all affect the growing child.

Adolescence, during which numerous biological, psychological, and social changes occur, presents additional developmental challenges. Identity development is a core task (Erikson, 1968), and youths seek to develop new relationships as their identities further develop. Early disruptions that limit the ability to form long-lasting connections can be detrimental to a youth's ability to cultivate positive lifelong relationships (Bowlby, 1983). Attachment problems can also affect relationships with people who interact with the child in later roles and can thus negatively influence a variety of outcomes in later life (resulting, for example, in difficulties at school or work). Cushing et al. (2014) discussed how youths transitioning out of foster care deal with both a sense of mistrust in relationships and a desire for permanent relationships. Thus, a major developmental challenge for these youths in early adulthood is "learning to negotiate their own capacities and comfort for interdependence and independence in the context of complex and often disrupted family histories involving birth parents and other potential parent figures" (p. 74).

Theories of resilience attempt to explain why some individuals, despite serious adversity, are able to attain a reasonable degree of well-being. Such theories are particularly relevant to children receiving child welfare services because they nearly all have experienced adversity. A range of adversities exist, some mild and shared with other young people (for example, starting in a new school), some severe, traumatizing, and catastrophic. Children and youths also experience varying degrees of support to combat these adversities. Some receive multiple supports from a wide variety of people over a long period of time. Others receive inconsistent or intermittent support. Some receive no support but, tragically, only further hostility or abuse.

The research on resilience undergirds various strengths-based approaches. Classic studies by Masten (2001), Rutter (1987), and Werner and Smith (1982) articulated core attributes of this theoretical framework. Although some elements of resilience may have internal psychological components (for example, temperament), many elements are social. Masten (2001) described resilience as class of phenomena characterized by "good outcomes in spite of serious threats to adaptation or development" (p. 228), and said that the study of resilience requires two major judgments: one related to the threats to development (resilience does not occur if there are no significant threats) and the second related to the quality of the adaptation or developmental outcome.

According to Werner and Smith (1982), developmental outcomes are determined by the balance between risk factors, protective factors, and stressful life events. This balance is determined not only by the number of risks and protective factors but also by their relative duration, frequency, and severity, and the developmental stage at which they occur. Resilience can be developed by promoting protective factors and reducing risk factors that threaten healthy development. Summarizing 40 years of research, a recent report (Mathematica Policy Research, 2011) identified three broad categories of protective factors: (1) individual characteristics, such as cognitive ability, temperament, and social skills; (2) characteristics of the family and home environment, including parental discord and monitoring; and (3) community or school characteristics, such as external support systems, peer associations, and community resources. Although early perspectives on resilience implied that there was something about the inherent nature of extraordinarily resilient children, more recent empirical research suggests that nearly all children who are at risk have the capacity to be resilient (Masten, 2001).

This fuller, developmental perspective, taking account of attachment and resilience, must be kept in mind when reviewing outcomes data and considering interventions. It is not surprising that outcomes for the population are poor and that many short-term and minimalist models of intervention are unlikely to be effective in most cases. It is not the specific transition point that is likely problematic (or not by itself in any case), but rather the cumulative disadvantages and traumas encountered over a long period in substitute care.

Despite the disadvantages they face, it is not appropriate to stereotype and stigmatize the aging-out population. They face a wide diversity of family circumstances, experiences before entering foster care and while in care, and risks and opportunities associated with exiting from the child welfare system. The examination of the literature on outcomes that follows is intended to further a conceptual understanding of the research rather than to provide a complete review of the literature, which has now become extensive.

Outcome Studies

The study of outcomes is critical, both to document the basic problem and to help measure the potential effectiveness of policy and program interventions. Over time, this research has grown increasingly rigorous. The initial wave of outcome research was characterized by small and localized studies (for example, Barth, 1990; Mallon, 1998). Although limited in methodological rigor, these studies provided crucial early information that set the stage for attention to the issue by demonstrating the need for intervention.

National-level outcome data remain limited. Over 20 years ago, Cook (1994) conducted the only national study on this population and focused primarily on assessing the impact of independent living services. The study is quite dated now and reflects the experiences of young people before enhanced policy attention. But it documented on a national scale several of the challenging outcomes that have continued to be identified in more recent work. Although independent living services (and the policies that fund them) have developed since the study was conducted, it still provides some lessons (reviewed in chapter 10) that remain valuable today.

National-level data are now becoming available through the NYTD, which was established to track the services received and outcomes attained by foster care alumni (ACF, 2012). The NYTD requires states to collect data on youths who received independent living services paid for or provided by a state agency, as well as demographic and outcome information for some youths in foster care whom the state will follow over time. States are expected to survey youths in foster care (at baseline and follow-up) regarding six outcomes—financial self-sufficiency, homelessness, educational attainment, positive interactions with adults, high-risk behavior, and access to health insurance—on or around their 17th birthday and again when they are 19 and 21. States with a large foster care population may use a random sample rather than surveying the entire population. All states will collect and report outcome information on a new baseline population cohort every three years. States began collecting data for NYTD on October 1, 2010.

Currently, the most substantial source of information on youth outcomes is the Midwest Study of Adult Functioning of Former Foster Youth, which has tracked youths formerly in foster care in three midwestern states (Illinois, Iowa, and Wisconsin). Youths were eligible to participate in the study if they were in the care of a public child welfare agency at age 17, if they had entered care prior to their 16th birthday, and if the primary reason for their placement was not delinquency. Youths were not included if they had a developmental disability or severe mental illness that made it impossible for them to participate in the initial interviews, were incarcerated or in a psychiatric hospital, were missing from their care placement, or were in a placement out of state. The final sample of 732 young people included all of the eligible youths in Iowa and Wisconsin and two-thirds of the Illinois youths. Baseline interviews were conducted between May 2002 and March 2003 with 96 percent of the eligible youths. Four additional waves of survey data have since been collected, the most recent focused on outcomes at age 26 (Courtney et al., 2011). This longitudinal follow-up study of a large number of youths has contributed invaluable knowledge of the life circumstances of aging-out youths.

A second regional study, the Northwest Foster Care Alumni Study, conducted in Washington and Oregon (Pecora et al., 2006), has also provided useful findings. Case record reviews were conducted for 659 alumni (479 of whom were interviewed) who had been in the care of Casey Family Programs or the Oregon or Washington state child welfare agency between 1988 and 1998.

Several other studies have reported outcome findings at the state or local level (Collins, Spencer, & Ward, 2010; Daining & DePanfilis, 2007; Festinger, 1983; Reilly, 2003). These studies also contribute to the knowledge base, can help focus attention on the issue at the local level, and could be used in planning.

The more methodologically rigorous studies compare outcomes of youths transitioning out of foster care with the general population of youths and young adults in national data sets such as Add Health and the National Longitudinal Survey of Youth. These studies allow comparisons between foster care alumni and other youths, particularly other disadvantaged youths. Challenges such as homelessness, unemployment, and involvement in the criminal justice system may be a function of low income and other vulnerabilities that are not particular to the foster-care or aging-out experience.

Outcome Findings

Common domains in outcome studies have included housing, education, employment, financial self-sufficiency, and absence of negative outcomes such as involvement in the criminal justice system. Key findings in these outcome areas are reviewed in the following sections.

Housing

Housing issues have received prominent attention in most outcome studies. Homelessness, a well-recognized threat for youths who have left foster care (Park, Metraux, & Culhane, 2005), has been a primary focus. Other relevant housing-related issues include housing independence, stability, and satisfaction, and community context. Each of these issues, while far less studied, can be critical to a young person's well-being.

Homelessness. A national study (Cook 1994) found that about one-quarter of youths formerly in foster care had experienced at least one night without a place to stay. Of participants ages 23 and 24 in the Midwest Evaluation of Adult Functioning of Former Foster Youth, 24 percent had experienced homelessness (defined as "sleeping in a place where people weren't meant to sleep, or sleeping in a homeless shelter, or not having a regular residence in which to sleep") (Courtney et al., 2009). The Northwest Foster Care Alumni study found that 22 percent of participants "experienced homelessness for one day or more within a year of leaving foster care" (Pecora et al., 2006, p. 1471). Reilly (2003) reported that 36 percent of foster care alumni in Nevada stated "there had been times when they did not have a place to live" (p. 736). Daining and DePanfilis (2007) found that 28 percent of foster care alumni in Maryland reported homelessness. Collins, Spencer, and Ward (2010) reported that 37 percent of foster care alumni (currently age 19–20) in Massachusetts described having been homeless at least once since age 18.

Studies vary in many ways, including their definitions of homelessness and the extent of the follow-up period under examination. All the data indicate that the threat of homelessness is real; however, much more information is needed to fully understand how the issue affects this population. In particular, it would be helpful to have additional information about the processes by which young people become homeless after leaving care. In some cases, homelessness may occur suddenly, but in many cases there might be predictive factors such as unstable social networks. Qualitative studies that follow young people over a longer period of time could uncover the details of how some of them become homeless, information that could be used to help prevent homelessness.

Housing Independence. Some data are available on whether young people live independently or with others and the types of relationships they have with other household members. The Midwest Evaluation (Courtney et al., 2011), conducting follow-up at age 26 with 595 young people, found that 31 percent were living in their own place, 18 percent with biological parents or other relatives, 36 percent with a spouse or partner, and 4 percent with a friend. Smaller numbers were living with a nonrelative foster parent (2 percent) or in group quarters

27

(1 percent). Unfortunately, 5 percent were in jail or prison, and 1 percent were homeless; both of these percentages were higher than comparable data from Add Health (less than 1 percent in each case).

Another follow-up study found 29 percent of youths formerly in foster care were living with a spouse or partner; 24 percent with friends; 11 percent alone; 22 percent with birth parents, siblings, or other relatives; and 3 percent with former foster parents. Seven percent were incarcerated; 2 percent were homeless; and 2 percent were in the military (Reilly, 2003). Collins, Spencer, and Ward (2010) reported that the largest single group of youths (32 percent) were living on their own, but many were living with relatives, some with their birth parents. A fairly large percentage of young people (12 percent) were living in a group home or residential setting.

Although jail, institutionalization, and homelessness can be presumed to be bad outcomes, evaluation of the other housing situations would require more information about the preferences of the youth. The studies generally do not ask whether a situation is the young person's preferred living situation. Some young people may want to live on their own, others may want to live with relatives, and others may want to live with friends or partners.

Housing Stability. A few studies have reported data on the stability of places lived since leaving care. Cook (1994) reported that one-third of youths interviewed two and a half to four years after discharge reported having lived in five or more different places. Of participants in the Midwest Evaluation, at ages 23 to 24, over two-thirds had lived in at least three different places, including 30 percent who had lived in five or more places (Courtney et al., 2009). Reilly (2003) found that 35 percent had moved five or more times since leaving foster care.

Very few data are available on the reasons for or consequences of housing instability. Change may be needed, and frequent moves may be developmentally appropriate in some cases (Collins & Curtis, 2011). But given the common experience of instability in foster care placements, further housing instability in early adulthood is likely unhelpful in securing steady employment and support networks.

Frederick, Chwalek, Hughes, Karabanow, and Kidd (2014) put the measurement of housing stability among homeless young people at the forefront of their research. They recognized that although housing stability is often a key concept in the research, it is poorly defined and conceptualized. Thus, they conducted qualitative interviews with over 50 currently homeless young people. They defined housing stability as "the extent to which customary access to housing of reasonable quality is secure" (p. 965) and argued that stability is best understood as a continuum. As it may be constantly under threat, the most accurate way to measure stability is to assess the threats to it. Thus, they defined housing security along eight dimensions, including known threats: housing type, recent housing history, current housing tenure, financial status, standing in the legal system, education and employment status, harmful substance use, and subjective assessments of housing satisfaction and stability. Further inquiry along these lines would be useful in deepening our understanding of threats to the housing situation of vulnerable young people.

Housing Satisfaction. To my knowledge, no studies have examined either youth's choice of living situation or its quality (either objectively or subjectively measured). This type of information is critical to a realistic understanding of the housing of youths who have left the foster care system. Because they had almost no choice in their housing environment while in care, helping them obtain their desired housing as young adults might be a particularly helpful step toward success.

Community Context. Finally, housing issues differ from one location to the next. Yet there is an astonishing dearth of information about the community settings to which youths go upon leaving care. Even if they move to a different physical setting, some protective factors (for example, ongoing access to mentors) might be maintained by continuity in the same community setting. This is discussed further in chapter 9.

Education

Comparing data from several states and using Add Health, Pecora (2012) examined educational outcomes for young adults at approximately age 24. Add Health data indicate that 92.7 percent of 23-year-olds had a high school diploma or GED. The rate was 75.6 percent for youths formerly in foster care in the Midwest Study (Courtney et al., 2009), 69.2 percent for those in Michigan, and 84.8 percent for the Northwest Study. The proportion of study participants who reported completing a bachelor's degree was 24.2 percent in the Add Health data set, 3 percent in the Midwest study, 7.7 percent in Michigan, and 1.8 in the Northwest study. The evidence is clear that youths leaving care lag behind the general population in educational outcomes.

There are numerous potential reasons why these disparities in education exist. Pecora (2012) argued that much of the disparity in educational outcomes can be attributed to factors such as placement changes throughout a child's lifetime that decrease school stability and make educational performance more difficult. This can lead to being held back in school, and can contribute to stigma surrounding learning (Pecora, 2012). On a more positive note, Unrau, Font, and Rawls (2012), found that youths with a foster care background, once in a college environment, are more motivated socially and academically than other students and more likely to seek support through student services. Although academic performance was found to be lower than for other youths, the discrepancy in grades parallels their academic starting points, having entered with lower grade point averages and lower scores on standardized college-readiness tests (Unrau et al., 2012). To keep students engaged, support in the college environment is critical to success.

Employment and Financial Self-Sufficiency

Overall, employment has been given less attention than education, perhaps reflecting an emphasis on education at this developmental stage and recognizing the economic benefits of postsecondary education.

One study of employment outcomes (Stewart, Kum, Barth, & Duncan, 2014) compared foster care alumni and other youths in three states (California, Minnesota, and North Carolina). Examining their sample longitudinally (up to the mid-20s in California and Minnesota, and up to age 30 in North Carolina), the study found that youths who had aged out of foster care had poorer employment and earnings outcomes than other low-income youths and the general population. In addition, the study used the National Longitudinal Survey of Youth 1997 for comparison. Youths who aged out of foster care experienced lower than average rates of employment and low earnings through age 24 compared with similar-age youths nationally and those from low-income families in their respective states. However, in all three states, the majority of the youths did work at some point between the ages of 18 and 24.

Because of the challenges they face in education and employment, foster care alumni are more likely to receive public assistance. Byrne et al. (2014) examined public assistance receipt among older youths exiting foster care. Using data from Los Angeles County, they found that 28 percent of foster care alumni received cash forms of public assistance—either Temporary Assistance for Needy Families or county-based general relief. The likelihood of initial receipt of public assistance was highest within the first 18 months of leaving the system. Crossover youths (those involved in both the child welfare and juvenile justice systems) were even more likely to receive public assistance. An earlier study reported that 21 percent received public assistance within four years of leaving care (Festinger, 1983), 30 percent were receiving public assistance when they were interviewed two and a half to four years after leaving care (Cook, 1994), and 50 percent of a foster care alumni sample received public assistance between ages 18 and 33 (Pecora et al., 2006).

Involvement in the Criminal Justice System

Of participants in the Midwest study, between ages 17 and 19, 28 percent had been arrested; 12 percent had been convicted of a crime; and 19 percent had spent time in detention, jail, or prison (Courtney et al., 2005). Offense rates were higher among youths in foster care than in the general population (Cusick & Courtney, 2007). McMahon and Fields (2015) conducted a cluster analysis of data from the Midwest Study to identify subgroups of youths in foster care in regard to criminal involvement. In this sample of 730 youths who had aged out of care, 12 percent reported frequent criminal conduct. In comparison, 28 percent reported no criminal conduct; 41 percent reported moderate criminal conduct; 19 percent engaged predominantly in group fighting, minor stealing, and selling drugs.

Analysis by Vaughn, Shook, and McMillen (2008) of youths in Missouri identified four subgroups of aging-out youths on the basis of their legal involvement: low risk, moderate risk, high risk with externalizing psychopathology, and high risk with participation in the drug culture. One positive finding was that the low-risk group was the largest, making up 69 percent of the sample. Nonetheless, 31 percent of the youths in the sample were at moderate or high risk of involvement with the criminal justice system, suggesting that overall, the population of youths aging out are at greater risk for legal involvement than the general population of youths.

As these data indicate, there can be substantial crossover between youths involved in the child welfare and juvenile justice systems. Culhane, Metraux, and Moreno (2011) compared young adult outcomes for youths in Los Angeles County involved in the child welfare system only, the probation system only, and both systems, and found that youths involved in both systems were more likely to be involved in the criminal justice system as adults.

Additional Questions and about Outcomes

The research evidence tells a straightforward story that outcomes for youths leaving foster care, particularly when leaving without preparation or support, are poor. Studies conducted at different times, in different regions, and using different methodologies have yielded largely consistent findings. Despite this evidence, substantial gaps remain in knowledge about outcomes. It is a positive development that the research on this issue has extended beyond simply identifying poor outcomes, yet much more remains to be learned.

How Do the Poor Outcomes Relate to Each Other?

Little in the research literature explicitly addresses this question, and theory does not make a consistent contribution. It would be relatively simple to help youths attain one essential outcome if they had little difficulty attaining the others. This is rarely the case, however. Some youths face challenges in virtually all domains. Others may have substantial strengths in some areas but struggle in others.

One avenue to better understanding of how outcomes relate to each other is the identification of youth profiles. Some analyses, as discussed above, have attempted this in relation to criminal justice outcomes for the aging-out population. Keller, Cusick, and Courtney (2007), analyzing Midwest study baseline data, identified four groups:

1. distressed and disconnected (those most likely to experience difficulty in the transition, as they are troubled and lack social connections with adults and formal systems of support)
2. competent and connected (those making progress toward successful adulthood)
3. struggling but staying (those who face numerous challenges but are more connected to the child welfare system than the first group)
4. hindered and homebound (those who appear connected to family but may have difficulty with adult self-sufficiency because of difficulties related to school achievement, employment, and early parenting)

Aging-out youths have a wide variety of experiences, and further research is needed to provide greater clarity about these differences, which could contribute to the development of more targeted interventions.

Outcomes are often interrelated. A significant amount of research has been conducted on the economic risks young people face. For example, there is clear evidence that not completing high school results in poor economic and social prospects (Belfield & Levin, 2007). Efforts to help youths earn a high school diploma imply that this accomplishment will lead to improved employment and earnings outcomes and forestall homelessness and criminal justice system involvement after leaving care. Circumstances that interrupt schooling or create barriers to higher education—such as early parenthood—are also recognized in the research literature (Hoffman & Maynard, 2008).

Some outcomes may have greater developmental or economic implications than others. Homelessness is particularly challenging because it makes it difficult to sustain other components of well-being such as education, employment, and social networks. All major studies of youths leaving care have measured their housing situation. There may be several reasons for this focus. First is the apparent over-representation of foster care alumni in homeless shelters (Park, Metraux, & Culhane, 2005).

Second, housing issues resonate with many constituencies. It is difficult to imagine anyone being able to meet other life goals without having stable housing. A longitudinal or "career" approach to understanding housing for young foster-care alumni (Collins & Curtis, 2011)—as other social science studies have used to examine, for example, an offending career or an illness career in terms of its transitions, trajectories, changes, and turning points—may provide new insight and lead to additional strategies.

Third, self-sufficiency is a widely promoted and often politicized goal for people receiving any kind of government assistance. Most notably associated with the 1996 reform of the Aid to Families with Dependent Children (AFDC) program, self-sufficiency is also a key concept of the FCIA. People who are homeless or experiencing housing instability often need government assistance. Therefore, a focus on the risk of homelessness may also be a focus on the risk of government dependency.

What Is the Reason for the Poor Outcomes?

Predominant theoretical models for explaining poor outcomes focus on developmental attachment and trauma. But other, more macro-oriented models that take accumulated disadvantage into account are also relevant. Poverty, with its many related disadvantages, is a major factor. Many of these young people are born into lives of disadvantage. Racism and classism are institutionalized within our systems and our society, leading to the overrepresentation of children of color (Hines, Lemon, Wyatt, & Merdinger, 2004) and poor children (Jonson-Reid, Drake, & Kohl, 2009) in child welfare systems. Sociological and political perspectives, discussed in chapters 3 and 4, help explain poor outcomes from these systemic perspectives.

How Can Our Policies and Programs Improve Outcomes?

To answer this question requires an evidence-based evaluation of current policies and programs. We are only beginning to understand the long-term trajectory of foster care alumni and how it might be affected by intervention. Chapter 10 discusses programming and evaluation.

Conclusion

Although the research methodology has improved, resulting in more sophisticated data that are able to tell a fuller, more complex story, the basic message has remained the same since early studies, in the 1980s and before, conducted follow-up with youths who had aged out of or otherwise left foster care. The outcome evidence has consistently shown the difficulties that these young people have in obtaining the elements of a safe, healthy, moderately secure life. Studies that have compared these youths with the general population indicate they are worse off in many ways.

Some researchers have used sophisticated multivariate techniques with large data sets to identify typologies of youths. This research, as well as the experience of those in the field, confirms that despite comparatively worse outcomes there is a range of experiences. Some youths who age out of care are successful in a variety of domains: They go to college or get good job training; are successfully employed and financially self-sufficient; have strong and healthy adult relationships and are good parents; and avoid legal trouble, substance abuse, and self-destructive behaviors. Many of these capable people are among us in the workplace and community. We know good outcomes can occur.

Other young people struggle greatly for a wide range of reasons. Some experienced sustained and extreme troubles before coming into care, leaving little potential for interventions to help. Perhaps better interventions could have helped, but the child welfare system was too overburdened and under-resourced to provide the right kind of services in sufficient amounts.

Finally, it is important to note that some young people who are not represented in these outcomes studies may be even more vulnerable. Runaways are not part of survey-based studies. They can have an elevated risk of several problems, particularly related to victimization and exploitation (Finkelstein, Wamsley, Currie, & Miranda, 2004).

Between those who do well and those who struggle intensely is a group of young people who have moderate struggles in their journey to adulthood. Their challenges are often shared with other vulnerable youths—those involved in the juvenile justice system or living with disabilities or poverty. Research tends to examine these outcomes individually, with little attention to the multiple and accumulated disadvantages that produced them. Moreover, many of our systems and programs were historically set up to deal with one type of problem (for example, child welfare, mental health, or juvenile justice). The existence of these siloes has been identified as a problem itself, and the provision of more comprehensive and integrated services has long been identified as a goal.

CHAPTER 3

Sociological Perspectives on Youth and Young Adulthood

The outcomes identified in the preceding chapter are related to common developmental goals of young adulthood—moderately stable housing, postsecondary education or employment, and the absence of serious problems such as incarceration. Although outcomes are measures of individual attainment, young people are not just individuals suffering trauma, demonstrating resilience, and achieving or failing to achieve outcomes. They live within a social context that may either help or hinder them on their life journey.

In some ways, youths leaving care experience life in the same ways that other young people do, with a combination of opportunities and constraints. As youths and young adults, they are a part of a generational cohort. Larger social forces affecting all youths may have a disproportionate effect on young people with long histories in substitute care, because the mediating institutional forces of family, school, and community are less available to them.

Theoretical frameworks based in sociology can improve understanding of the social context for transition. This chapter focuses on three (partially overlapping) sociological approaches relevant to young adulthood in general and youths leaving care in particular: the life course, emerging adulthood, and social capital frameworks. Each is discussed in turn below. Their practical implications are discussed further in later chapters on community practice and programming.

Life Course

The life course perspective has been widely used to examine the occurrence and timing of key events in human lives as well as the impact of those events on later life conditions (Elder, 1998). Its perspective on people's lives, structural contexts, and social change encompasses ideas and observations from many disciplines, including history, sociology, demography, developmental psychology, biology, and economics (Mitchell, 2003). It elaborates the importance of time, context, process, and meaning on individual development and family life (Bengtson & Allen, 1993). Mitchell (2003) listed several fundamental elements of the life course approach:

- ▲ sociohistorical and geographical location (individuals' developmental paths are embedded in and transformed by conditions and events occurring during the time and place in which they live)
- ▲ timing of lives (including chronological age, the generational cohort, and the historical time period)
- ▲ heterogeneity and variability within age cohorts (despite some shared social circumstances)
- ▲ social ties, especially interdependence and reciprocity
- ▲ human agency and personal control (individuals can affect social structures)
- ▲ the effect of early life course decisions, opportunities, and conditions on later outcomes

Although multiple components of the life course framework are relevant to youths leaving care, I primarily use information on the "leaving-home transition"—the point at which a young person leaves the family home for independent adulthood—rather than, for example, family formation. This transition to independent living partially mirrors the aging-out experience. Much of the sociological research on the leaving-home transition uses a multigenerational perspective as human development occurs within the context of family. Therefore, it also provides some relevant contrast to the aging-out experience of youths in foster care, a group with more complicated family histories.

The process of establishing residential independence varies widely among cultures and has changed over time. In some cultures, it is rare that young people would ever live independently of their parents except to move into marriage. In the United States, demographic evidence indicates that, until the later decades of the 20th century, the age at which a child left home and became independent was declining, but that this trend has reversed (Goldscheider & Goldscheider, 1993). Challenging economic conditions and the inability to secure a well-paying job that would allow the establishment of a separate household have been documented as reasons for delay in leaving home (Settersten & Ray, 2010).

Trends in the timing of leaving home (and of marriage and child-bearing) are influenced by a variety of factors including economic conditions; historical events; and ongoing social inequalities based on factors such as gender, race, and socioeconomic status (SES) that exist within historical cohorts (Shanahan, 2000). Summarizing the role of economic conditions, Shanahan (2000) concluded that previous research has tended to assess the economy in static, objective terms, to the neglect of dynamic, complex measures involving both objective (for example, the unemployment rate) and subjective (for example, perceived employment prospects) indicators. Shanahan also suggested that measures of the economy typically have emphasized the overall level of opportunity (for example, the unemployment rate) rather than how opportunity is distributed. Thus, while it is recognized that a poor economy keeps young people from moving out of the family home, the fact that economic prospects are different in different groups receives less attention.

In the general life course literature, the home-leaving process intersects in critical ways with educational attainment, employment, and marital and parenting decisions, all of which affect self-sufficiency. The timing of these processes is a key factor. A successful transition from youth to an independent and productive adulthood is related to the opportunities that exist for young people and the public and private resources that help them attain transition-related outcomes (for example, housing stability, appropriate level of education for career goals, and stable employment and income). These processes are more likely to succeed if they occur in a certain order. For example, moving out before completing an education and getting a stable job can lead to further challenges. Family conflict and other adverse family circumstances have been found to be related to young people leaving home at an earlier age than the norm (Aquilino, 1991; Goldscheider & Goldscheider, 1999).

The life course perspective reflects not only how people formulate and pursue their life goals, but also how they are constrained and enabled by socially structured opportunities and limitations (Shanahan, 2000). Research on the individual life course examines change and development as individuals age within their social and cultural context. The meaning of age is shaped by the culture; societies divide the life span into recognized stages (for example, childhood, adulthood, and old age). These socially constructed life stages are not fixed; rather, they have expanded and contracted in length and new ones have emerged in response to broader social changes. Changes in mortality have greatly influenced the concepts of young, middle, and older adulthood, for example.

The increased heterogeneity in life course transitions related to living arrangements, marriage, parenthood, school, employment, and careers results in widely disparate ages and sequences for these transitions. Some of these transitions were once markers of young adulthood but are now much less predictable in their meaning. This has led to the articulation of "emerging adulthood" as a life stage (and as the focus of a separate theoretical framework, discussed in the next section). A successful transition is likely related to many factors: opportunities, family influence, and individual decisions. Both opportunities and constraints can add up, leading to cumulative advantages and disadvantages. Its ability to link macro and micro levels of study (for example, the impact of public policy on youth and young-adult decision making) is a key strength of the life course framework.

Alwin (2012) discussed the concepts integral to the life course perspective and distinguished between life course and life span. What is particular to the study of the life course is the recognition of complex trajectories influenced by context and choice. The life course is not fixed at birth. Studies of the *life span* focus more on biologically determined changes and the aging process. *Life course* studies recognize these physical stages but also recognize that their meanings, and the social roles that are taken within each stage, can vary.

One reason for the influence of life course studies is their recognition that events that occur early in life have great influence on what occurs later. This knowledge, for social workers and other helping professionals, can guide interventions to improve the chances for good life outcomes. Many social work interventions for youths have emphasized the importance of early life decisions on later outcomes (for example, early childbearing, leaving school, and engaging in risky behavior).

Transitions are particularly important in life course studies. Transition to another life stage can engender a number of stressors, particularly if appropriate preparation and supports are not in place. Common stressful transitions include starting school (in childhood) and retirement (in adulthood). The transition from foster care to independent adulthood has many challenges articulated throughout this book. But transition can also be an opportunity to get on the right track toward better outcomes.

Also relevant is the concept of a "turning point," which can be linked with resilience. During times of transition, it may be particularly advantageous to intervene, because people might be more willing to take advantage of resources and supports offered to them. Fear of the future as well as self-reflection regarding needs may be key factors leading people to accept help during a transition. Turning points are experiences that move a trajectory forward. Often they occur when new opportunities emerge during a life transition (Werner & Smith, 2001). The perception of such events as life altering is important, because it is the subjective nature of the event that makes it a significant turning point.

Although turning points can also be harmful and lead to a negative developmental trajectory, substantial attention has been focused on their relation to resilience. Masten (2001) argued that much of the early work on resilience was misleading in its focus on "invincible" or "invulnerable" children—those who succeeded despite adversity. A better conceptualization is of resilience as a common phenomenon, a self-correcting developmental process at work in all children, which she called "ordinary magic."

How can this approach be adapted for young people transitioning on their own? In nearly all cases, the more typical life course has been disrupted by a range of circumstances that brought the young person into care. Many youths in foster care have experienced critical transitions that are not developmentally appropriate (for example, separation from family) and over which they have little control (White & Wu, 2014). Youths aging out of foster care left the family home earlier and under circumstances involving family stress, trauma, and loss. Typically they had little choice in the decision to separate them from their family. Some ran away from home; though this is an exercise of choice, it entails so many risks that it is almost never an optimal way to leave home.

Furthermore, many normative transitions have not occurred at the point when youths leave foster care. The typical manner of leaving the family home is gradual, moderately planful, and often with the knowledge that return home is possible if necessary. This has historically not been the case for youths leaving foster care at age 18. Geenen and Powers (2007) called this experience "instant adulthood"; these youths are not afforded the luxury of a gradual transition to adulthood. Although federal policy now requires transition planning for youths leaving care and allows states to extend care beyond age 18, the transition to independence can still be abrupt.

Turning points have particular resonance for youths leaving care. Hass, Allen, and Amoah (2014) conducted a qualitative study of turning points and resilience among academically successful youths in foster care. Interviews were conducted with 19 foster care alumni making the transition to adulthood who were identified as having achieved postsecondary educational success. Findings suggested the turning point toward academic success required the interaction of three factors: (1) a sense of autonomy in decision making, (2) availability of instrumental and social support systems, and (3) environmental factors such as access to safe havens and opportunities to demonstrate competence. Individuals who provide support have been described as "turnaround people" (Werner & Smith, 2001).

Emerging Adulthood

Arnett (2000, 2004) proposed emerging adulthood as a new concept of development for the period from the late teenage years through the 20s (with a focus on ages 18 to 25) that allows young people a prolonged period of independent role exploration. This developmental period is situated within a social context and in relation to larger social forces, particularly demographic change, industrialization, and modernity (Côté, 2000).

The emerging adulthood framework is based on demographic studies that identified changes in family formation, dissolution, co-residence, employment, and SES. Traditional markers of adulthood vary in different historical and cultural contexts. In the United States, some of these markers have included leaving the family home, marrying and having children, and completing school followed by full-time employment and financial self-sufficiency. This normative understanding of transition for young people has been based primarily on mid-20th-century American life. Later in the 20th century, demographic evidence clearly showed numerous changes in the timing of these indicators of adulthood. Many have been delayed, and some of the ordering has changed.

Arnett (2000) argued that emerging adulthood is the "only period of life in which nothing is normative demographically" (p. 471). Almost all Americans age 12 to 17 live at home with one or more parents, are enrolled in school, and are unmarried and childless. In contrast, emerging adults' lives are characterized by diversity. The home-leaving experience and the living situation in young adulthood are highly variable. Goldscheider and Goldscheider (1999) found that recent cohorts of young adults most frequently left the home to be independent or because of school or marriage. Some left for a nonmarital living situation (cohabitation or single parenthood), for a specific job, or to join the military. Reasons differed for men and women; women were more likely than men to leave the family home for marriage (33 percent and 10 percent, respectively), whereas men were more likely than women to leave for school (36 percent and 28 percent, respectively). In addition, emerging adults often change residence, including temporarily moving back into their parents' home (Goldscheider & Goldscheider, 1999).

Like other development concepts, the identification of a normative period in life raises questions about the extensiveness of its normativity—to whom does it apply and under what conditions? Who benefits, and who is placed at a disadvantage? Psychological research on changing adulthood (Arnett, 2000; Côté, 2000) emphasizes individual issues—responsibility for oneself, separation from one's parents, and decision making. But social conditions also play a critical role. Public policy can affect the diverging pathways of young adults over time. For example, higher education policies may either increase prospects for equitable access to a high-quality education or perpetuate inequality by fostering high-quality postsecondary education for privileged young people and low-quality education for those in lower social strata. Federal financial aid policies that have shifted toward loans rather than grants are one example.

Social class advantages and disadvantages are transmitted from parents to children in many ways. Approximately two-thirds of young adults in their early 20s and 40 percent of those in their late 20s received financial assistance from parents (Schoeni & Ross, 2005). Other researchers have found similar patterns of parental financial and emotional support for young adults (Fingerman, Miller, Birditt, & Zaritt, 2009; Swartz, Kim, Uno, Mortimer, & O'Brien, 2011). Other methods by which social advantage is passed from parents to children include access to resources such as schools, communication patterns, engagement in beneficial social networks, and socialization regarding aspirations and values (Swartz, 2008). Thus, the advantages of social class are not only financial but also include housing stability and quality, access to education and job networks, community safety, and quality of public services.

Arnett (2000) briefly addressed social disadvantage, noting that limitations in educational and occupational opportunities do influence the extent to which young people can experience their late teens and 20s as a volitional period (a time when a young person can make choices about his or her life). He suggested that these explorations about school and work are different (but not necessarily fewer) for the working class, with the emphasis on exploring work options rather than educational options. He also recognized that fewer opportunities are available in minority communities.

Berzin and DeMarco (2010) used the National Survey of Families and Households to examine the impact of poverty on key markers of emerging adulthood, and found significant impacts of poverty on critical events of emerging adulthood (home-leaving, marriage, and parenthood). Poor youths were more likely to leave home before age 18, but their likelihood of leaving home decreased after this age. The researchers noted that early home-leaving may critically influence a young person's ability to complete an education and build up the resources needed for successful independent living. In addition, a high percentage of poor youths did not leave home at or after age 18, potentially affecting their chances of ever moving to an independent situation and leaving poverty. Findings also indicated that poor youths were less likely to marry at all ages, and more likely to become teenage parents, than nonpoor youths. Because early parenting is related to lower educational rates (Hoffman & Maynard, 2008), this may lead to further disadvantage and decrease chances of exiting poverty.

Settersten (2007) focused on the impact of social inequality on transition and suggested two distinct processes: "exploration" and "drift". For young people from relatively privileged backgrounds, highly variable patterns may be created by the luxury of exploration in regard to higher education, employment, romantic relationships, and activities aimed at personal growth. Personal or family resources enable them to take the time for exploration. For those from less privileged backgrounds, however, patterns of drift are related to limited opportunities, fewer resources, and restricted social networks. People with less privilege may start down a path (college, for example) but may have to drop out

41

because of a lack of resources or a need to work to support themselves or family members. They may take jobs they do not really want, for financial reasons, but then move on to something else as soon as they can.

The sociological literature on early adulthood suggests that as the period of young adulthood has lengthened, families often bear some of the cost. If this material support is occurring in middle- and upper-class families, "societies must be concerned about the plight of the sizable proportions of young people whose parents are largely absent from their lives" or are unable to provide this level of support (Settersten, 2007, p. 265). This argument did not address youths leaving foster care specifically but would apply to their circumstances.

In addition to the effect of family resources on the process of entering adulthood, Settersten (2007) also tied the differences between young-adult "exploration" and "drift" to provisions (that is, government-funded supports such as food stamps, housing, and tuition assistance) made available within welfare states, characterizing the United States as a liberal market state in which support for vulnerable populations is minimal and temporary. Thus the life course is "characterized by significant discontinuity" as a result of the emphasis on using personal resources to navigate life and individuals' unequal access to resources. The ongoing privatization of social risks (Hacker, 2008) is another force in the declining welfare state that exacerbates the challenges facing vulnerable young people.

Lee (2014) offered a framework that takes into account the institutional influences that affect emerging adulthood, noting the long-term forces that operate through institutions, resulting in advantage for some young people and a disadvantaged ("accelerated") adulthood for others. Lee referred to youth as "marginalized" rather than "vulnerable," drawing attention to the structural forces that lead to their disadvantage.

A related area of work has examined the meaning of young adulthood to young adults themselves. If the traditional markers of young adulthood have become less relevant, what markers does the current generation understand to be symbols of adulthood? Furlong, Woodman, and Wyn (2011) contrasted "transition" and "cultural" perspectives to the study of the sociology of youth and young adulthood. Transition perspectives such as those reviewed above tend to be used in large-scale, quantitative, longitudinal studies. Cultural perspectives have been primarily ethnographic to understand the relevant meaning of adulthood.

One example of this type of ethnographic work described a therapeutic model of selfhood in the young adult years among the working class that is "inwardly directed and preoccupied with its own psychic and emotional growth [and] has become a crucial cultural resource for ascribing meaning and order to one's life amid the flux and uncertainty of a flexible economy and post-traditional social order" (Silva, 2012, p. 506). In part because young people's lives are less determined by external gender, religious, moral, and legal codes than they were in previous generations, a traditional model of selfhood based on external norms is less relevant (Silva, 2012). Silva's (2012) own study focused on working-class young people, for whom traditional markers of adulthood have become increasingly unattainable or undesirable, and addressed questions concerning class, the transition to adulthood, and cultural models of selfhood. She found that respondents embraced an inwardly directed self, preoccupied with its own psychic development. This therapeutic narrative allowed working-class men and women to redefine competent adulthood in terms of overcoming a painful family past. Specifically, working-class youths "are haunted by the meanings and rituals of traditional adulthood even though they see this model as unattainable, inadequate, or simply undesirable" (p. 518). Her data revealed that the working-class discourse related to adulthood is ingrained in the institutions that shape this generation's lives, including social services, school psychologists, self-help literature, free drug trials, the Internet, and Alcoholics and Narcotics Anonymous. One additional point is related to the need for witnesses to one's story to legitimate the self-perception of adulthood. But for the majority of respondents, finding witnesses proved difficult. Without a witness to legitimate their story, the young people became "suspended in a narrative of suffering, and the ritual failed to produce a newly adult self" (Silva, 2012, p. 519).

How can this approach be applied to youths aging out of foster care? The broader sociological literature on home-leaving (for example, Goldscheider & Goldscheider, 1999) may note that an adverse family climate is related to early home-leaving, but this literature is not specific to the foster care experience. Consistent with the emerging adulthood concept, youths may not be developmentally ready to be on their own. Often, they have not attained some prerequisites for securing stable housing, such as completing schooling or maintaining stable employment and income (Pecora et al., 2006).

The process of constructing a therapeutic narrative of adulthood might be applicable to many foster care alumni. These youths have engaged with a variety of institutions (not just child welfare) that have defined their story. Searching for their own story and overcoming their past is a part of many youth narratives. Samuels and Pryce (2008) suggested that similar forces were at work among their study participants. Their qualitative data on 44 young foster care alumni suggest a strong desire for self-reliance. Participants in their study emphasized their perseverance through hardship and expressed pride in their self-reliance. This also speaks to the importance of listening to youths' experiences and providing opportunities for them to tell their stories.

43

Youths leaving care fit the emerging-adulthood group in terms of age. The more fluid understanding of adulthood during these years also affects the aging-out population. In the dichotomy of explorers and drifters, the lack of social privilege would, in most cases, relegate aging-out youths to the second category.

Social Capital

Although there are many definitions of and controversies about the concept of social capital (Lin, 1999; Wacquant, 1998), it is increasingly being applied to vulnerable youths and other disadvantaged populations. Bourdieu (1984), Coleman (1988), Putnam (2000), and Portes (1998) are some of the most well-known theorists of social capital, which has been defined as resources that result from membership in a social network or are based on relationships (Bourdieu, 1984). These networks are not static; they must be constructed and maintained and activated when needed. Coleman (1988), who focused on the family unit, described social capital as both a relational construct and a facilitator of action in providing resources to others through relationships based on shared values and norms. Reciprocity and trust are key elements within the social network. Lin (1999) argued that social capital is inherently network based; from the social-capital perspective, investments in these networks result in dividends just as economic investments in human capital through education and training result in economic benefits.

Portes (1998) distinguished three basic functions of social capital: social control, family support, and generation of benefits through extrafamilial networks. People can accumulate social capital and might do so in a planful manner. The more social connections people have, the more likely it is that their social capital will grow (Portes, 1998). Unfortunately, the converse may also be true; those who begin with few connections start at a disadvantage. In this way, social capital (or its absence) becomes another mechanism by which advantage (or disadvantage) accumulates.

The prevailing assumption that social capital is good and, consequently, deficits in social capital are not good, leads to intervention strategies that help people get more social capital. But the positive effects of social capital are not assured. Portes (1998) conceptualized "negative social capital" as detrimental consequences that derive from social capital; networks can create demands, cause restrictions, or lead to one person's gain at another's expense. Although the positive effects of social capital receive extensive attention, these positive effects are not apparent in all cases or for all individuals. Portes (1998) referred to the "exclusion of outsiders" as a disadvantageous consequence: Group solidarity generates access to resources for members of the group but can lead to the exclusion of people outside the group.

Briggs (1997) distinguished between social capital that people use to "get by" (cope with life challenges) and social capital that helps people "get ahead" (enter networks with more resources and opportunities). Both strong and weak ties can be helpful in different ways, with strong ties providing a sense of inclusion and solidarity and weak ties providing access to outside resources and opportunities (Granovetter, 1973). Social networks with some weak ties allow permeability—new information sources that may lead to opportunities not otherwise accessible.

Wacquant (1998), analyzing the black urban ghetto, linked the focus on social capital with broader social issues related to distribution of resources. He argued that policies and public sources of support for urban communities are a critical element of social capital that has deteriorated. In addition to the focus on direct, interpersonal relationships among residents, the focus should also be on those indirect social relations "mediated by public organizations and by the private institutions that these in turn support. *For state structures and policies play a decisive role in the formation and distribution of both formal and informal social capital"* (p. 35).

The social capital concept been applied to a variety of areas, increasingly including youth issues. A recent analysis (Mathematica Policy Research, 2011) applied both resiliency and capital development frameworks to factors leading to adverse adult outcomes, particularly in self-sufficiency, and found that many vulnerable youths lack one or more of four key types of capital: human (individual-level skills), social (connections focused on educational and employment opportunities), cultural (knowledge of how educational and employment systems work), and economic (financial resources to pursue education or job training). Although, like the resiliency perspective, the capital development perspective emphasizes multiple levels (individual, family, community) of risk factors, the capital development perspective focuses primarily on the resources and knowledge needed to succeed in education and the workplace. The importance of adults, therefore, is largely related to their role as connectors to educational and employment opportunities. The social networks of vulnerable youths (formed through family and community) are often lacking in economic resources. The implication is that interventions, therefore, should emphasize connection to resource-rich networks.

Furstenberg and Hughes (1995) used Coleman's concepts of social capital to examine the extent to which social capital within the family and community has a positive effect on the life chances of disadvantaged children. Using a longitudinal data set, they examined the extent to which later adjustment was linked to the family's social capital: "the degree to which parents and children were embedded in a protective social network and were themselves a closely bonded unit with mutual expectations, trust, and loyalty" (p. 589). They found that most of the measures of social capital were related to markers of socioeconomic success in early adulthood and not to other key outcomes such as early parenthood for girls or legal problems for boys. The relationships examined were complex, and the authors suggested that the general concept of social capital is less useful than examination of different kinds of social capital and their potential links to specific outcomes.

How does this apply to foster care alumni? In a general sense, disadvantaged individuals are likely to benefit from social capital resources that help them to get by (social support) and get ahead (social networks). Youths leaving care need both of these resources during their transition to adulthood. Ward (2009) used the social capital framework to explore the reasons young people return to child welfare agencies after age 18. She noted that while in care, youths are not able to build much social capital, and thus when they leave care, they have very little capital on which to draw. Even as youths build economic and social capital, a return to the state child welfare system gives them, at minimum, access to information.

Ward (2009) found that youths in care do not seem to accumulate capital among family, friends, or community networks. Rather, family and friends may offer them limited sources of social capital (for example, small loans or emergency housing) but are not able to help them with social leverage. Also, family tensions influenced youths' access to social capital. Unresolved family conflicts continued when they returned home and sometimes resulted in a resource drain for them. Ward also noted that organizational networks and neighborhood institutions that could act as resource brokers were absent from youths' lives.

Similar findings were reported by Perez and Romo (2011), who used a social capital framework to examine the experiences of 32 young foster care alumni. They found that many attempted to reunite with family as they aged out of care and that they sought family relationships as a source of social capital before they sought out friends or shelters for assistance. The authors described attempts by young people to seek shelter in their family networks and the many difficulties that they encountered. Friendship networks, therefore, were used as another source of social capital to obtain shelter. This results in the practice of "couch surfing," often among peers who have similar disadvantages.

Social networks have been described as having both bridging functions (linkage to resources) and bonding functions (building solidarity) (Putnam, 2000). Overall, the bridging function of social networks may be limited for youths in foster care because of the resource deficits identified earlier. Furthermore, because of their histories of movement and instability, they have had to work constantly to bridge every time they are faced with a new situation. Like for many disadvantaged populations, therefore, opportunities for bonding may be particularly important. Further discussion of the application of social capital concepts to developing social connections in the community is provided in chapter 9.

Conclusion

Although youths aging out of care have faced particular experiences that make their life trajectories more challenging, they are part of a cohort of young people, all of whom are moving toward adulthood in a specific social place and time. Understanding this broader sociological picture and its specific application to youths leaving care can be useful. Particularly because they have generally lacked the profound social advantages of strong families, and are nearly always burdened by poverty, the broader social context may have an amplified impact on their lives.

The three theoretical frameworks reviewed in this chapter are interconnected in many ways; they all speak to the social context of the transition from youth to adulthood. As this sociological literature primarily addresses normative lives of youths within families, it requires some adaptation in its use for vulnerable youths with extensive child welfare system involvement.

The life course framework is particularly useful for thinking about trajectories and transitions, linking earlier life experiences with later outcomes, and understanding how larger systems of culture and social policy affect life trajectories. It recognizes that timing of transitions is critical in the life course; transitions that occur either too early or too late in life may lead to further challenges. Youths aging out of care face many challenges precisely because they are entering adulthood in ways that are not developmentally normative. Some may need to mature further physically before they can make better decisions. Some may need to struggle first before they can use assistance. Turning points may be particularly central to social work interventions; often this is exactly what intervention aims to achieve: helping youths get onto or move toward a positive trajectory.

The emerging-adulthood framework was developed, in part, on the basis of demographic evidence. Understanding normative trends in emerging adulthood and comparing them to the experiences of youths aging out of foster care can help highlight the serious disadvantages that the latter group faces. This can provide the moral impetus for policy changes that can align the transition experiences of aging-out youths with the norm. This can include, for example, extending time in foster care, allowing re-entry to care after an initial exit, and emphasizing higher education.

Initially, accounts of emerging adulthood primarily captured the experiences of more privileged segments of society, those young adults for whom an extended period of exploration had benefits and no serious repercussions. Comparative work with other youth populations has highlighted structural and institutional forces that exacerbate existing stratification (Lee, 2014) and has examined historical and cultural trends in the transition to adulthood. Some sociologists have criticized the emerging-adulthood framework because of its lack of attention to the varying opportunities and constraints that allow more privileged young people to take advantage of the benefits of this exploratory period and hinder less privileged young people from developing a secure foothold in adulthood.

The explanation for many of the poor outcomes witnessed among young adults formerly in foster care is the absence of transfer of social resources of all types. The families from which they come are mostly poor. Temporary or permanent separation from parents may preclude the transmission of even meager social resources. Social policies can have a critical role in providing some opportunities and resources for those youths who do not have the advantages of family to buffer them from harm and provide the resources and connections described by the term "social capital."

Because social capital involves social connections, it also has a conceptual relationship to engagement with civic issues and government systems. This is explored further in the next chapter, which examines political theories relevant to youths leaving foster care.

CHAPTER 4

Political Perspectives on Youth and Young Adulthood

This chapter reviews research on young people as a political entity, including their actual and potential influence on the political world, where decisions are made that affect their welfare. This includes their participation in formal political processes and their ability to influence decisions as an interest group.

Those who work in youth services understand the potential for including youths, as a group, in programming, service delivery, and policy making. Although youth participation remains to be institutionalized in many settings, youths have successfully participated in several roles. Formal entities such as youth councils, advisory boards, and commissions exist in many programs, organizations, agencies, and governments. Youths have participated as trainers in a variety of initiatives at state, county, and municipal levels. Student councils have long played a role in schools. Group homes and other congregate settings might incorporate input from young people in programming and rules. Within the policy realm, youths can organize to give testimony and speak in public forums during consideration of legislation that affects them. In essence, youths might be involved as an organized entity in any decision-making endeavor in which adults might similarly participate.

Several successful examples suggest that youths and young adults as an interest group can be organized for effective political action. Particularly since young adulthood allows for participation through voting, might the extension of support to young people over age 18 increase prospects for political action? To what extent can and should youths leaving foster care function as a unique interest group? Might they also benefit from collaboration with other youth-focused groups? This chapter will apply insights from the literature on youth organizing to youths leaving care. Consistent with a social work perspective emphasizing empowerment of disadvantaged populations, youths leaving care can advocate for themselves and work collectively to achieve policy goals.

The aging-out population, like the youth population more generally, has a flexible age range but generally includes adolescence and young adulthood. This includes both those below age 18 and those above. Although adolescents are different from children, they frequently operate under shared policy frameworks. Thus, to some extent, the policy environment for children is also relevant to adolescents, and, consequently, to the aging-out population.

There is evidence that concerns of young people are not a top priority of policymakers. An Urban Institute analysis found that federal expenditures on children in 2013 totaled $464 billion, up slightly from the $460 billion spent in 2012, but below a peak of $499 billion in 2010 (Hahn, Isaacs, Edelstein, Steele, & Steuerle, 2014). The "kids' share" of the total federal budget was 10.2 percent in 2013, a half-point increase from 2012. The kids' share of tax expenditures (tax breaks to families with children, the nonrefundable portions of tax credits, and other tax provisions) fell by a half point to 8.8 percent of all tax expenditures. The kids' share of the economy dropped in 2013, with total expenditures on children falling slightly over the past year from 2.9 to 2.8 percent of the gross domestic product (Hahn et al., 2014).

Comparisons with the Elderly

Further insight is gained from a comparison of spending on youths with spending on the elderly, which is higher in both total and per capita spending. Per capita federal spending on the elderly rose from about $4,000 in 1960 to $27,975 in 2011 in inflation-adjusted (2013) dollars. Over the same period, per capita federal spending on children rose from $270 to $4,894. While the federal government spent nearly six times more on the elderly than on children in 2011, but state and local spending is heavily slanted toward children, particularly through public schools. Combined federal, state, and local spending on the elderly was just over twice the combined spending on children in 2011 ($28,754 versus $12,770) (Hahn et al., 2014).

Researchers have examined the divergent levels of social spending on children and the elderly and their consequent levels of economic well-being. Preston (1984) examined this divergence through the 1970s and 1980s, during which time the well-being of children deteriorated while that of the elderly improved. Political power was identified as a key factor; the growth in the elderly population contributed to their power and their ability to secure beneficial social spending, policies, and programs. Newacheck and Benjamin (2004) also identified divergent trends in social welfare spending for children and elders between 1965 and 2000. Ozawa and Lee (2011) found that the ratio of social transfers (for example, social insurance benefits and social assistance transfers) for elderly people to those for children was 5.80 around 1990 and grew to 8.12

around 2000. Their analysis included other countries, and they concluded that the United States spends less for both elderly people and children than other rich countries, the amounts of public resources allocated to children and their families are disproportionately low, and this is the main source of generational imbalance in U.S. social spending. In thinking about the future, Newacheck and Benjamin (2004) argued that "leaving the future welfare of children and elders to the caprices of politics and the vagaries of larger economic forces is morally bankrupt and fiscally irresponsible" and called for a new fairness doctrine based on need rather than historical entitlement (p. 145).

Children and the elderly have historically received specialized policy attention. This is culturally ingrained in many societies; moral commitments to widows and orphans, for example, stem from the Bible and other foundational religious texts. Yet at least within the United States, the elderly have been more successful at claiming policy attention than have children and youths.

Lessons can be drawn from the elderly's enhanced political power to analyze prospects for youths' potential political gain. Grason and Guyer (1995) identified similarities between children and the elderly: both groups are easily identifiable based on age; both have particular development vulnerabilities; as individuals at the ends of the age spectrum, both are characterized by a certain level of dependency; and this vulnerability and dependency have traditionally prompted varying degrees of special social protection for both groups.

Grason and Guyer (1995) compared Title V of the Social Security Act (aimed at children) and the Older Americans Act of 1965. They argued that the service system for children and families, in contrast to that for the elderly, "lacks a core structure and uniform services, resulting in great variability and inequities" (p. 577). Features of the Older Americans Act that are needed for a strong policy response (but are missing from Title V) include assurances that the concerns of the population will have high-level national visibility; specification of organizational structures and functions at the national, state, and local levels that include the horizontal and vertical coordination of all policy development, planning, and service delivery by the multiple public programs that address the concerns of this population; definition of a national core uniform set of community-level services and activities; and legitimized advocacy and participation by consumers and the community in policy development and program implementation. Within elder services, self-advocacy by consumers and participation in program planning and oversight are widely accepted as standard practice. This is not the case for services aimed at children, youths, and families.

The United States does not have strong government institutions designed to protect the interests of young people. Gormley (2012) provided several examples of this: there is no cabinet-level department for children; although there is a Children's Bureau within HHS, it has been transferred from one department to another over the years and is relatively small; the House of Representatives created a Select Committee on Children, Youth, and Families in 1983, but it was abolished in 1993. In comparison, the Senate Special Committee on Aging, which was created as a temporary committee in 1961, is still in existence.

The Older Americans Act established a range of supportive services for the elderly. Comparable legislation for youths, the Younger Americans Act, was introduced in Congress in 2001 but was never passed despite multiple attempts over several years. Modeled on the Older Americans Act, it would have established a comprehensive and coordinated national youth policy. Built on a youth development model, the Younger Americans Act was community based, focused on children ages 0 to 19 years, and sought to shift funding focus away from youth problems and toward developing youth capacities. It would have established an Office on National Youth Policy within the White House, a Council on National Youth Policy within HHS, and formula-based state block grants to support community-based youth development programs and services. Youths would have been the central force in planning.

Bork (2012) provided another example of the lack of sustained federal commitment to youth policy. She characterized President George W. Bush's 2003 convening of the White House Task Force for Disadvantaged Youth as a turning point in youth policy because it assessed federal youth policy and developed recommendations to strengthen it. The task force found that federal youth policy, administered across several departments, lacked coordination and focus. On the basis of the task force findings, the Federal Youth Coordination Act was introduced in 2005. After negotiation, the Act was modified slightly and attached as Title VIII of the Older Americans Act reauthorization bill. It passed the House and the Senate with no opposition at the end of September 2006 and was signed into law by the president on October 17, 2006. It was then renamed the Tom Osborne Federal Youth Coordination Act (PL 109–365), after its key sponsor. It established the Federal Youth Development Council, which was to be made up of 11 federal department secretaries and heads of agencies; representatives from youth-serving nonprofit organizations, foundations, and faith-based organizations; and young people themselves. Funding did not follow, however. Although the federal government devoted attention to the issue of youth, it still has not followed through with implementation (Bork, 2012).

Although there are numerous policies applicable to youths and young adults, unlike older people, this group does not benefit from specific social policies that can unite them as a political force. In contrast, scholars have argued that old age policies create beneficiaries who then form political interest groups to defend the policies that support them (Hudson & Gonyea, 2012). Two policy areas that may have this potential for young adults are college financial aid and health insurance through the Affordable Care Act. Organized policy action groups are working on these issues. For example, the organization Young Invincibles (http://younginvincibles.org) was founded in 2009 to provide a voice for young people in the health care reform debate. In addition to health care, the organization works on issues related to higher education and employment. The Roosevelt Institute (http://www.rooseveltcampusnetwork.org), with a campus network of more than 120 chapters in 38 states, advocates for young people in local and national policy debates. The organization's *Blueprint for Millennial America* (Roosevelt Campus Network, 2015) articulates policy proposals in the areas of education, the environment, the economy, health care, social justice, and diplomacy. Efforts such as these are needed to advance the standing and institutionalization of policies that benefit young adults.

Youths and Young Adults as Political Actors

The core explanation for the difference in policy attention to youths and the elderly is the difference in political power between the two groups. The elderly have power and express it through voting, financial contributions to campaigns, interest group and lobbying activities, and myriad other forms of influence that occur in the context of broad civic engagement.

Voting and Civic Engagement

In every presidential election since 1964, voters ages 18 to 24 have consistently had lower turnout than any other age group. In contrast, Americans 65 and older consistently vote at higher rates than any other age group (File, 2013). Voting does tend to increase at later stages of the life cycle, as young adults move into more stable phases of employment and family formation (Flanagan & Levine, 2010).

Voting is only one manifestation of civic engagement, of course. A recent study of civic participation by people ages 18 to 29 found that the majority of young people had experienced some level and mechanism of civic engagement. Focused on the presidential election year 2008, the study identified six categories of young people in regard to their civic engagement: political specialists (19.3 percent), broadly engaged (19.0 percent), only voted (17.9 percent), civically alienated (16.1 percent), engaged nonvoters (14.4 percent), and politically marginalized (13.3 percent) (Center for Information and Research on Civic Learning and Engagement [CIRCLE], 2011). According to this research, young people express their civic engagement in a variety of ways; the picture of civic engagement is more optimistic than when assessed by voting patterns alone.

Only a fairly small minority (16.1 percent in 2008; 23.2 percent in 2010) were considered to be civically alienated (CIRCLE, 2011).

Civic engagement is thought to serve multiple purposes. For the individual, it can contribute to development and personal growth. In some models, it is considered part of the transition to adulthood (Flanagan & Levine, 2010). But it is also critical in the building of a community and is necessary for democracy. Flanagan and Levine (2010) also reported that over several decades, both forms and patterns of civic engagement in this age group have changed, with contemporary young adults engaging in more short-term and episodic periods of civic engagement rather than sustained commitments to organizations.

Once again, social class plays a key role. Rates of both voting and volunteering are lower for young adults without college experience (Flanagan & Levine, 2010). This is partly attributed to cumulative disadvantage over the course of childhood and adolescence and is exacerbated by unequal opportunities to practice civic engagement (Flanagan & Levine, 2010). One study based on data from California reported that high school students attending higher SES schools, those who are college-bound, and white students have more such opportunities than low-income students, those not heading to college, and students of color (Kahne & Middaugh, 2008). Flanagan and Levine (2010) found that dropping out of high school and being arrested are related to reduced rates of adult civic engagement. These are two disproportionate risks for poor and vulnerable youths, such as those leaving foster care.

Power and Interest Groups

In addition to broad activities related to civic engagement, youths and their allies may aim to directly influence policy by engaging in various interest-group organizing activities. Because vulnerable youths typically lack political power, numerous efforts are needed to develop empowerment-based approaches to help them claim their power.

Several theories related to power, and its impact on public policy, have been articulated. Perhaps most well known is the dichotomy between theories based on the power of elites (for example, Mills, 1956) and those based on pluralistic models of multiple group influences (Dahl, 1958). In contrast to overt, observable power in the decision-making process, Bachrach and Bartz (1962) identified "two-dimensional power," which can prevent challenges to power, including nondecisions, which can prevent other issues from being raised. Because there is no conflict, because an issue is not raised, it is presumed that there is consensus on the status quo.

Additional manifestations of power occur when large groups of people remain passive; they do not claim and use the power they potentially have

(Gaventa, 1980). This type of power results in a number of institutionalized processes that prevent vulnerable populations, particularly poor people and people of color, from gaining victories in the policy process. Parenti (1970), for example, examined efforts to exercise power within lower strata, urban, primarily black community groups, concluding that political decision making resembled a more elite than pluralistic model. Black urban residents who attempted to claim power through organized action to secure modest changes (for example, installation of a traffic light) found that "the visible agents of the ruling world" (government officials, the private sector, existing policy structures) "displayed a remarkable capacity to move in the same direction against some rather modest lower-class claims" (p. 519). Public officials' delaying tactics were effective because of the protests groups' inherent instability due to their dependence for resources on outsiders.

Birkland (2011) noted that the American system of democracy, with its constitutionally protected freedom of association, does not put a legal burden in the way of organized interest groups. The major barriers are not political but rather related to the costs of organizing and generating resources. Effective interest group activity can be expensive. Thus, while groups are easily formed, their ability to effectively influence policy is variable. Some groups are viewed by policymakers as having more legitimacy, which allows them more strength in their dealings (Maloney, Jordan, & McLaughlin, 1994). Knowledge is a critical attribute of a group that can influence its ability to become a policy insider (Howlett & Ramesh, 2002). Communication with decision makers requires resources that established groups often have but emerging groups do not (Birkland, 2011). Scholars have suggested that public interest groups play an important role in Washington politics as a result of the breadth and durability of their organizations, especially as some have developed into large organizations supported by membership and corresponding budgets (Berry & Wilcox, 2009).

Groups that want their issue to reach the public agenda must gain the attention and support of others; they often must expand the scope of conflict to draw others into the effort (Schattschneider, 1960). Advocacy coalitions (Sabatier & Jenkins-Smith, 1999) form that focus on policy subsystems (for example, child welfare or youth services) and involve multiple individuals and organizations who hold a shared belief system and advocate for shared policy goals.

The field of youth services has had some specific challenges related to strong interest group advocacy. Scott, Deschenes, Hopkins, Newman, and McLaughlin (2006) noted that organizations advocating for youths vary across many dimensions: target (children versus youths), stance (problem-oriented versus preventive versus supporting positive development), focus (general versus specific), and mix of advocacy and service provision. Overall, the field is "relatively unsettled and contested" in comparison to some other subfields (for example, child development). In terms of policy, youth services are contesting several existing (and highly institutionalized) fields such as education, social services, and juvenile justice. Thus, most of the work has taken place within local communities.

Youth Empowerment

Often missing from policy discussion is a sustained role for youths in the process. If power is important for influencing public policy, and youths lack power within political systems, how can youths organize to be more powerful and able to influence policy? Empowerment is a core concept in efforts to be inclusive of service populations in service delivery and organizational decision making. Pearrow (2008) defined *empowerment* as "a process of increasing personal, interpersonal, or political power so that individuals, families, and communities can take action to improve their life situations" (p. 202).

In regard to a youth voice in policy making, Faulkner (2009) distinguished "consultations," in which young people's views are gathered to be used in decision making, and ongoing projects, in which there is a process that involves some discussion on decisions. She noted that the literature on involving young people in consultations is much better developed than that on ongoing projects, and that reports from projects with ongoing participation have documented problems. For example, criticism of the composition of ongoing-participation initiatives is commonplace; policymakers can be impressed by youth participants in the political process but often assume that they are not representative of youths in general (Faulkner, 2009).

The potential benefits of youth participation can accrue to an individual participant, a group of participants, and the broader society. Thus, individual youths may gain from participation by learning skills and self-confidence; a group of youths may gain by obtaining resources, programs, or other favorable treatment; and society may gain by hearing and addressing youths' views and developing more effective programming and policy. Various studies have evaluated these effects of participation (Checkoway, 2011).

Youth involvement was characterized by Hart (1992) as occurring along a continuum with eight levels:

1. manipulation (children are engaged in issues but have no real understanding of the issues or their actions)
2. decoration (adults use children to support their cause)
3. tokenism (children are said to have been given a voice but in reality have little or no opportunity to formulate their own opinions)

4. assigned but informed (children are assigned a project role, but they understand the project and have voluntarily consented to be a part of it)
5. consulted and informed (children have some understanding of the process and their views are taken into account, at least to some extent, but adults design and run the project)
6. adult initiated, but decision making is shared with children
7. child initiated and directed (ideas are both generated and implemented by children)
8. child initiated, shared decisions with adults (usually achieved only by older teenagers; rare, largely because of the "absence of caring adults attuned to the particular interests of young people") (Hart, 1992, p. 14)

Adu-Gyamfi (2013) described several adaptations of Hart's continuum (Kirby, Lanyon, Cronin, & Sinclair, 2003; Treseder, 1997) that articulate the appropriateness of different types of participation in different circumstances. Checkoway and Richards-Schuster (2003) offered an alternative typology distinguishing between breadth and depth of participation: youths as subjects, consultants, partners, and directors. At one end of the continuum (subjects), youths are objects of adult-driven research but have no role in the process. At the other end (directors), youths are at the center of all decision making.

Klindera and Menderweld (2001) offered a set of strategies for promoting youth participation in decision-making forums: viewing young consumers as advocates and educators, treating youths on advisory boards in the same way that other members are treated, scheduling meetings at times convenient for youths, valuing youths for their experience, and promoting equal partnership and respect. Those interested in youth participation have been encouraged to pay particular attention to the youth–adult relationship and the institutional or organizational context in which these activities take place. Combating "adultism," or helping adults develop perceptions of youths as capable of being partners and decision makers, is seen as an essential element in successful efforts. Morse, Markowitz, Zanghi, and Burns (2003) noted that adults need to assess their own attitudes and behaviors when they work with youth participants. Elements of organizational culture, which include shared values and beliefs about partnering with youths, and resources such as money for space, food, and professional development, are deemed essential components of successful adult–youth partnerships.

Efforts to encourage youth participation in programming and policy must continue to examine the role of power. Adu-Gyamfi (2013) conducted research on participation and empowerment with young people involved in participatory initiatives in Ghana and concluded that youth participation did not lead to empowerment. The interviewed youths had a voice to discuss issues of concern to them but did not have the power to influence policy decisions on those issues. This was true despite the project's aim of empowering young people to influence policy making. The study found that young people's participation and influence during the course of policy implementation was very limited and at some point nonexistent. Adu-Gyamfi concluded, "There is an implied but inadequately explored conceptual link between participation, self-confidence and empowerment" (p. 1771). Whereas the scholarly literature related to youth studies frequently uses the concepts of participation and empowerment, theory in this area remains inadequate and conceptually flawed.

Adu-Gyamfi's (2013) study offered intriguing results and consequent cautions regarding assumptions that youth participation will naturally lead to empowerment. More intentional and vigorous efforts are needed, centered on organizing youths to achieve their own goals. Youth organizing is a specific intervention methodology that involves "a process that brings young people together to talk about the most pressing problems in their communities, conduct research on these problems and possible solutions, and follow through with social action to create community-level change" (Christens & Dolan, 2011, p. 529). A commonly used definition of *youth organizing* is offered by Funders' Collaborative on Youth Organizing (2009): "an innovative youth development and social justice strategy that trains young people in community organizing and advocacy, and assists them in employing these skills to alter power relations and create meaningful institutional change in their communities."

Christens and Dolan (2011) identified four distinguishing characteristics of youth organizing initiatives (compared with other models for youth community engagement):

1. They concentrate on the conditions faced by young people, the systematic nature of these conditions, and the role of power in creating and maintaining these conditions.
2. Youths learn strategies for collaboratively harnessing their collective social power to challenge powerful people and institutions to make community-level change.
3. Youths choose the issues that are most important to them through a collective decision-making process.
4. Adults support youths in organizing, but youths often take the lead in decision making about issue selection and strategy.

Youth Empowerment in Child Welfare Systems

For several reasons, youths in child welfare systems are particularly disempowered. Hegar and Hunzeker (1988) discussed characteristics of child welfare agencies that make empowerment-based practice both difficult and necessary: Clients of child welfare systems are often disempowered in multiple ways (poor, minority, and single female parents are disproportionately represented); these clients become further disempowered in the course of the investigation and subsequent processes in the child welfare system and courts; serving a socially devalued group leads to stress within the work settings (for example, lack of resources); and characteristics of bureaucracy include rigid lines of authority, hierarchy, and inertia.

Dupuis and Mann-Feder (2013) also reported some of the challenges to youth empowerment in a child welfare context. There are inherent contradictions between the goals of youth protection and those of youth empowerment. Child protection systems operate from an authoritative stance, work with clients (both young people and their parents) whose involvement is often involuntary, prioritize child safety over other important outcomes, and have legal responsibilities related to child protection that allow interventions—especially child removal—that may be highly unwelcome by parents and children. Best practices in child welfare emphasize partnership and collaboration with families, as well as youth-oriented policies that foster empowerment. Yet these principles remain difficult to achieve: "This commitment would entail sustained efforts to transform the culture of care to a culture of collaboration, where policies and procedures stress partnerships with clients" (pp. 374–375).

Other characteristics of child welfare systems also contribute to youth disempowerment, particularly the deficit-based nature of intervention and the bureaucratic orientation of systems (Dupuis & Mann-Feder, 2013). The deficit-based nature results from the fact that families typically enter the child welfare system through failures in parenting. The bureaucratic orientation results in organizations that are "large, complex, and hierarchical," decision-making processes that are "most often top-down," and services that "are provided in separate departments that function as silos" (p. 375). Dupuis and Mann-Feder (2013) therefore concluded that although there is great interest in a youth empowerment approach in child welfare, agencies often underestimate the amount of change that is needed to make this shift. Organizational cultural change to achieve this goal requires extensive commitment, and adults must be ready to cede their own power. Similar observations are made throughout the literature (for example, Clay et al., 2010) that empowerment-based practice requires fundamental organizational and structural change.

Aiding foster youths with the transition after care also occurs in a wide variety of community settings, both formally (in collaboration with child welfare agencies) and informally (in the multitude of voluntary programs and services offered in community-based settings). By their nature, community-based settings may have more potential to support the empowerment of young people. Some examples of efforts to empower transitioning youths are provided below.

Empowering Youths Aging Out of Care

Youth Participation in Case Planning

Federal law governing the transition from foster care to independent living requires states to involve youths in the design of independent living programs and to give youths a voice in their case plans (Morse et al., 2003). At an individual case level, there has been a focused policy response to ensure youth's voice in case planning.

This is also articulated in international conventions. Article 12 of the United Nations Convention on the Rights of the Child states that "States Parties shall assure to the child who is capable of forming his or her own views the right to express those views freely in all matters affecting the child, the views of the child being given due weight in accordance with the age and maturity of the child" (General Assembly of the United Nations, 1989). Because of their older age, participation in planning is particularly relevant for youths leaving foster care.

Although youth participation in their own case planning is an essential element of good practice, my focus on youth participation in on the systemic issues: youth advisory boards, youths as trainers, and youth involvement in policy development.

Youth Advisory Boards

Dupuis and Mann-Feder (2013) suggested that youth advisory boards were the earliest manifestations of youth empowerment in child welfare and that in recent decades they have been the only visible form. But they noted a number of problems: The boards were poorly run and often understaffed or staffed by individuals with inadequate training; transportation and meals were not provided for the youths sitting on the boards, and their school or work schedules were usually not taken into account; there was a lack of funds for projects that youths wanted; the collaborations were experienced as tokenism rather than as active partnerships; collaboration and advice were sought from youths, yet little was done to implement any of their suggestions; and only youths considered to be doing well were chosen for these boards (Dupuis & Mann-Feder, 2013). The problems continue to be a common experience.

According to the National Resource Center for Youth Development (2014), 42 states and the District of Columbia reported some form of youth advisory board that related to adolescent foster care. The amount of information provided is variable. Some reported just the name of the organization (for example, Delaware has a Youth Advisory Council). Most provided a brief description—for example, "Arkansas' Youth Advisory Board has been in place since October 2000. The board is involved in discussions of policy, procedures, legal issues, and special projects and some of its members serve on other boards and advisory groups." Some (for example, Alaska, Florida, and Iowa) provided a more extensive description of the board's history, mission, and activities. This information suggests that many states aim to have a youth advisory board; there is, however, little evidence of the accuracy of the description and effectiveness of advisory board activities. California Youth Connection (Box 4.1) is the largest and most fully developed state-level youth organization devoted to foster care issues.

Box 4.1: Practice Highlight—California Youth Connection

According to the organization's mission statement, California Youth Connection (CYC) is "a youth led organization that develops leaders who empower each other and their communities to transform the foster care system through legislative and policy change" (http://www.calyouthconn. org/mission). CYC is involved in numerous initiatives. A recent policy success was its involvement in the passage of the California Fostering Connections to Success Act, which allows youths in foster care to have access to services until age 21 (discussed in chapter 7). CYC youths train each other and provide trainings in the community for policymakers, social workers (and social work students), foster parents, and other key stakeholders in foster care. Topics have included youth empowerment, legislative advocacy, and community organizing. The training projects, such as the Y.O.U.T.H. training program (discussed in chapter 8), use innovative youth-led approaches.

Given CYC's significant influence on policy and practice in California, can this model be applied in other states? CYC started out small and had limited impact, but the organization has now been active for many years. California also has a large number of youths in foster care. The large number of youths available ensures that the type of work CYC does can be spread across many people and can be sustained over time. Some states are replicating the model, but it will take a while to achieve the same level of success. The national organization Foster Youth in Action, which was started by a

(continued)

former executive director of CYC, supports the development of youths in foster care in more states. Current locations in addition to California are Florida, Georgia, Indiana, Iowa, Massachusetts, Nebraska, New York, Oregon, and Washington (personal communication with J. L. Evans, director of trainings, California Youth Connection, San Francisco, April 3, 2015).

Youths as Trainers

Clay, Amodeo, and Collins (2010) reviewed nine of 12 national projects focused on training workers to help youths transition out of foster care, which included youths in six ways: (1) key informants in needs assessments, (2) advisory committee members, (3) curriculum developers, (4) trainers, (5) participants in videos and other media performances, and (6) conference presenters. Existing youth advisory boards did not appear to play a major role in these projects.

Benefits to the youths who participated included skill building, increased confidence, a sense of identity, and a sense of self-worth associated with being heard and valued. As a group, youths also identified several challenges similar to those identified by project staff. These included their inability to participate consistently due to scheduling difficulties or life issues, logistics such as transportation, lack of clarity about their role, and lack of confidence in their ability.

Overall, representatives of the projects that participated in the study concluded that the benefits of youth involvement far outweighed the challenges. When youth involvement was implemented fully, consciously, and with focused resources, youths could contribute in meaningful ways. The authors concluded that youths are still an untapped resource in child welfare training, waiting to be engaged and empowered for the mutual benefit of the various child welfare constituencies. An ongoing challenge is to scale up such efforts so that more young people can be involved and more training audiences can have access to the benefits of youths as trainers.

Morse et al. (2003) provided a practice guide for engaging youths in foster care in child welfare training projects, which offers numerous lessons culled from all 12 projects. They identified potential roles for youths as advisers, trainers, and curriculum developers and offered specific ideas to consider (for example, offering youths opportunities to disseminate their experiences in a variety of ways) as well as challenges (for example, youth recruitment and retention, stereotypes held by adults and youths about each other, challenges of sharing power, and providing constructive feedback) and recommendations to address these challenges.

Youth Involvement in Policy Development

Courtney, Dworsky, and Napolitano (2013) described the involvement of youths in foster care in California in the passage of legislation extending foster care beyond age 18. They noted that important contributions were made by youths currently or formerly in foster care to passage and implementation of the California Fostering Connections to Success Act. The California Youth Connection was often mentioned as a key player, but there were other sources of youth input in planning and implementation across the state. The authors also noted that some youth advocates thought that the process could have been more youth friendly; meetings were often held at times that conflicted with school or work, and some youth populations (for example, system-involved youths) were not always represented.

Policy Forums

Day, Riebschleger, Dworsky, Damashek, and Fogarty (2012) reported on youths in foster care who participated in policy forums in Michigan regarding access to higher education, held under the auspices of Michigan's Children, a private nonprofit legislative advocacy organization that brings young people to speak to policymakers and community leaders. In summer 2010, Michigan's Children convened two forums to give high school students who were currently in foster care and college students who had been in foster care the opportunity to talk about barriers to completing high school and attending college. Before the forums, youths participated in advocacy and media training.

The researchers reviewed the transcripts of youth testimony and, although they did not identify a causal link with the youths' testimony, they reported the following policy actions: school supplies were purchased and delivered to attendees; the State Court Administrator's Office facilitated placement changes for a number of youths who had voiced concerns about the safety of their current placements; Michigan's Children partnered with the State Court Administrative Office to train judges, attorneys, and child welfare workers on educational disparities between youths in foster care and their peers; the Michigan Supreme Court agreed to update an education resource book for judges; the Child Welfare Services division of the State Court Administrative Office established a work group focused on building on partnership with the Detroit public schools; the state's consent decree was revised to prioritize the educational needs of children in foster care; and resources were appropriated in the state budget for six colleges and universities to adopt college access and retention programs.

Critical Importance of the Youth Voice

Empowerment of youths to participate in systems-level change requires listening to them. There are many ways to do this. Like all other individuals, young people can decide how they would like to engage, when they would like to speak, and what mechanisms they would like to use. Written products, some produced by youths, can help to tell their story, including books such as *The Heart Knows Something Different* (Youth Communication, 1996), magazines such as *Represent* (http://www.representmag.org/), and blogs such as the one produced by the Court Appointed Special Advocates (http://blog.casaforchildren.org/blog/tag/foster-youth/). Young people can also make presentations at public forums and training events. Telling their story to adults who are listening may be part of their own transition to adulthood. Audiences provide needed witnesses to the story of overcoming (Silva, 2012).

In addition, hearing the youth voice has a role in policy. The policy-making literature has been underused in furthering understanding of youth participation projects (Tisdall & Davis, 2004). The basic premise of youth participation is clear: "Without hearing and heeding the voices of those affected by the policies and practices we create, our efforts to improve the systems designed to help them are doomed to failure" (Liebmann & Madden, 2010, p. 255).

One expert (personal communication with A. Barrows, vice president, ideas42, Boston, December 15, 2014) said that efforts to include a youth voice often use a "tokenizing" approach, but there are instances when youths have been given legitimate power and voice. Moreover, people who have experienced foster care can provide a valuable reality test in policy making. They can stop or slow down the implementation of a policy that sounds good but may not reflect the reality of the lived experience of youths. Barrows offered an example related to permanency. States had to implement federal mandates regarding permanency without hearing from youths about this, many of whom may have a different view. He continued,

> There is also a significant paradox regarding youth voice. Those most in need are heard the least and are least well positioned to advocate for themselves. We usually hear from those who have benefited the most. Depending on how youth-led groups are formed, they may tend toward the more vulnerable or the better positioned. This also has challenges for large-scale political advocacy efforts by youth. One of the most successful ways of utilizing youth leadership is to make it about the collective, not the individual, and move toward a broader vision. But it remains important to hear the voices that carry more

pain and resentment toward the system. It is a challenge to get these two parts of the youth voice together: those who are more resentful can serve the role as prophet (they are unconstrained by the system and tend to speak more stridently and/or are more impolitic) whereas those who are more positive may bring more social capital. Both voices have merit but it can be hard to keep them together. (personal communication with A. Barrows, vice president, ideas2, Boston, December 15, 2015)

Conclusion

Adolescents have more autonomy and capacity than young children; consequently, there can be room for them to participate in policy and programming. This is even more the case for young adults. This chapter has focused on youths as a real and potential political force and has identified some of the challenges inherent in this: the ill-defined age group; the diverse range of issues that might be of concern; the fact that some are under the age of 18 (and therefore cannot participate in some processes such as voting); and that for those over 18, voting and other aspects of civic action are inconsistent across the age group.

Youths and young adults, unlike older people, do not have specific social policies that can unite them as a political force. Youths are developmentally busy; education and early-stage employment may be their prevailing focus. It can be difficult to engage them in organizing activities because of their already full lives. Moreover, in terms of their own development, there may be a risk that participation in organized youth political action will distract them from the education- and career-related tasks needed for a successful transition to adulthood.

Among more vulnerable youths—those involved in the child welfare, juvenile justice, or another system—the sense of potential political power is likely further eroded. The systems are inherently disempowering as a result of the impersonal and routinized nature of large bureaucracies. Those who have suffered from abuse or neglect may be particularly disempowered as a consequence; not having control over their bodies and having their voices silenced certainly is detrimental to developing a sense of voice or agency.

Yet clearly youths, youth advocates, and various allies recognize the need to change this. Numerous but largely diffuse efforts are occurring. There is clear evidence that youths, including youths leaving care, can have some influence on policy and programs. What would it take to move from small-scale organizing to greater influence and impact? Can they join with other vulnerable youths, and youths more generally? The benefits of a coalition approach on behalf of all young people offers strength in numbers. It also moves beyond a "vulnerable youth" label to potentially create more political heft. Higher education and health care are two primary areas in which large coalitions of young people might be organized to obtain better support in policy systems. The Young Invincibles organization has prioritized these two issues.

The concept of "targeting within universalism" (Skocpol, 1991) (finding ways to offer specialized assistance within universal programs) is appropriate in these broader policy efforts. Increasing supports and transitional services for the wide variety of youths in the country, not just those in care, would help all youths, but perhaps disproportionately benefit youths with extensive child welfare system involvement. This decreases the stigma associated with supports and increases the political sustainability of programs. More universal approaches to funding higher education, providing job training and employment opportunities, and health insurance, with specific or enhanced services for particularly vulnerable populations such as youths in foster care, are likely to have the most success in the long term. Several examples exist in areas of health equity (National Collaborating Centre for Determinants of Health, n.d.).

Throughout all such efforts, the integrity of the youth voice must be maintained. This serves the dual purpose of providing witnesses to stories of youths overcoming difficulties and facilitating policy development and systems change that reflects the realities of young people's experience.

PART II

Fundamentals of Policy

Policies Related to Leaving Care, Child Welfare in General, and Other Social Welfare Issues

Policies relevant to youths leaving foster care are nested within child welfare policies, which in turn are part of broader social welfare policies and need to be understood in that context. Stronger social welfare policies would likely reduce the need for child welfare policies, and better child welfare policies could avoid the need for youths to leave foster care to begin adulthood on their own.

Attention to the needs of children has waxed and waned through the years. The needs of youths have received less attention (outside the juvenile justice system), and the needs of young adults are nearly invisible in policy. Historically, care of children, like other forms of social welfare, was provided informally by extended family and community networks. Religious congregations often played a primary role, particularly in the care of orphans. In many parts of the world, these networks remain the primary providers of care. Times of social reform in the 20th century—including the Progressive Era early in the century, the New Deal of the 1930s in response to the vast social problems brought on by the Great Depression, and the Kennedy-Johnson years in 1960s (Jansson, 2015)—saw greater attention to the needs of vulnerable populations.

For example, during the Progressive Era, which saw attention to regulations protecting health and safety, there was also increased focus on to children's needs. The first White House Conference on Dependent Children was held in 1909. Other efforts during the Progressive Era included attention to working children, juvenile courts, and establishment of the Children's Bureau. Similarly, as part of the Roosevelt administration's response to the Great Depression and the enactment of foundational legislation to develop a social welfare safety net, children's needs were addressed as part of the Social Security Act; Title IV established the Aid to Dependent Children program to provide some federal assistance to low-income families with children. Often unrecognized in the current policy environment, which emphasizes getting families off public welfare, was the initial intent that financial assistance to poor families would help keep families together. Parents would not need to give up children to public authorities because they could not care for their basic needs. The 1960s saw greater expansion of the social welfare safety net. Following on the heels of the civil rights movement and the renewed acknowledgement of poverty in the United States, the federal government advanced several social reforms including medical insurance for the poor, community development, and attention to the needs of youths.

Additional policy progress has been made in recent years, most notably passage of the Affordable Care Act, which aimed to broaden health care coverage. On the other hand, there have also been numerous efforts to restrict access to public assistance programs, most notably through the Personal Responsibility and Work Opportunity Reconciliation Act of 1996 (PRWORA) (P.L. 104-193). Overall, although policy histories can trace many advances in social welfare, the United States lacks a firm commitment to broad social welfare provision, particularly in regard to family and youth policy, which have great import to the aging-out population.

Child Welfare System

In the United States, as well as other countries of the industrialized, developed world, formal systems of child welfare are guided by complex policy arrangements. In the United States, within federal guidelines, states have authority to define child abuse and neglect, develop systems of responding to maltreatment, implement programs, and develop specific policy responses. State and county systems are a major force in policy development.

Federal child welfare policies typically have ambiguous goals, have greater aspirations than are supported with funding, and can direct actions to be taken at lower levels without sufficient attention to implementation. Many of these policy challenges can be attributed to the challenging nature of the work and the vulnerability and lack of political clout of the populations the policies are intended to serve.

The existing system is a collection of programs and policies established incrementally through the years. There has been little attempt to plan a comprehensive system based on the best available evidence. The current child welfare system began to emerge as a major public institution during the 1950s. It grew in size, particularly in its investigative aspects, as child maltreatment came to be identified as a social problem requiring intervention. Many of the services provided by public child welfare systems, and their private contracted agencies, aim to keep families together and strengthen them so that children do not need to be removed from their homes. McGowan (2014) provided a detailed history of child welfare policy development.

Although it is not the preferred course of action, removing the child from the home is necessary in some cases. Substantial research has recognized the importance of family and home environment to children's development and the potentially traumatic effects of separation. This is the case even when a family is troubled and cannot provide an optimal environment for development. When a child is removed from the home and placed in substitute care, the state agency has an obligation to fulfill certain roles that go beyond ensuring child safety. The agency takes full responsibility for the children and youths in its legal custody; this includes responsibility for ensuring that they are safe; that they receive adequate physical, emotional, and educational care, including for any special needs; and that efforts are made to reunify them with their families or, when that is not possible, to develop and implement plans for a permanent and safe home (Mallon & Hess, 2014). Title IV-E of the Social Security Act authorizes federal funding to states to help cover the costs of operating their foster care and adoption assistance programs.

After passage of the Child Abuse Prevention and Treatment Act (CAPTA) (P.L. 93-247) in 1974, child protective service responsibilities began to over-whelm the child welfare system because many more children and families came to its attention. Often this worked to the detriment of supportive or preven-tive services provision and changed the relationship of worker and client to an adversarial one (Waldfogel, 1998). To receive funding under the act, states had to establish a definition of maltreatment and have a system for receiving and investigating reports of maltreatment. This resulted in a flood of reports that required investigation. Funding for services and treatment was not attached to the legislation. Hence, child welfare systems became unbalanced, addressing reports of maltreatment but limited in their ability to address the needs of fam-ilies. Many subsequent reform efforts have aimed to minimize the intrusiveness of the investigation and reorient the system to be more family centered (Wald-fogel, 1998).

As research began to identify problems with the foster care system—partic-ularly long stays in care, lack of planning for the child, and limited attempts to work with the family toward reunification (Fanshel & Shinn, 1978)—programs and policies were developed to reduce placements in foster care (by provid-ing more in-home services and more intensive casework to help families to reunify) and to work toward more permanent solutions for children in care. The major federal policy response was the Adoption Assistance and Child Welfare Act (1980) (AACWA) (P.L. 96-272), which led to several critical changes. It implemented the concept of permanency planning to end foster care drift and required states to engage in reasonable efforts to prevent foster care placement and to reunify families. It also required detailed case plans with permanency goals and six-month case reviews. Title IV-B of the Social Security Act was amended to provide more money for services to prevent placement, and Title IV-E was created to provide funding specifically for permanency planning and reunification. The legislation also aimed to reduce financial barriers to adoption by providing adoption subsidies for special-needs children. This provided uncapped entitlement funding for foster care and adoption assistance for children whose families were eligible for AFDC.

The AACWA had some initial success in reducing the number of children entering foster care and their length of stay. But in the 1980s, some troubling trends were identified: The numbers of children entering care were rising, very young children were entering care, re-entry (after reunification or adoption) was increasing, and foster care caseloads began to see more children and youth with difficulties (for example, being older or a minority member or having special needs).

As part of the 1993 Omnibus Budget Reconciliation Act (P.L. 103-66), the Family Preservation and Support Program was enacted. This program reiterated the principles of the AACWA and created a new provision in Title IV-B of the Social Security Act that provided the first funding source for family preservation and support programs to prevent the need for placement in foster care. Thus, there was a clear policy movement toward avoiding out-of-home placement whenever possible, and some attention to family-based services (albeit small federal funding compared with funding for out-of-home care).

The Adoption and Safe Families Act (ASFA) 1997 (P.L. 105-89) revised and clarified AACWA (P.L. 96-272), improving child safety and further promoting permanency options, including adoption. Impetus for the legislation was largely related to concern over high reentry rates, continued foster care drift, and growing caseloads (Simmel, 2012), as well as concern that the predominant goal of family reunification had some negative effects on child safety (T. J. Stein, 2003). Therefore, while ASFA reauthorized the Family Preservation and Support Program, it was renamed Promoting Safe and Stable Families. ASFA established timelines and conditions for terminating parental rights, authorized planning for alternative permanent options concurrent with efforts toward reunification, and shortened the time to permanency hearings from 18 months to 12 months. It also encouraged adoption. New guidelines were established for the time children should spend in out-of-home care before termination of parental rights and freeing the child for adoption. States must file for termination of parental rights when the child has been in care for 15 of the most recent 22 months (although some exceptions are allowed). The realities of families engaged with the child welfare system related to poverty, housing, incarceration, substance abuse, and many other issues make the timeline problematic.

In terms of permanency, ASFA identified preferential options for those in foster care: (1) safe reunification with their parents or relatives, (2) adoption by relatives or another family, (3) permanent residence with relatives or another family serving as legal guardians, (4) legal guardianship or permanent custody with another adult, and (5) safe placement in a permanent living arrangement not enumerated in the statute.

The general child welfare policies reviewed above, if they were more successful, would substantially reduce the number of youths aging out of foster care by strengthening families and avoiding foster care altogether; reunifying families after shorter stays in foster care; and, when that is not possible, establishing other forms of permanency (particularly adoption). Attention to these issues is as important as improving the policies that govern aging out of care.

Although not specifically aimed at older youths, ASFA has had several implications for them. Simmel (2012) examined the implications of ASFA for adolescents. The accelerated timelines for terminating parental rights and freeing children for adoption might particularly benefit infants and toddlers—those most likely to be adopted and those whose development most urgently requires attachment and bonding. Adolescents, however, are more likely to have attachment to their biological parents and to prefer long-term foster care to maintain some of that attachment. Terminating parental rights is less likely to result in adoption and may foreclose any possibility of reunification. ASFA led to an almost 73 percent increase in adoptions within the decade after it was enacted, but youths ages 11 to 19 represented only 17 percent of all children adopted in 2010 (HHS, ACF, Children's Bureau, 2011, cited in Tao, Ward, O'Brien, DiLorenzo, & Kelly, 2013).

ASFA also supported guardianship as a permanency option. Relatives were increasingly recognized as a potential permanency option that may be particularly appropriate for young people who have been in foster care a long time. Moving a safe and stable kinship foster placement into a legally permanent arrangement allows the guardian to make appropriate decisions for the child (regarding health care, supervision, and other issues), without the need for oversight by the court or the child welfare agency. Guardianship might serve the needs of the African American community, in particular, which has traditions related to informal adoption rooted in the response to slavery and postslavery migration (Leashore, 1985).

A critical challenge, however, was that although ASFA recognized legal guardianship as a permanency option, it did not provide for guardianship assistance payments. Without subsidies, kin might be unwilling to serve in the role of guardian. In the 1990s, federal waivers were granted to states to conduct demonstrations of the use of Title IV-E funds to finance legal guardianships for foster children. The waiver demonstrations, particularly in Illinois, demonstrated some success in achieving permanency and influenced federal law, which created the Adoption and Guardianship Assistance Program within the Fostering Connections Act. Many (but not all) states have since developed these programs. Early impediments included inaccurate information regarding affordability (from states) and views that guardianship was a lesser form of permanency than adoption; the biggest obstacle has been reconciling bureaucratic and cost issues with the traditions and customs of informal kinship care (Testa & Miller, 2014). Also, to avoid creating a financial disincentive to guardianship and adoption, some supports for aging-out youths (for example, higher education financial aid and some transition services) have been extended to youths who are in guardianship arrangements or have been adopted (Testa & Miller, 2014).

Significant effort has been undertaken to change individual mindsets and agency practices to continue to aim for permanent family-based solutions for adolescents in care. And there has been some success in this area. The National Resource Center for Permanency and Family Connections (http://www.nrcpfc.org) offers numerous resources for pursuing permanency options, including adoption, for older youths in foster care. But despite many efforts to reunite children and their families, find extended-family members who can fulfill a parental role, or facilitate adoption, some children remain in foster care or an alternate setting for long periods of time; as the age of leaving care approaches, they need to prepare for adulthood and be supported in their transition from care.

Policies Affecting Youths Aging Out of Foster Care

Enacted in 1986, Independent Living Initiatives of Title IV-E of the Social Security Act was the first federal policy designed to address the specific needs of youths aging out of care. This legislation was a partial response to the recognition that young people leaving foster care at age 18 were ill prepared for life on their own and clearly struggled. Before this, some states and localities may have provided some supports for youths aging out of care, but the lack of federal legislation and reimbursement for independent living services gave states no incentive to provide them.

This legislation provided federal funds to states to help adolescents in foster care age 16 or older develop independent living skills. States received federal funding according a formula based on the percentage of children in the state who received federal foster care assistance in 1984, the most recent year for which data were available when the program was established. States were allowed flexibility in the design and implementation of their independent living programs. The services outlined in federal law included outreach programs to attract eligible youths, education and employment assistance, training in daily living skills, individual and group counseling, integration and coordination of services, and a written plan for transition to independent living for each participant.

A critical restriction was that these funds could not be used for housing, despite the serious housing challenges facing these youths. Funding was also limited to services for youths age 16 and older whose foster care placements were reimbursed through Title IV-E. Other youths transitioning from foster care could not receive these services unless they were paid for by state funds. Subsequent reauthorizations allowed services to be provided to an expanded range of youth (for example, up to age 21, not limited to those with Title IV-E eligibility, for up to six months after discharge) and incrementally increased funding.

The few studies conducted on youths leaving care continued to find that they struggled to achieve a stable adulthood. Consensus was that a much greater level of support was needed. In 1999, the next piece of federal legislation specific to youths leaving care was passed. The Foster Care Independence Act amended Title IV-E to provide states with more funding and greater flexibility in carrying out transition programs. The (FCIA) established the Chafee Foster Care Independence Program, which included a $140-million-capped entitlement requiring a 20 percent state match, an updated funding allocation formula based on the proportion of a state's children in Title IV-E and state-funded foster care, and expansion of eligibility to age 21 for those likely to remain in foster care until age 18 and those who have aged out of foster care without regard to their eligibility for Title IV-E–funded foster care (previous eligibility was focused on those 16 to 18 years of age in Title IV-E–funded foster care). Also, states could now use up to 30 percent of funds for room and board for youths ages 18 to 21 who left foster care because they reached age 18, and states could extend Medicaid coverage to young people ages 18 to 21 who were in foster care on their 18th birthday.

Additional provisions included the requirement to involve young people in planning program activities, a 1.5 percent set-aside of program funds for evaluation and technical assistance, a requirement that benefits and services be available to American Indian children in the state, emphasis on accountability and outcome measures, the use of funds for training, and the requirement that state plans certify coordination among key stakeholders.

The states could use the Chafee funds in any manner that might reasonably accomplish the purposes of the program, which were to (1) identify children who are expected to be in foster care to age 18 and help them make a transition to self-sufficiency; (2) help these children get the education, training, and services necessary to obtain employment; (3) help them prepare for and enter postsecondary training and education; (4) provide them with personal and emotional support; (5) provide a range of services and support to complement their own efforts to achieve self-sufficiency.

Chafee funding could be used to serve three eligible groups: youths in foster care who are likely to remain in care until they are at least 18 years old, youths who left foster care when they were age 18 or older, and youths formerly in foster care who exited care for adoption or to live with a relative legal guardian when they were at least 16 years old. Eligibility for youths formerly in foster care extends to their 21st birthday.

The legislation stated that establishing permanency for these youths should remain the priority and reinforced this emphasis in four ways: stating that independent living services are not an alternative to adoption; requiring states to train both foster and adoptive parents about preparation for independent living; reinforcing the importance of personal and emotional support for young people aging out of care; and specifying that independent living services can be provided to young people at various ages and stages approaching independence (National Foster Care Awareness Project [NFCAP], 2000). A critical gap in regard to permanency, however, was that the legislation and its programs provided no specific focus on assisting youths to connect with family members or other adults who can provide permanency.

States that receive Chafee funding are required to provide financial, housing, counseling, employment, education, and other services to youths formerly in foster care up to age 21, although the law does not specify how much of the funding should go to these services. The only restriction is that no more than 30 percent can be used for room and board. There is no statutory definition of room and board; states can adopt a reasonable definition of room and board, which generally includes housing but may also include rental deposits, utilities, household start-up purchases, and food, for example. Agencies that receive Chafee funding are expected to coordinate with other federal and state programs for youths.

Before the development and expansion of transition-focused policy and programs, the aging-out experience was fairly standard and largely lost from view. But with the increased policy focus and the varying efforts within states, there is now much greater variability in the aging-out experience. Under the Chafee programs, states offer different levels of support and types of programming and use different eligibility criteria. In some states, youths over 18 years of age who had been in foster care can remain in the care of the state, receiving various supports with defined eligibility criteria. In other states, these young adults might be referred to independent living programs, which might be primarily housing based with potential links to other services (for example, employment). In some states, young adults transitioning from care still receive little support.

Two provisions in the FCIA of 1999 pertain to evaluation: the creation of the NYTD and the requirement for a randomized study to evaluate programming. More information on these provisions is provided in chapter 10.

A new purpose was added to the CFCIP with the Promoting Safe and Stable Families Amendments of 2001 (P.L. 107-133). The objective of the Chafee Education and Training Voucher (ETV) program is to fund states to make available vouchers for postsecondary training and education to youths aging out of the foster care system or adopted from public foster care after age 16. States may allow youths participating in the voucher program to remain eligible until age 23 as long as they are enrolled in a postsecondary education or training program and are making satisfactory progress toward completion of that program. The voucher is to be used for the cost of attendance at an institution of higher education and can be up to $5,000 per year for each student. Funds can be used for expenses such as tuition, room and board, books, and transportation.

Another policy support aimed at helping youths in foster care succeed in college is the Higher Education Opportunity Act (P.L. 110-315) of 2008, which amended earlier legislation to enable children in foster care to participate in federal higher education support programs such as Talent Search and Upward Bound and to claim independent status when they file a Free Application for Federal Student Aid. Okpych (2012) articulated two areas of weakness related to support (financial and other) for youths in foster care in postsecondary education: It ends too soon, and it varies substantially from one state and educational institution to another. All youths can apply for federal income-based grants and loans, but other sources of financial aid and support can vary.

In regard to more general assistance to transitioning youths, some states now extend foster care to age 21, providing for basic needs (such as housing) that enable youths to attend a postsecondary institution, while others do not. States have substantial discretion regarding the type and amount of services they provide through the Chafee program. Further, some states support postsecondary education using state resources in addition to the ETV, while others do not, and some postsecondary institutions offer financial assistance or other supports to youths in foster care, while others do not. Finally, there are some privately funded scholarships for youths from the foster care system that have state residency requirements (Okpych, 2012).

In regard to premature expiration of support, Okpych (2012) documented the fact that many students who enter a four-year college take longer than four years to complete their education and that foster care alumni may have particular life circumstances (such as unstable housing and the need to work) that further influence the likelihood that they will need a longer time to complete their education. Many sources of assistance for foster care alumni end at age 21, thus leaving these young people to finish their education with less or no support. Okpych made three policy recommendations: extend FCIA funding to age 25, establish campus-based support programs funded by FCIA, and increase ETV funding to reflect the cost of college.

The Fostering Connections Act (P.L. 110-351) was signed into law on October 7, 2008, by President George W. Bush. In addition to its focus on adoption, it included three provisions that affect older youths in foster care. First, youths 16 and older who were adopted or placed in a legal guardianship after the age of 16 can remain eligible for Chafee-funded independent living programs and ETV financial assistance.

Second, young adults ages 18 to 21 can remain eligible for support under Title IV-E if the state chooses to continue to receive federal matching funds for licensed placements for young adults up to the age of 21. Also, supervised independent living settings can be approved placements for youths for the purposes of Title IV-E eligibility determination. The Title IV-E eligibility provision also allows states to continue to provide adoption subsidies and kinship guardianship subsidies to providers who entered an adoptive or guardianship agreement with a youth over the age of 16 until the youth is age 19, 20, or 21, at the state's discretion. There are conditions for the young adults' continued eligibility for Title IV-E reimbursement: They must be in school, employed at least 80 hours a month, participating in a program that facilitates their employment readiness, or unable to participate in any of these activities as a result of a documented medical condition. The legislation allows states to take these steps but does not require them to do so. The states have discretion in multiple areas—setting the conditions of continued eligibility, determining eligibility, and allowing young people to reenter foster care between the ages of 18 and 21—thus increasing interstate variation in supporting foster care alumni.

The third provision of the Fostering Connections Act that affects transitioning youths is a mandate that caseworkers create a transition plan for youths within 90 days before their 18th birthday or other emancipation date. The plan should be individualized; involve the youth; and identify resources for housing, education, employment, health care, and other necessary supports.

Extended time in foster care is highly important given the known challenges these young people face when beginning independent adulthood. The Midwest Study found that youths who lived in Illinois (which allowed staying in care past age 18) had better outcomes than youths in states that did not allow this (Courtney, Dworsky, & Pollack, 2007)—evidence of the potential protective benefit of extended time in care. But it is not just the extension of time in foster care that is important. Foster care for youths ages 18 to 21 should be developmentally appropriate: geared toward permanency, client directed, and informed by brain development research using a positive youth development approach (focused on connections, high expectations, allowing youths to make their own decisions and learn from mistakes, and having meaningful opportunities to contribute to the community) (Jim Casey Youth Opportunities Initiative, n.d.). The option to return to care is also important. Young adults who return to care after aging out can have very different and more positive perceptions about their experience with the foster care system because they are choosing to engage with it (Ward, 2009).

Another recent piece of federal legislation that is relevant to youths aging out of foster care is the Preventing Sex Trafficking and Strengthening Families Act of 2014 (P.L. 113-183), which is designed to encourage states to combat sex trafficking among youths in foster care, promote normalcy for youths in foster care, help move more children from foster care into adoptive homes, and increase the amount of child support provided to families when a parent lives outside the United States. Particularly relevant is Title I, which requires state child welfare agencies to promote normalcy for youths in foster care, allowing them to more easily participate in age-appropriate social, scholastic, and enrichment activities. Absence of such opportunities has long been identified as a barrier to appropriate normative growth opportunities for young people in care.

The law requires states to support the healthy development of youths in foster care by implementing a "reasonable and prudent parent standard" for decisions made by a foster parent or a designated official for a child care institution. This standard provides designated decision makers with the latitude to make parental decisions that support the health, safety, and best interest of the child. These include involvement in extracurricular, cultural, enrichment, and social activities, including opportunities for safe risk-taking, like those typically made by parents of children who are not in foster care. Through this standard, the act intends to promote normalcy—the ability to engage in healthy and developmentally appropriate activities that promote well-being—for all youths in care (Center for the Study of Social Policy [CSSP], 2015).

Core Policy Issues: Permanency and Disproportionality

Although many policy issues require further attention, two are inherent within the child welfare system, receive significant attention, and have particular relevance for youths leaving care: young people's need for permanency, and the disproportionate presence of different racial and ethnic groups in the foster care system.

Permanency

Most relevant to the aging-out population is the extent to which permanency has guided policy and practice for older children and adolescents in care. The AACWA and ASFA provide a legislative framework that emphasizes permanency, and the FCIA states explicitly that preparation for independence does not take the place of efforts to establish permanency for youths. However, the FCIA's real emphasis is on skill building, not permanency, reflecting a 1990s approach to independent living. Permanency efforts have been targeted more to (and more successfully with) young children than older youths, whose needs in regard to permanency have not been sufficiently addressed (Avery, 2010; Renne & Mallon, 2014).

Renne and Mallon (2014) pointed to the overuse of the "another planned permanent living arrangement" (APPLA) category of permanency goals, noting that this has become the default for adolescents. The regulations give three examples of a compelling reason for APPLA: (1) an older teenager specifically requests emancipation as his or her permanency plan; (2) a parent and youth have a significant bond but the parent is unable to care for the youth because of an emotional or physical disability and the youth's foster parents have committed to raising the youth to the age of majority and to facilitate visitation with the disabled parent; (3) a Native American tribe has identified APPLA as appropriate.

Overreliance on APPLA in practice is partially attributable to guidance from the FCIA, which, as described earlier, focuses on preparing older youths for transition rather than on permanency. One study of caseworker perceptions of APPLA (Tao et al., 2013) found that often individual-level factors (resistance to adoption or mental health or behavior issues) and family-level factors (unwillingness to work on permanency planning) resulted in an APPLA designation. Caseworkers could not specify many strategies used in their practice for securing legal permanency for older youths in foster care. Instead, they focused on the need for better independent living services.

Legal permanence is not the only issue. Also critical is young people's sense of themselves as having permanent relationships. Cushing et al. (2014) examined relational permanence by analyzing a sample of youths who had been in a specialized foster care program serving older youths with histories of multiple failed foster home placements and residential treatment. The sample included youths who were adopted, reunified, and aged out. Statistical analysis identified four distinct patterns of relationships with parents and parenting figures. Those young adults who reported connections to both birth parents and parental figures showed higher levels of competence and lower vulnerabilities in young adulthood relative to the other groups. Having both a supportive relationship with a birth parent and a relationship with a parental figure seemed to confer an advantage over having one parental relationship. Conversely, young adults with minimal connections to parents and parental figures exhibited the greatest risk in antecedent experiences (for example, multiple placements) and the most vulnerability in early adulthood outcomes. The authors concluded:

> *Legal permanence was neither necessary nor sufficient alone in determining whether young adults were connected to birth parents or parental figures during young adulthood. Yet positive perceptions of parenting figures, the sense of belonging to a family while in care and consistency of parental figures over time significantly distinguished groups who were connected from those who were not.* (p. 80)

The implications are that practice must focus on the qualities of the relationships youths have with families—the relational dimensions of permanence—not solely achieving legal permanence.

Disproportionality

Children and youths from some racial and ethnic groups are overrepresented in the foster care population compared with their percentage in the general population. At the national level, this includes African American, Latino, and Native American children and families; local patterns might vary. McRoy (2014) provided a comprehensive account of issues of disproportionality for African American children, in part noting that issues of disproportionately are observable at each stage of child welfare system involvement: higher maltreatment investigation rates, case substantiation rates, and likelihood of being removed from the home, longer stays in care, less likelihood of returning home or being adopted, and greater likelihood of aging out of care and experiencing challenges after aging out.

The reasons for disproportionality are many. Families of color face higher levels of poverty, single parenting, and parental challenges related to substance use and incarceration. In addition, they are more likely to encounter racism and bias in reporting and other service decisions (for example, removal from the home) and to lack community and culturally appropriate resources, among other challenges (McRoy, 2014; Roberts, 2002). In her analysis of bias in child welfare policies, Gainsborough (2010) raised questions regarding efforts to preserve families of color through supportive services, suggesting that policies and resulting decision making regarding removing children from the home and failure to successfully reunify indicated a belief that such families were not worth saving.

Legislation has aimed to address some aspects of these disparities. For example, the Indian Child Welfare Act of 1978 (P.L 95–608) aimed to address disparities related to Native American children, who were disproportionately removed from their families and frequently placed in nontribal homes. The Multiethnic Placement Act of 1994 (P.L. 103-382) aimed to decrease the length of time that children wait to be adopted; prevent discrimination on the basis of race, color, or national origin; and facilitate the recruitment and retention of foster and adoptive parents who can meet the distinctive needs of children awaiting placement. Yet disparities related to race and ethnicity are still highly visible.

Efforts to address disparity require attention to cultural practices embedded in the system. In one example from research on African American families and the child welfare system, Jimenez (2006) found that the concept of legal contract (unitary responsibility) that undergirds child welfare may not fit with the history and culture of African American families, which approach parenting as more of a shared responsibility among kin. The tradition of kin and community responsibility is situated within West African culture and further developed in the United States as a way of protecting families devastated by slavery and as a response to employment fluctuations after slavery and migration to the north. The church community also had a key role. Thus, informal adoption of children and a voluntary agency (not public system) response were the mechanisms of addressing child welfare needs. The implications for child welfare policy have been the need for more flexibility regarding informal adoption and guardianship; the importance of kinship care and hence the need for reimbursement of relatives who serve as guardians; and the use of family- and community-based care (models such as family group conferencing and the use of churches).

There has been surprisingly little attention to disparity in regard to leaving-care experiences and services. Some evidence from outcome studies has suggested greater disadvantage among black foster care alumni compared with others (Dworsky et al., 2010). Variations in help-seeking behavior have also been identified (Scott, McMillen, & Snowden, 2015). Avery (2010) suggested the transition to independence may be especially difficult for members of racial and ethnic minority groups. For these youths, "a sense of membership in an ethnic, racial, or cultural group is an underlying issue that pervades and influences progress toward adulthood. In addition, these youths are frequently faced with discriminatory attitudes and evidence of their lower status and power in society which forces them to have to continually negotiate their sense of self in relation to other groups" (p. 403). According to recent analysis of the NYTD, black youth in urban areas received fewer services, whereas female youths and youths with disabilities were more likely to receive services (Okpych, 2015). All of these areas (outcomes, help-seeking patterns, and service availability) require more intensive attention to black youths and other demographic populations to ensure both equity and a culturally competent range of services.

Other Federal Policies

The prospects for young people aging out of the care system may also be influenced by the numerous wide-ranging policies that affect life prospects for a much larger population. These might include broad preventive and normative developmental policies that support the well-being of families and individuals as well as high-quality school systems, access to preventive and specialized health care, safe housing and communities, and economic and employment mechanisms. Numerous young people would be better off if they had all these things that supported families in the first place.

Young-adult-oriented policies need particular attention in assessing the potential development of this group. In addition to the Chafee program, Mares and Jordan (2012) identified four other federal programs potentially relevant to this and other vulnerable groups of young people: Temporary Assistance for Needy Families, TRIO Student Support Services (to help disadvantaged students complete postsecondary education), the Second Chance Act of 2007 (P.L. 110-199) Prisoner Reentry Initiative, and the Transitional Living Program (for homeless youths ages 16 to 21). These are just a few of the larger federal policies that can sometimes assist youths leaving foster care, as well as other vulnerable populations of youths engaged in state service systems.

A few transitioning youths may benefit from the federal Department of Housing and Urban Development's (HUD) Family Unification Program. Launched in 1992, this program was designed to provide special housing vouchers and supportive services to families involved in the child welfare system to prevent children from entering or remaining in foster care because of families' housing problems. Under the program, federal funds are competitively awarded to local partnerships; public housing authorities provide vouchers, and child welfare agencies provide case management services. Congress made young people aging out of care eligible for the program in 2000. Eligible youths include those who were in foster care any time after the age of 16 who are currently between the ages of 18 and 21 and are homeless or at risk of homelessness. An average of 3,560 vouchers was awarded each year between 1992 and 2001. Then, after a period of reduced funding, in June 2011, HUD awarded 1,900 new vouchers through this program (National Center for Housing and Child Welfare, 2013). Although this assistance can be helpful to youths in need of housing, it is an unstable source of funding and clearly not sufficient to meet the housing needs of the 23,396 youths who left foster care in 2012.

The ACA is a massive piece of legislation with potentially far-ranging impact, aiming to improve access to health care for large segments of the U.S. population. It requires states to provide, as of January 2014, Medicaid benefits to all youths who were in foster care on or after their 18th birthday in their state until age 26. This applies to all youths currently in care and those who would have been eligible any time since January 1, 2007. At the time of this writing, this legislation is in the critical implementation stage. The CSSP (2014a) has made the following recommendations to state child welfare agencies: Elect the option to cover youths formerly in foster care regardless of where they were in care; automatically enroll youths before they age out of care; implement a one-time eligibility determination; engage foster care alumni in designing a campaign to reach all youths formerly in foster care who may be eligible for Medicaid coverage; select the most appropriate managed care program for this population when possible; educate all child welfare agency representatives; and work with Medicaid agencies to coordinate enrollment and eligibility of foster care alumni after their 26th birthday.

Employment policies specific to transition-age youths are particularly lacking. Henig (2009) suggested that states incorporate employment programs for youths in foster care into the local employment and training programs funded by the Workforce Innovation and Opportunity Act (formerly the Workforce Investment Act). With partial implementation taking effect July 1, 2015, the act aims to increase investments in addressing the needs of disconnected youths as well as other vulnerable youths through the use of proven service models, more work experience activities (summer jobs, pre-apprenticeship programs, on-the-job training, and internships), and, for example, requirements for local areas to increase the percentage of youth formula funds used to serve out-of-school youths to 75 percent (from 30 percent under current law).

Youths with disabilities face unique challenges. When they age out, they may be eligible for benefits under the Supplemental Security Income (SSI) program if they meet its income and disability criteria. Adult disability (required for SSI) is an inability to engage in substantial gainful activity because of a medically determinable physical or mental impairment that has lasted, or is expected to last, for at least 12 months. This is a different definition than that applied to children. Children in the foster care system typically do not get SSI benefits because their federal foster care payments exceed the income limit for SSI eligibility. Thus, the SSI system would be new to most youths aging out of foster care.

Until recently, the Social Security Administration (which administers SSI) accepted applications from youths no more than 30 days before their 18th birthday (King & Rukh-Kamaa, 2013). Processing often took longer than 30 days, however, so many SSI-eligible youths leaving foster care at 18 faced a gap between leaving care and receiving SSI payments. The Social Security Administration has since changed its policy, allowing youths to apply 90 days before turning 18. King and Rukh-Kamaa (2013) evaluated this policy change using administrative data and found that the policy change may have led to earlier SSI applications among foster care youths with disabilities and shortened the time between reaching age 18 and receiving an SSI determination. Variation in state policy regarding both foster care and SSI are important. Some states allow an extension in foster care only for youths with disabilities.

Finally, there are many other policies the United States might adopt that would support family life in general. Both family policy and social welfare policy are less well developed (and have less political support) in the United States than in other industrialized countries. The United States is one of the few industrialized countries that do not have explicit universal family policies (such as parental leave and publicly funded child care) for working parents and their children (Ozawa & Lee, 2011).

Conclusion

Policies to help youths transition from foster care have developed and expanded. Not long ago, young people received almost no assistance when they turned 18 and left the child welfare system. Individuals who experienced this transition are still with us and can attest to their experience of beginning adulthood on their own without preparation or support. We have made some policy advances; funded efforts targeted to this population; engaged in substantial program development (but limited program evaluation); brought significant attention to the plight of these young people; and, overall, articulated the ongoing need for additional resources.

Improvements in supports for youths leaving care must also be considered in the context of overall improvements in the child welfare system. More stable foster home placements, greater connections to family, and culturally competent service delivery are all fundamental improvements in the child welfare system that would aid the success of youths aging out of care. This is particularly visible in discussion of enhancing youth education and employability. The foundation for success in these domains is laid earlier in life. Ensuring that the educational needs of all foster care youths are met in primary and secondary schools would likely result in improved economic well-being for youths aging out of care.

The United States has neither a robust family policy nor a policy for supporting young adults. In current social policy, neoliberal perspectives dominate, with a near-total emphasis on outcomes related to self-sufficiency. Some have asserted that self-sufficiency has become so dominant in policy discourse that it is no longer even questioned (Hawkins, 2005). Self-sufficiency and independence are frequently articulated values in contemporary American culture and are fully woven into the policies and resulting approaches. Language tells the story: the FCIA. If independence and self-sufficiency are the outcomes we are trying to achieve, a much larger, systemic, and well-funded approach is needed.

Issues important to preparing youths for adulthood are not limited to vulnerable young people or those involved in the child welfare system. More universal approaches to funding higher education, providing job training and employment opportunities, and health insurance, with specific or enhanced services for particularly vulnerable populations such as youths in foster care, may provide the most successful strategy in the long term.

Numerous policy-oriented theories and frameworks may be of use for further understanding and improving policies related to transitioning from care. Although other policy sectors make extensive use of various theories of the policy process (for example, agenda-setting, decision making, implementation, evaluation), these are seldom applied to child welfare policy and almost never to policies on transitioning out of foster care.

Chapter 6

Agenda-Setting and Policy Formation: Framing Problems and Populations

How can the challenges facing youths leaving care get more attention from policymakers? What causes policymakers to pay attention to an issue? Why do policy improvements take certain forms but not others? What factors influence the timing and form of policy changes? This chapter addresses these questions using theoretical approaches related to problem and population definition, the process of framing, and the impact of framing on policy development. This includes the social construction of target populations and the impact of that construction on policy. Institutional constraints that limit policy change are also discussed.

Very little of this rich theoretical literature has been applied to child welfare generally or to youths aging out of foster care. Yet understanding these theories is not just an academic exercise; they have implications for how policies are designed and what policy options are considered feasible. Understanding the reasons for this determination may facilitate further policy development and adoption.

Constructions of Children, Youths, and Youths Aging Out of Care

Anglin (2002) argued that "child" and "family" are social constructions: "Societies construct their understandings of the nature of 'the child' and 'the family' through a system of social customs and laws that evolve over time within the changing broader philosophical and cultural context" (p. 233). Childhood has also been described as "the consummate social construction," which developed based on the beginning of a caring concern for children (Shanahan, 2007, p. 411). Aries (1962) argued that the concept of "child" is a modern invention that did not exist before the 17th century. More recently, Zelizer (1985) argued that society's emotional sense of childhood is fairly new and directly related to the decline of the child's role as an economic producer.

Shanahan (2007) reviewed much of the theoretical and empirical work on childhood and children, particularly within sociology. Although attention to children was initially marginal in much of the sociological scholarship, both the need to protect society from deviant and delinquent children and the need to save children from social evil were core themes in the sociological scholarship of the 1900s. These themes have had an impact on the development of social policies related to children (for example, juvenile courts, child welfare systems, compulsory schooling, and labor laws).

Shanahan (2007) also noted that childhood is framed in relation to adulthood. Children are "human becomings" rather than human beings (Holloway & Valentine, 2000, p. 5). This construction of childhood informs numerous approaches to professions that work with children. Shanahan observed that the boundary between adulthood and childhood is often manipulated by adults—"children may have voice, but adults control the conversation" (Shanahan, 2007, p. 415)—and that the maintenance of childhood and particular images of childhood are important to adults: "Since the Progressive Era... healthy, happy childhoods have been equated with prosperous adults and harmonious societies" (p. 415).

The broader implication of this is that any human developmental period can be defined in various ways and is related to a larger context. Stages of development have been identified that previously were not seen to exist—recently, emerging adulthood (Arnett, 2000, 2004), and before that, adolescence (Hall, 1904). Description of children, youths, and adolescents as "adults in the making" is fitting for a population defined as "aging-out youth" or "transition-age youth." Their entire identity is defined by outsiders as "adults in the making." The often explicit link with self-sufficiency in adulthood reinforces this perspective.

Constructions of Social Problems

Social problems are also constructions. Nelson's (1984) rich study provided compelling evidence that child abuse was deliberately framed solely as physical abuse committed by pathological parents. This was necessary to gain attention in the political arena that eventually resulted in the passage of CAPTA. More divisive issues such as child neglect (related to inequitable social resources) and corporal punishment (related to parental control) were purposefully marginalized during policy discussions.

"Aging out" is also a construction. In regard to youths aging out of care, exactly what is the problem? Collins and Clay (2009) found different definitions of the problem and different potential solutions emerging from those definitions. They divided problem descriptions into two broad categories: system oriented and individual oriented. System-oriented descriptions focused on issues such as lack of provision for transition-age youths, problems with inter system collaboration, difficulty implementing new programs in complex bureaucracies, and lack of accountability. Individual-oriented problem descriptions focused on young people's challenges, such as a lack of permanent relationships, traumatic experiences, and lack of knowledge about how to live as an adult. Perceived solutions could similarly be categorized as focused on systems or individuals.

The problem of youths leaving care has often been defined sympathetically: the system's inability to adequately address transition, lack of permanent relationships, history of trauma, lack of adult living skills, and lack of resources. But there are politics involved as well. Gainsborough (2010) made the critical point that child welfare tragedies only become scandals when the public agency is perceived to have been at fault for failing to protect the child. In their study of stakeholders in Massachusetts, there was some indication that framing the problem of the public agency doing a poor job was motivated by the private agencies' interests in being able to directly access federal (Chafee Program) funds (Collins & Clay, 2009).

Broader scholarship has examined the construction of social problems (for example, Best, 1995). This emphasizes the framing of the problem to achieve agenda status (Baumgartner & Jones, 1993; Best, 1995; Cobb & Elder, 1983). Problem definitions are not objective; they are matters of interpretation and social definition (Cobb & Elder, 1983, p. 172). Best's (1987) analysis of the "missing children" problem found three different scenarios: children kidnapped by strangers, children snatched by one parent, and runaway children who sometimes returned. Although child kidnapping by strangers is rare compared with the other categories, emphasizing this scenario led to the missing children problem receiving greater prominence in the public mind and on the political agenda. On the basis of this analysis, Best (1987) identified three common techniques used to get attention to social problems: horrific stories, exaggerated statistics, and arguing that anyone could be affected.

Advocates portray social problems as affecting us all to gain attention for the issue and support for a solution. In regard to child maltreatment, this resulted in a "myth of classlessness" (Pelton, 1978), that is, the belief that the problem is evenly distributed and not related to social class. Gainsborough (2010) described how politically powerful but potentially inaccurate frames (for example, "we are all affected") can lead to ineffective policy solutions; the "myth of classlessness" ends up harming poor families who are more likely to be affected by child abuse and neglect because the remedies for child maltreatment have been focused on psychological treatment (for example, parent training) rather than antipoverty efforts. The reliance on parent training as a solution—it is a popular service offered to families engaged in child welfare systems—does not have a strong evidence base, but it is far less expensive than other interventions with a stronger evidence base (Barth et al., 2005)

Gainsborough (2010) argued that social programs focused on helping low-income individuals are not generous in scope and are politically vulnerable to reduction or elimination, and that therefore, although the myth of classlessness "may encourage a policy focus on individual pathology rather than on social structure or institutions, critics of the current child welfare system also suggest that the reality that those involved with the child welfare system are disproportionately poor and African American shapes the politics of child welfare" (p. 9).

Youths aging out of care are all poor and nearly all come from poor families. They are disproportionately youths of color. These facts are not usually in the forefront of discussion of the problem or potential solutions. Public support for addressing the problem may be eroded with a focus on race and class (as well as poor outcomes in the areas of homelessness and welfare use). Yet without acknowledgement of these facts, it can be easy to hide the root causes in social injustice and rely on individually focused solutions.

Construction of the Population

Further insights might be gained using Schneider and Ingram's (1993) focus on the social construction of populations targeted by policy initiatives, which they argued is particularly needed because of its relevance to "agenda setting, legislative behavior, and policy formulation and design, as well as studies of citizen orientation, conception of citizenship, and style of participation" (p. 334). Thus, construction of populations affects the likelihood of their receiving either beneficial or punitive policy action. Again, frames are purposefully used; political actors use frames and design policy proposals differently depending on the population.

The core dimensions identified by Schneider and Ingram (1993) are the perceived power of the target group and its basic construction as either positive or negative. Using these two axes, they identified four groups: the "advantaged" are positively constructed and have strong power; the "contenders" are negatively constructed but have strong power; the "dependents" are positively constructed but have weak power; and the "deviants" are negatively constructed and have weak power (see Table 6.1). Obviously, the "advantaged" are in the best position and the "deviants" are in the worst position in regard to policy treatment. The two core dimensions are premised on a set of assumptions related to the individual, the nature of power, and the political environment summarized by Pierce et al. (2014).

Table 6.1: Social Construction and Political Power—Types of Target Populations

		Construction	
		Positive	Negative
Power	Strong	Advantaged	Contenders
	Weak	Dependents	Deviants

Source: Reproduced with permission from Schneider, A., & Ingram, H. (1993). Social construction of target populations: Implications for politics and policy. *American Political Science Review*, 87(2), 334–347.

Schneider and Ingram (1993) argued that policies targeted at negatively constructed groups often attempt to modify behavior through coercive means, while those targeted at more positively constructed groups tend to rely on incentives. In addition, they noted that politically weak target groups who are negatively perceived by the remainder of society will be consistently disadvantaged in the policy process, for example, through lower spending (Nicholson-Crotty & Nicholson-Crotty, 2004). "Advantaged" groups have considerable control and can easily get their issues onto the legislative agenda. They are the recipients of much beneficial policy, and they have the resources and capacity to shape their own constructions and to combat attempts to portray them negatively. Conversely, for "dependent" groups, officials want to appear aligned with their interests, but their lack of power makes it politically difficult to direct resources to them. This results in symbolic policies that allow leaders to show concern but do not require allocation of substantial resources. Policy design and implementation also tend to be left to lower levels of government or to the private sector. This reinforces Gainsborough's (2010) point about ungenerous and politically vulnerable policies for the poor.

Scholars from many disciplines have used Schneider and Ingram's theory to examine a wide variety of populations and policy domains. In a recent review of this body of research, Pierce et al. (2014) identified 111 studies that have conducted empirical tests of the theory. Studies of children and child-related policies were few and primarily related to child poverty (located within the "dependent" group). One study examined providers of child care (Hynes & Hayes, 2011) identified as in the "contender" group.

Where might youths aging out of care fit into this typology? At first glance, children in child welfare systems are in the "dependent" category, with a generally positive social construction but little political power. Schneider and Ingram themselves put children in this quadrant (along with mothers and disabled people), but provided little exposition of the meaning of this to child policies.

There is an extensive scholarly and practice tradition that would indicate children are rightly situated in the "dependent" category. Their age contributes to this designation, and for abused and neglected children, their victim status reinforces it. Orphans have traditional religious claims to assistance. Children were identified within Elizabethan Poor Laws as a group deserving of assistance. The major U.S. program providing financial assistance to poor families with children was originally named Aid to Dependent Children. Once removed from their home, children's dependency status increases as they become fully dependent on government assistance.

Older children, adolescents, and transition-age youths may not be as positively constructed, however. There is clear evidence that infants and younger children are widely preferred for adoption and that older children are far less likely to be adopted (Barth, 1997). Experiences in foster care can carry stigma and the sense of being harmed by the system experience. Further, as children become older, any problem behaviors may be viewed less benevolently; they can trigger fear if they demonstrate aggression or blame if they demonstrate irresponsibility. Child welfare populations and juvenile justice populations are sometimes merged in the public mind and in state service systems. So as vulnerable abused children become troubled adolescents with poor social outcomes, their social construction likely leans toward the negative.

There is also some overlap with homelessness, both in reality and in the problem construction. There are at least two reasons for this. First, much of the attention to this problem initially came from research demonstrating foster care alumni were a substantial component of the homeless population (Park et al., 2004). As noted in chapter 2, nearly all follow-up studies of foster care alumni inquire about their housing. Such portrayals may be effective in underscoring the need to intervene to prevent these later negative outcomes. Yet these portrayals may also run the risk of leading to a negative social construction of the population and thus risking further disadvantage in the policy process. Second, it is not unusual for advocates for homeless people to state that some of them are youths formerly in foster care. This helps frame them in a more sympathetic light.

In addition, the social construction of people approaching age 18 and moving into young adulthood carries expectations of independence and self-sufficiency.

"Independent living" was long the goal of preparation for aging out. It now has a much more contested status (although it is still used in many policy and program documents), with interdependence, permanency, and community connection gaining in importance. Interestingly, the term "independent living" has a much more positive connotation in the disability community, where it is seen as emphasizing empowerment. Self-sufficiency has also received critical attention in regard to the aging-out population. Consistent with the welfare reforms under PRWORA, positive outcomes for youths leaving care include *not* receiving welfare. The emphasis on independence and self-sufficiency continues to be a key part of the policy environment, despite the contrast to the normative patterns of parental support identified in chapter 3. Poor and disadvantaged young people are expected to be self-sufficient in ways that more privileged young people are not.

Further challenges to a more positive social construction are posed by young peoples' links to families, communities, and the child welfare system. A young person might be viewed positively as worthy of intervention but damaged by the connection to family. Parental and family behaviors related to abuse, crime, addiction, and other challenges may lead to judgments regarding the worthiness of supporting families. Gainsborough (2010) noted that while we might expect the politics of child welfare to differ from the politics of welfare programs because abused children tend to evoke public sympathy, both areas of policy also focus on the behavior of parents. Negative views of poor families in general, and African American families in particular, encourage removal of children from their families. Powerful forces of racism and classism lead to judgments about the inherent worth of certain families; in practice, policies lead to consistent willingness to remove children from poor families of color (Roberts, 2002).

The entire system of child welfare was built on the need to rescue children from bad family and community environments. More contemporary efforts to reorient the system toward family support and community engagement move slowly. Potentially exciting strategies of family group conferencing and differential response remain to be fully integrated. The systems remain focused on child rescue, and suspicions regarding the families and community from which the child comes may still accrue to the child.

Child protective systems suffer from stigma as well. They are underfunded, politically vulnerable, and easily scapegoated (Gainsborough, 2010). A definition of *stigma* is "a mark or token of infamy, disgrace, or reproach" (American Heritage Dictionary of the English Language, 1980). One expert described the challenges that youths in foster care face in school systems, saying, "Society does not like teenagers or young adults." Add to this the stigma related to both a troubled family history and foster care placement and these young people face substantial stigma in various areas of their lives. Although they are entitled to an education, and need one to obtain critical outcomes, local school systems often do not serve them well (personal communication with D. Ferrier, executive director, Rediscovery and Youth Harbors, Justice Resource Institute, Boston, April 3, 2015). Commenting on recent newspaper coverage (Levenson, 2015) that described poor physical conditions (including roaches) at several local offices of the state Department of Children and Families, Ferrier asked, "What does that say about the value society places on our child welfare systems, the staff, and the families they serve?" (personal communication with D. Ferrier).

Although the positive nature of the construction may be fluid and contested, children and youth's weak power is very apparent. Young people, especially those who are poor and vulnerable, lack political power. This lack of power is further complicated in policy arenas by fear of government control and interference in private family matters (Minow & Weissbourd, 1993). Effective policy making for children and youths is complicated by other challenges: It is "difficult to disentangle children's problems from broader social problems that themselves seem insoluble"; efforts to address parts of these complex problems "run into ideological disagreements that permeate public policy discussion"; and "mobilizing constituencies for children requires eliciting a sense of self-interest that may contravene the concern for others necessary for sensible policies" (Minow & Weissbourd, 1993, p. 10).

Efforts to increase the power of young people in general and youths leaving care specifically are often case-specific initiatives that can achieve limited, well-defined goals. But vulnerable youths are still a long way from being a powerful force in policy making.

Shifts in Construction

Social constructions are not static. Hudson and Gonyea (2012) traced changing political construction of the elderly in the United States, which shifted from "dependent" to "advantaged" during the 20th century (based in part on the universal entitlement to the old age insurance program of the Social Security Act), but have more recently shifted to the category of "contenders." This, they explained, is due to weakened legitimacy of the population in the current social context, partly related to aggregate improvements in elder well-being in a time of fiscal restraints and concerns of intergenerational equity in social spending. As a population, the elderly continue to have power, but their social construction is less positive—they are deemed less entitled to benefits than they were in the late 20th century.

Change in social construction often occurs slowly and is influenced by two critical factors. The first is changes in social context (such as that which affected the construction of the elderly, as described above). The demographics of emerging adulthood are verifiable (for example, age at home leaving has increased). There was a time when young people with limited education and social advantage might have been able to secure an economic foothold. Because this is increasingly difficult, constructions of young adulthood are in flux.

The second key factor is that population members and their advocates actively seek to change their social construction, and that of the problems they face, knowing that this can influence their treatment in policy. Dependency status is highly precarious, with policy being defined by others while the target population lacks the voice needed to get beneficial treatment. A concerted effort to influence the social construction of vulnerable youths might be capable of shifting it to a category that would produce more favorable policy treatment. Although this goal is typically not explicit, numerous efforts to help children and youths gain their rights aim to shift the construction of the population to one with more power.

Outside of the United States, a rights-based approach, supported by the United Nations Convention on the Rights of the Child, is a primary mechanism for obtaining rights for children and is used in many countries to undergird policy and practice for children, youths, and families. The Convention has four core principles: (1) all rights apply to all children without exception or discrimination; (2) the best interests of the child must be a primary consideration in all actions concerning children; (3) states have an obligation to ensure every child's survival and development; and (4) children's views must be taken into account in all matters affecting them. Participatory processes are central to securing rights. Because of their age, participation in planning is particularly relevant for youths leaving care.

The United States is one of only two countries that is not a signatory to the Convention on the Rights of the Child. The reasons are complex and related to domestic legal, sociocultural, and political considerations (Scherrer, 2012). Nonetheless, a rights orientation is used in other ways. Recent legislation (the FCIA and the Fostering Connections Act) used similar language to convey the importance of youth participation in transition planning, for example.

Additional rights-based mechanisms are used in the United States. Class-action lawsuits aim to secure an improved response from large systems in response to infringement of rights. (These lawsuits are discussed in chapter 7.) A foster children's bill of rights, designed to inform foster children about their rights within a child welfare system, has been enacted in 15 states and Puerto Rico. During the 2014 legislative session, 10 states introduced 15 bills (of which, as of this writing, five have been enacted and five are pending) either seeking to establish a bill of rights or otherwise extending or defining the rights of foster children and parents, including independent living services for older youths, educational consistency and enrollment, foster child input into evaluations of out-of-home care placements, and extracurricular activities (Nowak, 2014). A children's ombudsman or child advocate currently exists in 22 states; another five states have a statewide ombudsman program that addresses the concerns of all governmental agencies, including children's services (Nowak, 2014). Although the specific responsibilities can vary by state, generally these offices investigate citizen complaints about government services and provide a systems-level approach to improving services for families.

Theories of Agenda-Setting

Constructions are only one part of the process for gaining positive attention in the policy environment. To be addressed effectively, a problem must first gain the attention of policymakers. Agenda-setting theories address how certain issues attain a place on the "list of subjects or problems to which government officials, and people outside of government closely associated with those officials, are paying attention at any given time" (Kingdon, 2003, p. 3). Kingdon's model identifies fairly independent processes, which he terms "streams," that, when they occur together, greatly increase the odds of a problem reaching the policy agenda: problem definition, policy selection, and political change.

Problem Definition

The previous section discussed how problems, and the populations affected by them, are intentionally framed to gain greater attention in the policy environment. Other aspects of problem definition are also important. These include empirical data about the problem and high-profile events (Kingdon, 2003).

Empirical data are typically necessary to focus attention on a problem. This is a part of the policy process particularly well suited to researchers. As advocates initially seek to focus attention on a problem, they typically collect data to demonstrate that the problem exists and is sufficiently serious to require public attention. The cause of youths leaving care was greatly advanced by data demonstrating their poor outcomes. These data continue to keep the cause in the policy spotlight.

Focusing events were defined by Birkland (2011) as "sudden, relatively rare, events that spark intense media and public attention because of their sheer magnitude, or sometimes because of the harm they reveal" (p. 180). The dramatic nature of these events cause the public and policymakers to pay attention and, thus, provide opportunities for interest groups to advance their political agendas. Child welfare policy can be influenced by focusing events—particularly child deaths or serious abuse while in foster care or by parents under the supervision of the system. Gainsborough (2010) noted that these high-profile cases affect agenda-setting but do not always affect policy making; occurring in a policy domain with a weak constituency (poor children and families), they may have less influence on policy than if the constituency had more power.

Discussion of the agenda-setting function of focusing events has not often been linked to issues of policy implementation. Gainsborough (2010) added this dimension by exploring the way in which focusing events can affect bureaucratic behavior as well as legislative behavior. For example, practices that minimize risk often result from focusing events. In Massachusetts recently, in response to a child tragedy in care partially due to a lapse in state oversight, there was a substantial increase in court petitions to gain custody, which caused an additional burden for the child welfare system (Schworn, 2014). A further result is that "fear of making such mistakes can create a culture of defensiveness, overprotectiveness, and reliance on procedural mechanisms rather than professional skill" (Collins, Kim, & Amodeo, 2010, p. 41).

Gainsborough (2010) also referred to Schneider and Ingram (1993) in her discussion, arguing that policymakers want to be perceived as responsive to the concerns of children, a "dependent" group; but at the same time, children's lack of political power means that policymakers do not want to spend resources to meet their needs. Consequently, symbolic responses are dominant. These characteristics also explain "the attraction of privatization as a policy solution for problems in the child welfare system. Privatization of child welfare services offers a clear policy response to perceived problems but at the same time does not necessarily commit the government to expending additional resources" (Gainsborough, 2010, p. 14). Other responses are also symbolic. Common actions following child tragedies including firing the commissioner of the public child welfare agency, forming an advisory group, calling for a report, and requiring additional documentation of case practices. A fundamental reorientation is rarely the result.

A further observation regarding focusing events in the foster care arena is that they typically involve young children. Focusing events involving youths leaving care are less common. Historically, agencies were not required to assist youths after age 18. Thus, if something happened to them after leaving care, the agency could not be held legally responsible. The factor of blame attached to the child welfare agency is less apparent. Youths who have aged out of care are largely invisible, and their suffering has not been noticeable. The data on their prevalence among the homeless population has been particularly critical for defining the problem, precisely because dramatic focusing events are rare.

Policy Selection

Policies are choices about how to address identified problems. Problems need to be coupled with feasible policy solutions to gain a place on the policy agenda (Kingdon, 2003). It is not in the interest of policymakers to select problems for attention that cannot be solved. Therefore, advocates who can propose a feasible solution for a clearly stated and compelling problem have a much greater chance of drawing attention to their issue.

Compared with the literature on problem definition, the literature on policy solutions is less well developed. It is partially covered in the wide-ranging policy analysis literature (Bardach, 2005; MacRae & Whittington, 1997). The policy analysis literature focuses on the systematic steps in the analysis of specific existing or proposed policies, whereas a more general focus on policy selection includes attention to political and institutional forces. Bardach (2005), for example, listed some solution categories—"things governments do"—including taxes (for example, change the tax rate), regulation (for example, change reporting and auditing procedures), subsidies and grants (for example, add a new one), service provision (for example, organize outreach to potential beneficiaries), education and consultation (for example, professionalize the providers of a service through training or certification), and financing and contracting (for example, change procurement practices). These solution categories are readily available and can be recommended to solve a problem by those wishing to advance their issue on the policy agenda.

Common solutions in the area of youths transitioning from care have included life skills; worker training; and, more recently, mentoring. Training in life skills was the first "solution" attached to the "problem" and resulted in the Independent Living Initiatives, the first federal policy focused on youth transition. More recently, as problem definitions have emphasized a lack of adult connections, more attention has been focused on solutions based on permanency and mentoring. These all basically fit with one of the ways in which the problem of youths leaving care is defined (for example, lack of skills, lack of relationships, and workers' lack of knowledge or skill). But they are also popular because they are feasible: They do not require a lot of resources or address systems-level change or social inequities. Mentoring, in particular, is advocated in many quarters to resolve a number of social problems. But cautions have been offered on mentoring as an overall approach to youths aging out of care:

> *The mentoring approach, particularly one-to one mentoring, remains an individual-level solution to what are inherently systemic problems. Families involved with the child welfare system struggle with poverty, mental illness, domestic violence, homelessness, and other social*

problems primarily rooted in systemic challenges related to social class, racism, and sexism....Disproportionate attention to mentoring as a solution might continue to prohibit the enactment of more comprehensive solutions to the problems plaguing vulnerable families. As is often the case in social work, both micro and macro efforts will need to occur simultaneously. (Spencer et al., 2010, p. 232)

More fundamental change is far more difficult in all program arenas; there is an inherently conservative nature to solutions proposed. Kingdon (2003) said that policies are more likely to be selected for consideration if they are technically feasible and congruent with the values of community members and accurately anticipate future constraints. In addition, theories that take into account policy histories (for example, Kay, 2005; Pierson, 2000) and institutional perspectives (for example, DiMaggio & Powell, 1983) help to explain the limited choices.

"Path dependency" refers to the influence that prior policy decisions can have on subsequent policy choices. "A process is path dependent if initial moves in one direction elicit further moves in that same direction; in other words the order in which things happen affects how they happen; the trajectory of change up to a certain point *constrains* the trajectory after that point" (Kay, 2005, p. 554, italics in original). Institutions are the mechanisms of path dependency that lead to multiply constrained choices. Kay (2005) focused on the policy level, noting that within the policy system, "there are various structures at different scales which act as institutions in shaping agents' decision making in the formulation and implementation of policy" (p. 557). Examples include budget rules, policy networks, and standard operating procedures in government departments and agencies. "Most importantly in terms of understanding policy development as path dependent, past policy decisions are institutions in terms of current policy decisions: they act as structures that can limit or shape current policy options" (p. 557). Thus, policy decisions have a cumulative effect; past policy decisions restrict current and future policy choices.

Several examples exist in child welfare. As noted earlier, the child welfare system was set up, and continues to operate, primarily for child rescue. Child safety is the first of the three goals of child welfare policy, and it receives the greatest attention. Risk and safety assessments, removal to foster care, and training about child protection continue to reinforce the child rescue priority. CAPTA emphasized reporting and investigation of child maltreatment and has had long-standing effects on the system, which led to the dominance of protective services, to the neglect of support services. Federal reimbursement for foster care has long outweighed spending for family-based services. All of these characteristics, based on prior policy decisions, continue to reinforce the child rescue ideology of child welfare. Reorientation of policies, systems, and services to support families within communities remains an ongoing challenge.

In regard to youths leaving care, some of the same forces are at work. Initial legislation focused on preparation for independent living. This led to nearly all the early work focused on this goal; independent living units, placements, and training were created, and specialized workers were trained. Now that systems have been built around this focus, it has become increasingly difficult to offer new ways of thinking to assist young people leaving care.

A related point about policy histories is that enacted policies create constituencies who then become actors in the policy system and contribute to further shaping of state and policy structures in new and consequential ways. As described by Schneider and Ingram (1993), policy motivates individuals to participate in the political process (if they are beneficiaries) or marginalizes them from the political system (if they experience the policy as threatening). For example, as discussed in chapter 4, the formation of old-age assistance policy within the Social Security Act played a key role in the creation of the elderly as a constituency; this, in turn, led to their organized presence as a critical factor in expansion and defense of these policy benefits (Hudson & Gonyea, 2012).

Additional institutional forces are found within organizations and organizational sectors. Characteristics of the "new institutionalism" (DiMaggio & Powell, 1983) include a tendency of organizations to persist rather than change, to conform to the larger field (for example, child welfare) rather than innovate, and to become increasingly similar to comparable organizations. The legitimacy of organizations is obtained from conformity to the overall field; innovations can present costs to legitimacy and should be avoided (Meyer & Rowan, 1983). The tendency is for institutional arrangements to preclude choices regarding course of action, leading to organizational inertia (DiMaggio & Powell, 1983). This is why state child welfare systems operate in some basically similar ways. Components of organizations (for example, protective services, independent living) also demonstrate homogeneity and stability.

This body of work speaks to the conservative nature of our policies in general. Policy approaches and organizational responses result from powerful forces that reinforce the status quo and lead to only incremental change. In many cases, proposed innovations are only slight deviations from existing approaches. Organizations are a key factor in policy implementation and are discussed further in the next chapter.

Political Change

Politics is the third stream in Kingdon's (2003) model. Key factors in this stream include elections, the political mood, and the influence of interest groups. In a general sense, sometimes the political environment is more open to taking action to protect vulnerable populations, children in foster care among them. Sentiment regarding the appropriateness of government taking action on social problems and its ability to do so varies over time.

Assessment of whether the political mood is propitious for advancing an agenda can be challenging. It is rarely a single factor that creates a political mood, but rather a confluence of political, economic, cultural, ideological, and sociological changes. Advocates do not passively wait for the right conditions but strategize as to the appropriate timing to capitalize on the conditions in the political environment. They also work with coalitions to influence the political mood and make it more open to social change.

Conclusion

Although the needs of youths transitioning out of foster care have become more apparent, this population remains comparatively small and marginalized within child welfare systems, which address many child and family needs and operate within highly charged political environments. Advocates need to constantly bring the needs of these youths to the attention of decision makers, otherwise they are at great risk of being overlooked within chronically overburdened systems.

Both the problem and population need to be framed in compelling ways to get policy attention. Doing this in a way that avoids pity and blame toward both the young person and the child welfare system can be challenging. Although child welfare systems do need to do more to support youths in transition, focusing blame on the system can result in more harm than good. Advocates should also be careful that the manner in which they describe poor outcomes for youths does not portray a population of unemployed, homeless criminals. The advocacy process must emphasize the need to support all young people in ways that enhance the full community.

Scholarship on the social construction of populations offers some crucial lessons. Most notable is an explicit effort to shift this population into a category that has more advantage in the policy process. Numerous examples identify the dangers of dependency categorizations. To some extent, this is the crux of the problem with the entire child welfare system. Efforts to claim power in some of the ways suggested (joining with other young people on some policy issues, exercising the youth voice in some of the ways identified in chapter 4, crafting messages in advantageous ways) may have particular potential for aging-out youths that are not available to younger children in care or their families. This is a population that is ripe for organizing itself and voicing its interests to control the way they and their problems are framed.

CHAPTER 7

Issues in Policy Implementation

Policy implementation is an essential piece of the policy process that tends to get less attention than agenda-setting (getting a problem recognized), policy formulation (developing the policy to address it), or evaluation (assessing the results of a policy). Multiple actors are part of the implementation process, which, for the most part, occurs out of the limelight.

Public child welfare systems, their private contracted agencies, and the workers who engage with youths are key actors in this part of the policy process. Many social workers work every day in a public or private agency (as administrators, managers, clinicians, and case managers) serving vulnerable populations. Their work occurs within the context of public policy decisions, and they have a critical role as policy implementers. Yet they often do not recognize that they play this vital policy role. For this reason, social workers may feel that policy work is foreign to their day-to-day responsibilities. Social work education aims to instill in future social work professionals the importance of engaging in the policy process, and policy practice is identified as a core competency by the Council on Social Work Education. Few social workers may be formal policymakers (such as legislators), but many advocate within their social work role. Use of policy implementation frameworks to conceptualize their role may be advantageous for scholarly study and practical service.

Although the real-world policy process does not fall into neat stages, the bulk of implementation generally comes after a policy decision is made through legislation or judicial review. Findings from implementation processes also provide feedback to inform policy development and lead to policy changes.

This chapter provides theoretical background on policy implementation, describes the federal–state relationship (primarily in regard to the Child and Family Review process), provides examples of policy implementation studies related to youths leaving care, and examines the core implementation concepts of collaboration and contracting. It also addresses policy change as determined by the judicial system through class-action lawsuits on behalf of children and families in child welfare systems.

Theories of Policy Implementation

Policy implementation "refers to the connection between the expression of governmental intention and results" (O'Toole, 1995, p. 42). The processes of implementation are complex, and a variety of adaptations can occur to address unintended consequences of the policy design as implemented in a particular context. Part of the reason for complexity is that numerous actors are involved. The study of policy implementation has been characterized as having an overwhelming number of variables; O'Toole (1986) identified more than 300 variables in his review of more than 100 policy implementation studies. Policy implementation theories cover the social sciences (for example, organizational sociology and political science) as well as the practice fields (for example, public administration, management, and social work).

Different types of implementation challenges may be related to different types of policies. Several implementation theorists have suggested that a classification of policy types is helpful in understanding implementation challenges. Van Meter and Van Horn (1975) offered a typology suggesting that policies with high consensus requiring small change are the easiest to implement, whereas those with low consensus and requiring large change are the most difficult. When examining implementation processes, certain variables have tended to receive more attention than others. Adequate resources are a perennial issue in achieving satisfactory policy implementation. For example, practice changes may not occur because needed resources (for example, treatment slots or reduced caseloads) were not provided by legislation. Clarity of legislation is another characteristic affecting success in implementation. Child welfare policy is recognized as sometimes advancing conflicting goals, most notably child protection and family support. In addition, key legislation has often included ambiguous phrases (for example, "best interests of the child"). In regard to youths leaving care, legislation has called for preparation of those likely to leave care at age 18 (without a great understanding of the ability to predict this) and for youth participation in planning for independence (without guidance on how to do so).

Scholars often refer to the implementation literature in a developmental sense: first generation (top-down), second generation (bottom-up), and third generation (hybrid or synthesis) (Hill & Hupe, 2002). Although these categories are recognized to be a simplistic rendering of complex phenomena, they can provide a tool for organizing this body of work. Top-down perspectives include the work of Bardach (1977), Pressman and Wildavsky (1973), Sabatier and Mazmanian (1979), and Van Meter and Van Horn (1975). These theories begin with a decision made by central government. They have assumed a direct link between policies and observed outcomes and tended to minimize the impact of implementers on policy delivery.

Bottom-up implementation theorists include Elmore (1980) and Lipsky (1980). Their theories focus on what is actually happening at the recipient level and understanding the causes that influence action "on the ground." The interaction between the worker and the client is central in defining the nature of policy implementation. Lipsky's (1980) work on the role of street-level bureaucrats in policy implementation is highly applicable to state and county child welfare and other human services bureaucracies. The street-level bureaucrat is in a position to interpret policy for the client, since the client typically is unaware of the rules and parameters of any particular policy. Organizations are often characterized by conflicting goals and time pressures within a context of strained resources. Thus, to conduct any work, frontline workers in these organizations use discretion to cope with the work pressures.

These theoretical foundations have been widely applied to public bureaucracies. B. D. Smith and Donovan (2003) applied Lipsky's theory to the everyday practices of frontline child welfare workers and found that workers were not able to use best practices because of organizational pressures (for example, time limits) and the need to conform to institutional expectations. For example, a critical best practice requires caseworkers to collaborate with parents in conducting assessments, arranging services, and providing supportive encouragement. But data indicated that caseworkers downplayed their role in helping parents change. Rather, bureaucratic pressures led to documentation-related tasks being considered core activities by the workers, and easily documentable activities dominated service plans.

Street-level bureaucrats operate with extensive discretion and may interpret policy favorably or unfavorably for a particular client given a variety of a factors, including their own views of the policy, explicit or implicit rewards existing in the workplace (for example, pressure to close cases or a focus on reducing risk to the agency), and personal biases. In helping youths access services, they are in a position to use discretion to help or create barriers. When well-intended but bureaucratic rules (for example, requirements for extending time in care) may foreclose options for youths, the street-level bureaucrat might advocate for a youth who technically may not qualify (for example, did not meet a specific goal related to school attendance) to be given another chance. Alternatively, the street-level bureaucrat may tell a youth that a specific program is not available (for a variety of reasons) when this may not technically be the case. Social workers are often street-level bureaucrats. Other street-level bureaucrats involved in youth transition include caseworkers, outreach workers, community youth workers, and foster parents.

More recent treatments of implementation add nuance to the top-down versus bottom-up dichotomy and may better reflect the realities of implementation. The majority of empirical experiences with implementation will have both top-down and bottom-up characteristics. Goggin, Bowman, Lester, and O'Toole (1990) focused on the communications between policymakers and implementers and found that policy does not typically result from commands (top-down) but rather from communication and negotiation among the actors. Goggin et al. also recognized the importance of "strategic delay" by states in response to some federal directives. Rather than being a mechanism to thwart implementation, strategic delay by states may lead to eventual successful implementation if it is used to engage in policy learning, organize resources, and encourage participation by affected groups.

Federal–State Relationships and Child and Family Services Reviews

O'Toole and Meier (2011) explicitly linked policy implementation and public management. The relationship between the federal government and state and county child welfare agencies is complex and involves various processes of reimbursement, planning, monitoring, and evaluation. Native American tribes also operate child protection systems, and many have their own administrative structure, court system, and programs.

At the federal level, HHS's Children's Bureau, within ACF, is responsible for administering and overseeing states' implementation of Title IV-E. Regional offices of ACF are responsible for reviewing state Title IV-E plans. ACF is also responsible for developing and distributing program guidance to the states. To help states with implementation ACF provides additional training and technical assistance through both the regional ACF offices and the Children's Bureau's Training and Technical Assistance Network.

In 2000, ACF began the Children and Family Services Review (CFSR) process to address federal requirements related to states' capacity to administer and deliver services effectively to children and families as well as outcomes of services for children in foster care and for children and families who receive services in their own homes (Milner & Hornsby, 2004). The CFSR process includes a statewide self-assessment and an on-site review (including reviewing a sample of cases and interviews with stakeholders). Each state receives a final report of the findings of the review and then develops a Program Improvement Plan to address any areas that did not meet national standards. If a state remains noncompliant, federal funds can be withheld.

The CFSRs have as a goal

> *to examine child welfare practices at the ground level, capturing the actual practice among caseworkers, children and families, and service providers, and determining the effects of those interactions on the children and families involved. The emphasis on child welfare practice is based on a belief that, although certain policies and procedures are essential to an agency's capacity to support positive outcomes, it is the day-to-day casework practices and the values on which they are based that most influence such outcomes.* (McGowan, 2014, p. 40)

Optimally, CFSRs provide an opportunity for the states and the federal government to jointly implement reforms at a systemic level that will lead to better outcomes.

The CFSR measures seven outcomes within three core domains:

1. *Safety*—children are first and foremost protected from abuse and neglect, and they are safely maintained in their homes whenever possible and appropriate.
2. *Permanency*—children have permanency and stability in their living situations, and the continuity of family relationships and connections is preserved for children.
3. *Well-being*—families have enhanced capacity to provide for their children's needs, children receive appropriate services to meet their educational needs, and children receive adequate services to meet their physical and mental health needs.

The CFSR also measures seven systemic factors: staff and provider training; statewide information system; case review system; quality assurance system; service array; agency responsiveness to the community; and foster and adoptive parent licensing, recruitment, and retention. Two full CFSRs have been conducted, and the Children's Bureau is planning a third round for 2015–2018.

Mitchell, Thomas, and Parker (2014) reviewed the second round of CFSR results and found that common challenges related to safety included the following: Medium-priority reports were not consistently investigated in a timely manner (24 states); effective services were not provided to families while children remained in the home (17 states); and some agencies did not consistently conduct adequate ongoing risk or safety assessments in the child's home (29 states). General challenges related to permanency included failure to file for termination of parental rights on behalf of children in accordance with ASFA (23 states). Challenges relevant to youths aging out of care included the following: When children were going to remain in foster care, they were not always placed in permanent living arrangements with families committed to caring for them long term (24 states); and young people either did not receive independent living services or the services available were insufficient (22 states). Challenges related to well-being involved many areas including insufficient mental/behavioral health services (32 states), insufficient dental health services (28 states), and insufficient coordination of educational services (28 states).

Mitchell et al. (2014) suggested that the impact of the CFSR is broader than its role in federal oversight. Other impacts include encouraging a learning environment involving federal, state, and county levels for continuous quality improvement; recognition of the need to simultaneously improve other related systems (for example, education, mental health, and the courts) to achieve better outcomes for children; increasing attention to implementation science for improving outcomes; and focusing on the need for high-level leaders (for example, state commissioners) to be engaged in vision and leadership for change to occur.

One clear observation of the CFSR process is the focus on children and family with no explicit attention to youths and young adults, another indication of the marginal status of these groups within the child welfare system. The CFSR has no specific focus on youth transition. One report that made suggestions for implementing the Fostering Connections Act (Commission on Youth at Risk, 2010) included some suggestions relevant to the CFSR: that it should encourage finding permanency for older youths; that Congress should require it to review elements of transition plans, such as housing; and that it must better involve youths in assessing child welfare challenges and crafting effective systemic solutions.

Implementation of Youth Transition Policies

There is a great deal to be learned in examining how specific policies related to youth transition are implemented. The study of implementation identifies potentially new issues to be addressed and shortcomings of the legislation that may not have been apparent earlier. Examples of lessons learned during implementation are provided in the next sections.

Implementing the FCIA

Collins (2004) discussed the implementation of the FCIA shortly after it was passed and identified several equity concerns, including highly variable state implementation, supplementation of services with state resources, varying eligibility criteria for state services, and lack of attention to understanding the characteristics of those served (versus all those who were eligible). This potential inequity continues to be a concern for the impact of federal youth transition policies at state and local levels.

Implementing the Fostering Connections Act

A recent (GAO, 2014) examined the implementation of specific components of the Fostering Connections Act: family connections, school stability, support for older youths, and states' savings from the change in income eligibility criteria for adoption assistance payments. In a nationwide survey conducted as part of this study, 49 states reported documenting youth input on the 90-day transition plan; 49 reported that the transition plan included ensuring that the youth had key documents; 36 required the plan to include intensive efforts to ensure that the young person had adult connections; 35 required the 90-day transition plan document to be separate from other planning efforts; and 28 required a transition planning specialist or outreach worker to assist the youth with the plan.

Examples of practices that worked in efforts to meet the 90-day plan requirements included prior transition planning efforts to lay the groundwork for the 90-day plan; permanency round tables (efforts to build stronger connections for older youths and increase older youth adoptions and reunifications); specialized units that handle older youth cases and receive training on the unique aspects of serving older youths in care; partnerships with the courts to train court staff in their roles; and a dedicated transition planning Web site.

Challenges to implementing supports for older youths included identifying appropriate housing for youths after transitioning from foster care (reported by 31 states); identifying supportive adults from the youth's life and engaging them in the transition planning (21 states); providing staff with the training and time to effectively engage youths in their transition planning (21 states); and arranging for stakeholders to meet for transition planning (10 states) (GAO, 2014).

In addition, the study found that 19 states had extended payments to youths age 18 and older but that budget constraints were a major factor preventing other states from doing this. Within the 19 states that had extended payments, there was also variability: 16 extended eligibility under all five allowable conditions: (1) completing secondary education or equivalent program, (2) being enrolled in an institution that provides postsecondary or vocational education, (3) participating in a program designed to promote or remove barriers to employment, (4) being employed at least 80 hours per month, (5) being incapable of doing any of these activities as a result of a medical condition; 17 provided options for supervised independent living; 17 allowed youths age 18 and older to leave and re-enter care; 12 allowed voluntary placement agreements to be made with youths; and 11 allowed foster care payments to be made directly to certain youths. Twelve of the states that extend federal foster care payments provided comments on challenges they faced in this regard. These included finding appropriate housing options; the cost associated with providing effective supportive services; the additional demand on caseworkers' time, and developing a program that meets the specific needs of older youths. States also reported challenges in designing policies to meet the needs of older youth, such as allowing youths to reenter foster care after leaving (GAO, 2014).

The study found that HHS has not yet provided sufficient oversight of the implementation of this legislation. Thus far, the department's main focus in overseeing state implementation has consisted of reviewing states' Title IV-E plans to ensure that they comply with federal requirements. The report also described the limitations of the existing CFSR process in regard to the Fostering Connections Act. It is not clear what indicators would be used to assess compliance with the new provisions. Adequate data are also lacking. HHS has not yet updated information collection requirements for case-level data for AFCARS (GAO, 2014).

The report provides recent and broad information about the implementation, thus far, of the Fostering Connections Act. I have primarily looked at its youth-related provisions and identified some of the challenges consistent with the scholarly literature on implementation. States are more successful at implementing the easiest provisions of the legislation (for example, documenting youth input to the 90-day transition plan). States are more challenged with the more resource-intensive provisions (for example, extension of foster care past age 18, which several states identified as a problem). Core mechanisms for ongoing monitoring of implementation are lacking. In particular, the CFSR process and the development of appropriate data systems have not kept pace with the policy. Finally, unevenness in policy implementation continues a pattern of inequity across states in their assistance for youths in transition.

Implementing the California Fostering Connections Act

Courtney et al. (2013) offered an extensive case study of the implementation of California state legislation to extend foster care to age 21. The California Fostering Connections to Success Act was passed by the state legislature and signed into law in September 2010. Sponsoring organizations included the Service Employees International Union (representing many of the state's public child welfare workers); the County Welfare Directors Association; the Judicial Council; California Youth Connection; and the California Alliance of Child and Family Services (an association of child welfare services providers), as well as several other youth-focused organizations (Courtney et al., 2013).

Stakeholders realized early in the implementation planning process that further legislation was needed to bring sections of the law into compliance with federal standards and to address some challenges that arose during implementation.

The resulting "clean-up" bill made changes, among other things, to provisions regarding youths returning to care after age 18. Under the original bill, youths could leave and reenter care an unlimited number of times before age 21, based on the assumption that the federal government would allow California to treat these absences from care like trial home visits for the purposes of claiming Title IV-E reimbursement. However, it became clear that federal requirements would create some complications (for example, requiring monthly visits with social workers and six-month court reviews) if the state wished to claim IV-E funds when young people reentered care. The clean-up bill addressed this problem by allowing cases to be dismissed and placed in "general jurisdiction" if youths decided to leave care. Youths could later reenter by signing a voluntary reentry agreement (Courtney et al., 2013).

This process well represents many of the complexities inherent to implementation. Legislation that appears fairly straightforward—extension of care to those older than 18—becomes complicated during implementation. Each state that extended time in foster care was required to engage in similar processes of amending state legislation and then putting in place the necessary rules, procedures, and structures. During these processes, numerous challenges might arise requiring additional attention and potentially further legislation.

Extending Medicaid Coverage

The ACA, as of 2014, made all youths who were in foster care on their 18th birthday eligible for Medicaid until age 26. To explore potential implementation issues, a recent study (Pergamit, McDaniel, Chen, Howell, & Hawkins, 2012) reviewed 30 states' earlier exercise of a federal option to expand Medicaid coverage to youths formerly in foster care until their 21st birthday (referred to as the Chafee Option) and applied lessons from that experience to state-level implementation of the ACA. In states that implemented the Chafee Option, a small number gave the entire authority for developing procedures to the Medicaid agency, with limited involvement from the child welfare agency. In these states, the Medicaid agency typically tried to make the enrollment and recertification process for these youths fit into the existing Medicaid framework. Pergamit et al. (2012) warned that, as states implement the ACA, foster care alumni (a fairly small group) may be incorporated in a way that minimizes the burden to the Medicaid agency at the group's expense. They also noted that one of the biggest challenges states will face in implementing the provision for youths formerly in foster care is keeping them aware of their eligibility. Youths who lose Medicaid eligibility under other criteria or who lose a job that had provided health insurance benefits remain eligible for Medicaid as foster care alumni until they turn 26 years old.

Implementing the Preventing Sex Trafficking and Strengthening Families Act

As mentioned in the review of policies, the Preventing Sex Trafficking and Strengthening Families Act (P.L. 113-183) was signed into law on September 29, 2014. This legislation aims to expand the opportunities for youths in foster care to participate in developmentally appropriate activities. Youths in foster care have often been unable to participate in the extracurricular, social, and cultural activities that are common to their age group. Exclusion from these activities can have a detrimental effect on development and increase feelings of stigmatization.

The CSSP (2015) offered the following suggestions for implementing this legislation: (1) Incorporate "nurturing" into the definition of a reasonable and prudent parent (because all youths in foster care have experienced some form of grief, loss, or trauma). (2) Include protective and supportive factors when establishing requirements for reasonable and prudent decision making. This includes providing guidance to caregivers on what should be considered when acting as a reasonable and prudent parent (for example, specific language that caregivers provide concrete support in times of need, and suggestions for building youth resilience). (3) Ensure that the healthy sexual development of youths in care is addressed in both formal and informal settings, including a youth's home environment. (4) Leverage existing financing structures (for example, Title IV-E waivers) to fund programs that support well-being for youths in care. Because the legislation was passed so recently, issues of implementation (for example, amending state legislation if needed, communicating across and within agencies, allocating needed resources, and training personnel) will receive primary attention in the next few years.

Collaboration and Contracting

Along with the public child welfare agency bureaucracy, the vast array of public and private organizations with which it collaborates and contracts are also part of the policy implementation process. Both formal contracted agreements and informal collaborations related to networks of services, shared resources, and shared problem solving are elements of policy implementation. The eventual interaction of (public or private) agency staff with the youth is an additional, and often critical, step in the implementation of policy. Regardless of any prior steps at the federal or state legislative level, and the administrative practices of the public agency and contracted providers, unless the staff act in concert with the policy as designed, the youth may never be affected (either positively or negatively) by the policy. This section focuses on collaboration and contracting as part of implementation. The next chapter examines training as one mechanism to facilitate implementation of policy.

Collaboration. Both top-down and bottom-up models of policy implementation suggest hierarchy. More recent scholarship has suggested that horizontal relationships as well as vertical relationships are important to the policy implementation process (Hill & Hupe, 2002). The concepts of "policy network" and "policy community" use this more complex model of relationships. Effective implementation often depends on a collaborative network.

Although there is extensive writing on the need for collaboration, experiences of collaborations, and challenges to collaboration, the empirical research base regarding interorganizational efforts in the human services is limited. Collaboration is defined and conceptualized in various ways. Moreover, it is often required by funding agencies and, therefore, organizations have an interest in it even if it entails challenges and its effect on outcomes is unclear. Chafee plans require documentation of collaboration in the planning process. The state plan must detail the planned implementation of the program and certify the collaborative process in the development of the application. In addition, collaboration should include input from youths in foster care and key stakeholder groups such as service providers.

The outcomes of interorganizational collaboration remain uncertain (O'Looney, 1997). Longoria (2005) suggested there are symbolic qualities to collaboration; organizations need to be perceived as collaborators to gain legitimacy.

> *The apparent popular notion that collaboration will enhance human service delivery systems is questionable at best and deceptive at worst. Although the concept offers promise on conceptual grounds, explicating specific outcomes and clarifying the process of an interorganizational collaborative relationship must receive the same enthusiasm, as promoting the popular and symbolically powerful phrase "let's collaborate" appears to garner.* (Longoria, 2005, p. 132)

Longoria (2005) traced some of the conceptual origins of collaboration in social welfare policy and found that much of it is related to an effort to better integrate services that are often provided and funded through a range of categorical and siloed streams that are inefficient, potentially redundant, and often leave significant gaps in services. A recent community study identified exactly this type of role for collaborations at the community level: Many helpful ways were identified in which state agencies, nonprofit organizations, and congregations worked together, and through networks of trust, organized services to meet needs not covered by more formal programs (Garlington, 2015).

Studies of collaboration within children's services have found mixed results. Glisson and Hemmelgarn (1998), in a Tennessee-based study, found that effort to coordinate public child-serving agencies was negatively associated with the quality of services provided. Palinkas et al. (2014) examined collaboration between public child-serving agencies in California to implement evidence-based practices. On the basis of interviews with several agency leaders, they found the collaborations did not hinder the adoption of evidence-based practices and in some cases were central to the adoption. Observing collaboration on training initiatives regarding transitioning youths, Collins et al. (2007) found no consistent evidence that selection, engagement, and maintenance of collaborative partners was done for well-defined purposes.

A feedback loop is an essential component of an implementation model (Goggin et al., 1990, p. 40). States and counties are part of the feedback mechanism. Gainsborough (2010) argued that although reforms implemented in response to a child welfare scandal may not always fix the problem they targeted, they alter the political trajectory of the policy area. Thus, policy feedback mechanisms are created that affect future policy making. Examples include formation of child advocate's offices, which lead to ongoing agenda-setting opportunities for advocates and movement toward privatization of services, which further engages numerous agencies in setting the policy agenda.

Client constituencies are also key collaborators that can provide feedback during policy implementation. Once again, power is a key concept. Powerful constituencies can effectively have input into the policy process in the implementation phase (as well as the agenda-setting and policy formulation phases).

In regard to feedback loops, classic work by Hirschman (1970) identifying the concepts of "exit," "voice," and "loyalty" is relevant. Young people in public systems rarely have the option to exit (except by running away) and have little voice to seek alternative placement settings. This reinforces the importance of voice in using the policy process to secure high-quality services and treatment. This voice is an important part of the implementation process. Although consumer satisfaction surveys have numerous limitations, measuring program satisfaction in meaningful and ongoing ways is particularly important in youth services because young people typically lack the power to express dissatisfaction in other ways and generally cannot display dissatisfaction by terminating services. Collins, Lemon, and Street (2000) argued that attention to increasing program satisfaction would keep young people in programs longer, which may be needed to attain important outcomes. Satisfaction is also related to participants' rights: "Consumers of services have a right to be treated in ways that they view with satisfaction. Programs cannot successfully affect outcomes unless program participants remain in the program for a sufficient period" (p. 293). Data regarding client satisfaction can also be used as part of the contract monitoring process to ensure that clients find services helpful.

Contracting. Contracting processes involve decisions regarding contract offers, monitoring mechanisms, and continuation or termination of contracts. Performance measurement is considered part of the contract process.

In recent years, the nonprofit sector has undergone substantial change, including a trend toward privatization of services, the increasing role of for-profit care, reforms of the welfare system, use of managed care models, and an increased emphasis on accountability. Historically, government, nonprofit (religious and secular), and for-profit organizations have all delivered social welfare services, albeit in different proportions, at different times, and in different sectors. For much of the last century, public child-welfare systems have relied on private non-profits to deliver services. What has changed in contracting processes has been the increased emphasis on managed care principles and contracting based on program performance and incentives (Collins-Camargo, McBeath, & Ensign, 2011).

Characteristics of managed care include gate-keeping and monitoring functions, capitation of payment related to predetermined units of service such as number of clients or number of days of service, assumption of financial risk by providers related to expenses not covered by contracted payment agreements, financial controls to limit benefits and use of services, and separate payment arrangements for costly specialized services (Quality Improvement Center on the Privatization of Child Welfare Services, 2006). Contracts identify both incentives and risks that induce the contracted agency to act in accordance with agency policy goals (for example, increased adoption). "Problems occur, however, when the lure to achieve contracted outcomes overrides the interests of individuals" (Zullo, 2006, p. 26). Both reunification and adoption are generally good outcomes, for example, but incentives to achieve them may cause contractors to promote them even when not in the best interest of a particular child or family. Monitoring of contracts is needed to ensure protection of clients, but rigorous monitoring increases administrative costs (Zullo, 2006).

Steen and Smith (2012) used a systems framework to compare public and private foster care agencies. They noted an increase in the use of private agencies for a range of foster care services and argued that this increase has been advanced by claims of the superiority of the privatization model without accompanying evidence. Reviewing published studies, they found little research and mixed results on the key child welfare outcomes of safety and permanency. They also found little evidence of cost savings.

They also found that public and private agencies differed in regard to their relationships with policymakers and funders. Private agencies generally have greater autonomy. When a large part of its budget is funded by a government contract, a private agency's autonomy may decrease; but even then, it has fewer restrictions on its ability to lobby policymakers. "Though there are no empirical comparisons of public and private child welfare agencies' relationships with policymakers, the private child welfare agency administrator appears to have a clear advantage over the public child welfare agency administrator" (Steen & Smith, 2012, p. 855).

In regard to relationships with funders, Steen and Smith (2012) reported that although public foster care agencies have the advantage of stable funding, private agencies have the advantage of negotiating power. Public agencies receive federal funding (primarily through Title IV-B and Title IV-E) as well as state funding. These are also sources of significant funding for private agencies, but the funding occurs through contracts, with payment mechanisms based on number of cases, outputs (for example, home visits), outcomes (for example, reunification), or a combination. Steen and Smith concluded that although private agencies have some leverage to attain favorable contracts, there are also disadvantages related to the unpredictability of case outcomes and case-related expenses.

Collins-Camargo et al. (2011) found, on the basis of interviews with key informants from child welfare systems in 2006 and 2008, that 18 percent of states in 2006 and 23 percent of states in 2008 had some privatized case management. Interviews in 2008 indicated that 27 of 47 states were using performance-based contracts that linked reimbursement to achievement of performance milestones. "One overriding theme that emerged from these study sites was *managers' deliberate efforts to develop interorganizational partnerships to improve child welfare service delivery*" (p. 505). The authors examined how managers initiate and respond in privatized and performance-based contracting environments, which have become highly complex as a result of the multitude of organizations and actors in social services delivery networks, and which influence multiple processes. They also reported that some public and private child welfare agency administrators developed interorganizational networks prior to contract implementation and used them to build alliances, clarify contractual goals and procurement strategies, and provide mechanisms for community input.

Performance measures must give the state enough information to determine whether a contractor is performing to standards. But identifying and using good outcome measures is challenging. There can be disagreements about performance standards; there is typically delay between an intervention and its expected outcomes; and contracted agencies do not have full control of conditions that affect outcomes (Romzek & Johnston, 2005). Networking issues are central. Although contract managers typically have training in hierarchical systems, the realities of current public management include horizontal relationships and systems of networks, which are far more fluid and difficult to manage (Romzek & Johnston, 2005).

Lynch-Cerullo and Cooney (2011) identified some of the challenges that managers face in regard to performance measurement. Resources are key. Citing Independent Sector (2009), they stated that about 75 percent of all nonprofit organizations have budgets of less than $500,000. Furthermore, they cite Carman (2009), who found that the majority of nonprofit organizations use internal funds to support evaluation and performance management, while one-quarter allocate no funds for these activities. This would greatly explain the challenges of evaluating aging-out programs. Another challenge is finding appropriate evaluation measures. Many factors outside program control also clearly influence client lives; multiple programs may be working with the same client, thus making it difficult to measure the effects of any specific program activity, and many clients may improve or attain outcomes without specific program help (Lynch-Cerullo & Cooney, 2011).

There has been little focus on the impact of contracting relationships on aging-out programs and services. One such study compared different means of providing services (predominantly private, hybrid, and predominantly public) in various locations and found that outcomes appeared unrelated to whether service was provided by a private or public entity or in a centralized or decentralized fashion, but rather to the direction and strength of leadership, measurable outcomes, and accountability (Han, Hsu, & Ishikawa, 2009).

Although there is no compelling evidence that privatized services are more effective in achieving outcomes, there can be other reasons for states to use them. The resulting web of relationships may expand the policy network, leading to more influence in policy processes. Increased privatization may also have symbolic value, indicating that change is occurring after a child-related tragedy in which the public system was perceived to be at fault (Gainsborough, 2010). Politics are also involved in regard to who gets to control the money associated with service provision (Collins & Clay, 2009).

Class-Action Lawsuits

Class-action lawsuits—alleging that a public agency has caused harm by failing to provide needed services—are another mechanism for achieving change in child welfare systems. A recent study by the CSSP (2012) found approximately 70 class-action lawsuits pending or having affected some aspect of child welfare practice in nearly 30 states, and almost 20 states currently working to implement consent decrees or other court orders. (In a consent decree, the agency agrees to take specific actions to improve the system but does not admit to fault for the harms alleged in the lawsuit. The court continues to provide oversight during the time the consent decree is in force, to ensure that the state agency complies with it.)

In child welfare, the primary class-action litigant is Children's Rights, Inc., an organization based in New York City. According to its Web site, Children's Rights is involved in 16 class-action lawsuits (see http://www.childrensrights. org/our-campaigns/class-actions/). Such lawsuits are often filed in regard to conditions such as abuse or neglect of children in foster care, lack of services or treatment for youths in foster care, untimely processing of youths within the system, multiple placements, lack of follow-up on cases, and problems with caseload size or case management. When successful, they can lead to implementable reforms to the state agency that oversees youths in foster care.

As is typical of class-action lawsuits, these 16 cases address numerous deficiencies in the child welfare systems' approach to addressing the needs of children in their care. Concerns related to youths aging out of care are not a primary focus but are often a part of the case. For example, in *Connor B. v. Patrick* (2011), among the many complaints, the class-action lawsuit alleges that "[a]pproximately 900 children 'age out' of DCF foster care every year with no permanent family, a substantial number of them inadequately prepared to live independently as adults" (p. 2). This case is currently on appeal, and hence, no remedy to this complaint has been implemented through the court system.

In cases in which a decision has been rendered, periodic monitoring reports provide extensive information regarding the child welfare system's efforts to meet the conditions of the court order and outcomes achieved. Review of the monitoring reports identifies some of the ways in which class-action lawsuits have led to efforts to improve youth transition experiences.

I provide three examples. In the District of Columbia, the 2010 court-ordered Implementation and Exit Plan includes requirements that the Child and Family Services agency develop policies and protocols for linking transitioning youths to needed adult services, employment services, and opportunities for mentors. It also requires that the independent living specialists provide consultation to social workers managing cases of youths ages 16 to 17 years to complete an assessment instrument and that youth transition conferences plan for transition to adulthood. The most recent monitoring report for the Michigan case *Dwayne v. Snyder* reported that the Michigan Department of Human Services agreed to provide increased higher education supports at Western Michigan University (through the Seita scholars program) and to ensure health coverage through the Medicaid program for the aging-out population. A recent monitoring report of the New Jersey case *Charlie and Nadine H. v. Christie* (CSSP, 2014b) similarly provides extensive documentation regarding a number of efforts to improve the child welfare system. In regard to youths leaving care, some of these services have included extending support and services to age 21, increasing attention to permanency for older youths, implementation of Permanency Roundtables, and reorganization of Youth Advisory Boards.

Such lawsuits can play an important role in shaping child welfare policy and ensuring appropriate services (Cohen, 2005; Mezey, 2000; Oppenheim, Lee, Lichtenstein, Bledsoe, & Fisher, 2012). But research suggests that they have a mixed legacy. Although some significant and lasting improvements have occurred, "there are also examples where expectations have exceeded results, where one problem has been solved only to create another, or where it has simply taken far too many years to achieve the anticipated improvements of the litigation" (CSSP, 2012, p. iv).

Conclusion

Implementation is a critical but complex process. Advocates have worked (and continue to work) to focus more attention on the needs of youths aging out of foster care, and to promote legislation that provides them more time in care, more access to resources, and more sustained efforts to achieve permanent connections. With hard-won victories come implementation challenges, often related to a host of complexities involving large state bureaucracies that work within federal guidelines. The manner in which policies are implemented affects workers' choices and clients' experiences. Workers, and to some extent clients, also have opportunities to influence policy and implementation.

Implementation is complex and involves numerous processes and participants, and it is not easy to understand or observe. Early conceptualizations of the policy process saw it as a series of stages (for example, agenda-setting, policy formation, implementation, and evaluation). The reality has been found to be far more complex—with blurred boundaries between stages, skipping or combining stages—and circular processes. Street-level bureaucrats craft policy on the ground during implementation. Implementation is also critically related to administrative practices such as contracting, performance monitoring, and training, and is frequently community based and requires collaboration. Implementation requires significant attention in any effort to create and sustain evidence-based policy interventions. Thus, improving outcomes for youths formerly in foster care requires attention to the practices identified in this chapter.

PART III

Furthering Best Practice

CHAPTER 8

Developing a Workforce to Assist Transition-Age Youths

All professions require training, but in the social services, training takes on particular importance, because the worker, and the relationship the worker is able to form with the client, are the essence of the service. Workers' effective "use of self" is critical to establishing a relationship to conduct the work leading to client attainment of goals. Any effective program model has the worker at the center, demonstrating knowledge of the content area, a supportive attitude toward the client, and skill in delivery of the specific service. The workforce is also critical to policy implementation. For effective implementation to occur, workers generally need to be knowledgeable about a policy, supportive of it, and capable of acting in accordance with its intent.

Two primary workforces are engaged in assisting youths with transition: the child welfare workforce and the youth services workforce. Although they overlap to some extent, they have very different traditions. Social work is closely aligned with the child welfare workforce but less fully visible in the youth services workforce, which has a wide variety of disciplinary backgrounds, of which social work is only one.

Professionals who help youths transition from foster care may work in a variety of settings. Those who work in public child welfare agencies operate within a bureaucratic context guided by substantial rules and regulations. Private agencies may have greater flexibility but, particularly if large and funded by government contracts, share much of the same organizational structure and operations. Organizations that operate within community settings may have greater informality and fluidity. Those who work with youths leaving the care system are found in all of these environments.

Topics relevant to the workforce assisting youths transitioning out of care include the differing traditions of the child welfare and youth services workforces, necessary competencies and attributes for assisting transitioning youths, and the workforce as a factor in policy implementation through its role in administrative practice.

Child Welfare Workforce

There has been consistent attention to the need to develop and support a high-quality workforce in child welfare, in large part through professional social work education. "The workforce is the most important and expensive resource that agencies must invest in to achieve their goals and objectives" (National Association of Public Welfare Administrators, 2011, cited in Munson, McCarthy, and Dickinson, 2014, p. 624).

Yet, despite its critical role, several authors have commented on the "deprofessionalization" of social work within child welfare through the decades (Blome & Steib, 2014; Ellett & Leighinger, 2007; Munson et al., 2014). Numerous forces have led to deprofessionalization, including the impact of CAPTA (which led to an influx of cases and the need to recruit more staff) and increasing regulation and administrative restructuring to reduce the complexity of the work (which allowed a less professionally trained workforce) (Ellett & Leighninger, 2007). Effects of this deprofessionalization have included segmentation of the work into separate program areas (for example, investigations and adoption), greater reliance on tools to support decision making, increased outsourcing of clinical services, and step-by-step policies and training curricula substituting for comprehensive professional knowledge (Ellett & Leighninger, 2007).

Recruitment and retention issues also receive substantial attention in the professional child welfare workforce (Alwon & Reitz, 2000). This includes understanding issues related to job satisfaction, the impact of low job satisfaction on worker turnover, and the negative implications of turnover for the quality of services (Faller, Grabarek, & Ortega, 2010). The organizational climate as perceived by workers in the child welfare system (for example, Glisson & Hemmelgarn, 1998) is also important. A positive organizational climate includes factors such as a sense of professionalism, opportunities for professional development and career advancement, effective supervision, and various administrative practices that support the work. There is widespread acknowledgement that developing mechanisms for hiring, training, supporting, and evaluating the staff members who deliver services are necessary components of an effective workforce and critical to the quality of services.

Morrison (1997) argued that the purpose of child welfare training has often been misunderstood by policymakers, senior administrators, and organizations as a whole. Misperceptions include "that training should deal with poor performance, resolve staff stress, act as a substitute for a lack of policy, or as a conduit for difficult messages" (p. 23). There may be demands for short-term training to solve organizational problems, or to put a large number of staff through training programs simply to show that something has been done.

If conducted for these purposes, training serves a symbolic purpose without affecting staff performance. This can damage the potential for training to be an effective instrument of change. In such a climate, management support for learning is equivocal, participants fail to engage, there are more frequent organizational intrusions into the learning environment, organizational problems are minimized or denied, training is not evaluated or followed up, and the overall credibility of training is reduced (Morrison, 1997). Training efforts can be wasted if the resulting knowledge and skills cannot be applied because of organizational constraints (for example, procedural demands, excessive caseloads, high staff turnover, insufficient supervision, or a poor organizational climate) (Gleeson, Smith, & Dubois, 1993). Numerous other barriers to the effective application of classroom training to the work setting have been identified (Curry, Caplan, & Knuppel, 1994).

There has been some federal support for child welfare training initiatives. Federal funding for child welfare originated under Title V of the 1935 Social Security Act. From 1935 to 1962, amendments were added enabling a variety of child welfare expenditures, including for training. In recent decades, federal funding for child welfare training has primarily been available through two amendments to the Social Security Act: Title IV-B (Section 426) and Title IV-E. Thomas (2012) reviewed the Children's Bureau's role in supporting the child welfare workforce from its origins early in the 1900s to the present day. This has included investing in a competent workforce; guiding professional development; and providing policy guidance, expert consultation, and funding to the states.

Critical innovations related to the child welfare workforce have included realistic recruitment that gives applicants an accurate description of work in child welfare, more effective screening and selection, competency-based child welfare training and specialized social work education, attention to the critical role of supervision, peer-to-peer models of professional support, and a positive organizational climate that supports a learning- and results-oriented environment (Munson et al., 2014). The last three of these are particularly important to policy implementation. Supervisors, for example, have a critical role as unit leaders. Their inclusion in initiatives related to policy and practice change requires involvement in activities related to quality assurance; program evaluation; redesign of information systems, forms, and procedures; and engagement in staff training (Hess, Kanak, & Atkins, 2009).

Another factor reinforcing the importance of child welfare training is the CFSR, which often stresses the need for staff development and training to improve program services. The state-developed Program Improvement Plans that result from the CFSR process frequently identify staff development and training as strategies to improve service delivery (Amodeo, Bratiotis, & Collins, 2009).

A recent study of child welfare training across the United States (Armstong, Coy, McNeish, Menendez, & Policella, 2013), which included a review of the second round of CFSR reports, identified 34 states in which staff training was found to be in substantial conformity with CFSR benchmarks. Although state curricula for specific job functions (such as adoptions, supervision, hotlines and intake, licensing, and children's legal services) varied, every state provided training for child protective investigations and ongoing case management and had training components for new staff (pre-service) and existing staff (in-service). Armstrong et al. found that most state training curricula provide opportunities for interpersonal skill building, practice-based course work, and instruction in promising or evidence-based practices, and include time frames for training completion and training delivery methods. All but three states provided a combination of classroom and field-based activities in their pre service training programs. Most states had an additional training component for supervisors. There was usually a mandated number of in-service training hours to be completed within a prescribed period; these requirements often differed on the basis of the position.

Sample training resources provided in this report suggest very limited attention to adolescents. Common themes included child development, court decorum, cultural competence, evidence-based practice, domestic violence, education needs, ethics and values, father engagement, LGBTQ youths, normalcy, permanency, placement stability, psychotropic medications, and co-occurring substance abuse and mental health disorders. One of the listed resources was explicitly related to achieving permanency for older youths, and one was specific to LGBTQ youths. None of the others were specific to a youth focus, although many of them were relevant to youths in transition. This suggests that transition-related issues are not receiving significant attention in many state training programs.

Youth Care Workforce

The youth care workforce is separate from the child welfare workforce. Although social work has a long history in child welfare and as a profession has been central to developing and leading the field, social work does not have primacy in the field of youth work.

Youth work in the United States is a "contested field" with "multiple competing definitions, disciplinary frames, and desired outcomes" (Roholt & Rana, 2011, p. 321). The career path of youth workers is highly variable; most do not set out to be youth workers. They have various backgrounds, educational qualifications, and disciplines; typically did not study in a youth-work-specific program; and have a variety of job titles of which youth worker is only one (Roholt & Rana, 2011). Community and social change is a recognized component of youth work, as well as changing misconceptions about youths, creating opportunities for youths, and expanding public roles for youths (Roholt & Rana, 2011). Like social work, youth work can be challenged by low pay and work conditions that result in burnout (Anderson-Nathe, 2008).

Roholt and Rana (2011) suggested that lack of clarity and definition concerns some in the field, leading to efforts to unify and define the field. A key effort to do so is the description of child and youth care practice:

> *Professional Child and Youth Care Practice focuses on infants, children, and adolescents, including those with special needs, within the context of the family, the community, and the life span. The developmental-ecological perspective emphasizes the interaction between persons and their physical and social environments, including cultural and political settings. Professional practitioners promote the optimal development of children, youth, and their families in a variety of settings, such as early care and education, community-based child and youth development programs, parent education and family support, school-based programs, community mental health, group homes, residential centers, day and residential treatment, early intervention, home-based care and treatment, psychiatric centers, rehabilitation programs, pediatric health care, and juvenile justice programs. Child and youth care practice includes assessing client and program needs, designing and implementing programs and planned environments, integrating developmental, preventive, and therapeutic requirements into the life space, contributing to the development of knowledge and practice, and participating in systems interventions through direct care, supervision, administration, teaching, research, consultation, and advocacy.* (Association for Child and Youth Care Practice, 2010, p. 2)

Given the importance of the work and the high variability in training and career trajectories, professional development of the youth workforce has become a critical focus of the field (Association for Child and Youth Care Practice, 2010; Quinn, 2004). Most professional development is organized as time-limited training for staff, often facilitated by senior agency staff (Roholt & Rana, 2011). Certificate programs in college settings have also been advanced as an option for increasing the professionalization of the youth workforce (Shockley

& Thompson, 2012). Professional development is considered a key factor in improving youth work practice and enhancing program quality. Curry, Eckles, Stuart, and Qaqish (2009) described a major initiative aimed at converting the workforce crisis into "an opportunity to transform the varied child- and youth-caring fields into a united profession based on a long-established, yet ever growing, developmental-ecological knowledge base and international collaboration" (p. 60).

Curry et al. (2009) described the North American Certification Project, administered by the Child and Youth Care Certification Board and sponsored by the Association for Child and Youth Care Practice. This certification effort is the first national effort to credential the broad group of professionals who work with children and youths. The process involved identifying relevant competencies for practice and organizing them into five domains: professionalism, cultural and human diversity, applied human development, relationship and communication, and developmental practice methods (Curry et al., 2009). Addition information regarding competency development, assessment procedures, a code of ethics, and other details is available (Mattingly, Stuart, & VanderVen, 2002).

Competency, assessment, and accreditation movements are part of the response to developing the youth workforce. Although there have been several efforts to identify a common set of competencies across the multiple aspects of youth work (for example, Vance, 2010, cited in Roholt & Rana, 2011), there has been some criticism that the competencies focus on therapeutic or recreational work with individual youth to the neglect of the more social justice or political aspects of youth work (Roholt & Rana, 2011).

Many of those who work with youths aging out of foster care come from the youth work tradition. This includes the large workforce in group and residential care, which should be fully engaged in preparing youths for transition, as well as community-based youth workers, who provide a range of supports to youths and young adults during or after their transition from care. Youth work's emphasis on community, social justice, and youth participation fits well with efforts to promote youths' leadership in advancing their own interests.

Training

Work with transitioning youths requires a specific set of skills that are not always explicitly recognized or prioritized during hiring and training. Some of these competencies may require a profound reorientation. For example, those working in child welfare systems who are engaged in youth transition may need to shift their focus from child protection to youth development. Among other things, this shift allows more developmental freedom and appropriate risk-taking. Those working in residential care who are engaged in youth transition may need to shift their mindset from structured settings to independence. All workers, regardless of setting, must be able to communicate positive attitudes toward youths and be skilled in helping with the transition experience.

Competencies needed in work with transitioning youths and young adults include clusters of tasks and skills that are derived from an analysis of a specific job and that determine the specific knowledge and skills necessary to achieve organizational and case-related outcomes in a manner consistent with best practice standards (Rycus & Hughes, 1998). To help learners meet competency standards, training usually includes specific learning objectives. These are often identified within domains of knowledge, attitude, and skill. Skill-based competencies are considered to be the most challenging; they require practice, feedback, and supervision in the work setting.

Training provides a key avenue for furthering worker competencies. In 2000, the Children's Bureau funded 12 three-year projects in the priority area "Training of Child Welfare Practitioners to Work Effectively with Youth Transitioning out of Foster Care through the Federal Independent Living Program" (HHS, ACF, Children's Bureau, 2014). Final reports from each project as well as training materials developed as part of the projects are available on the Children's Bureau Web site (https://www.childwelfare.gov/topics/management/training/curricula/caseworkers/core/outofhomecare/transition-living/transition-living-reports/). Each project had the purpose of developing and evaluating a competency-based training curriculum to strengthen staff intervention skills for working with older youths in foster care and independent living programs. In addition, several of the projects provided training to other relevant workers such as private agency personnel, group home staff, and foster parents. Because the projects all responded to the same request for proposals, the curricula they produced covered somewhat similar content. Content-delivery methods varied, however, and included community collaborations, experiential training exercises, and evaluation of training.

One of these projects, in which I participated (Collins, Amodeo, & Clay, 2004), emphasized the conceptual elements of positive youth development and the critical importance of paying attention to culture and understanding development theories of youth and young adulthood. Key areas of skill development included transition planning, engagement with youths, building youth skills for social functioning, and conducting groups with youths. Two additional areas of focus were using a youth development framework to address substance abuse and applying positive youth development to broader contexts of worker self-care, organizational environment, and community settings.

In 2004–2006, a team of which I was a member (Collins et al., 2007) conducted the National Evaluation of Child Welfare Training Grants, which examined the context, implementation, and outcomes of this cluster of training projects focused on transition to independent living. It examined how grantees implemented project activities, the extent to which they achieved immediate training outcomes, and site context factors that influenced achievement of outcomes. Evaluators reviewed each project's materials and visited the sites to observe their training and interview staff and collaborating partners.

Nine of the twelve original grantees participated in the evaluation. All had experience in child welfare training (a criterion for receiving the grant), several had designed youth-oriented training programs, and several had been recipients of previous Children's Bureau grants (Collins et al., 2007). The projects aimed to include a youth voice in different ways, and the evaluation found that the use of youths in delivering training was a critical strength. Watching youths as trainers increased participants' understanding of youths' strengths and resilience. "The youth were 'able to convey painful experiences and yet leave people feeling positive.' The youth trainers were professional, articulate, humorous, compassionate, and committed to improving the work of the social workers collaborating with them" (Collins et al., 2007, p. 5). There has been no formalized follow up to examine the extent to which these training projects were institutionalized in their settings or affected ongoing practice. The states and localities in which they were developed may continue to use them. Those that were produced under the auspices of a training academy are typically include among ongoing offerings. In addition, the project sites and the Children's Bureau make them available to other interested organizations.

One of these projects, the Y.O.U.T.H. (Youth Offering Unique Tangible Help) Training Project, was especially creative and committed to youth involvement. It has continued its efforts and is currently offering training in California. The organization is also developing the Foster Youth Museum (see Box 8.1). When it began work 15 years ago, the idea of youths as trainers was novel, and there was significant resistance from training audiences composed of child welfare staff. In one measure of progress regarding attitudes toward youths, it is now common for California youths to train social workers.

The youth voice in training can be inspiring to social workers. Project director Jamie Lee Evans quoted a training participant as saying, "it knocked the humanity back into my job." Social workers are bombarded with administrative work that takes their focus away from connecting with youths, and they appreciate the opportunity to spend time with young people in the training sessions (personal communication with J. L. Evans, director of trainings, California Youth Connection, San Francisco, April 3, 2015).

Box 8.1: Practice Highlight—Foster Youth Museum

The Foster Youth Museum began as a component of a federally funded training project for child welfare supervisors. The Y.O.U.T.H. (Youth Offering Unique Tangible Help) training project is a collaboration between current and former youths in foster care and child welfare professionals to deliver innovative training that is youth led in both design and delivery. In the process of developing and conducting training, youth trainers collected and displayed artifacts that represented their experience in foster care. The collection started small and was simply displayed on a table during the training. Eventually it grew into the Foster Youth Museum,

> *the largest collection of art, artifacts and video portraits about youth experiences in foster care. Conceived by current and former foster youth, the museum offers a unique opportunity to understand foster youth perspectives and how youth can heal and grow with supportive relationships, collaborative decision-making, positive encounters, and respect.* (Foster Youth Museum, 2015)

A recent exhibit, Lost Childhoods,

> *tells the story of loss and powerlessness in the foster care system—and the human capacity for resilience and connection. The exhibit includes art, artifacts and video portraits, and is organized by themes that characterize experiences in foster care and beyond: Loss, powerlessness, developmental disruption, institutionalization—and connection and achievement.*

Exhibits can be rented by other galleries, for training and other community events. By sharing the foster care experience and promoting dialogue in community settings, the Foster Care Museum aims to influence thought and action that promote the future childhoods of youths in foster care.

Web site: http://fosteryouthmuseum.org/

Workforce Development as a Factor in Policy Implementation

The previous chapter, on policy implementation, pointed to the link between implementation and training and to the centrality of individual workers in the implementation of policies related to service delivery. Thus, training is a major way of transmitting policy.

Several models of the policy implementation process acknowledge the role of training. Van Meter and Van Horn's (1975) model included variables such as the clarity of standards and objectives; adequacy of resources; level of interorganizational communication and enforcement; characteristics of implementing agencies (for example, competency and size of agency staff and vitality of the organization); disposition of implementers (for example, level of understanding of the policy and agreement with it); and the economic, social, and political climate. In this model, training can influence both the competency of staff in the implementing agency and the disposition of the implementers. Another model (Sabatier & Mazmanian, 1979) identified committed and skillful implementing officials as necessary for effective implementation. In this model as well, training can influence variables such as the competency of staff and the disposition of implementers. Copeland and Wexler's (1995) framework identified both professional orientation and training as characteristics of implementation officials within the larger category of organizational structure.

Other researchers noted: "A great deal of the more innovatory literature sets out to deal with questions about the role of staff at or near the bottom of the system or about how they receive and transform the efforts of others to 'mandate' them" (Hill & Hupe, 2002, p. 120). The same authors, discussing outputs and outcomes as important to the determination of successful implementation, refer to "attitude studies that identified changes of perspective on the part of street-level staff as their independent variable" (p. 122).

New policies are often accompanied by training programs so that managers, supervisors, and workers are able to implement the policy. If the policy is noncontroversial and easy to understand, training can be successful in facilitating its implementation. Many child welfare policies, however, are not like this. Policies often aim to reorient practice toward certain initiatives and use specific value orientations (for example, valuing youth participation, normalcy). Often these are not accompanied by the requisite resources and organizational change to support new ways of conducting the work. In these cases, training is not likely to contribute to successful implementation.

Policy implementation is likely to be more successful when the implementers support the policy and are capable of carrying it out. This is related to the attitudes and skills of workers; training is developed to influence their knowledge, attitude, and skills. If the policy is generally consistent with workers' attitudes and beliefs, it will be easier to implement. If a training program reinforces the attitudes and beliefs of workers, it, too, will be easier to deliver and more likely to be well received. But if the policy is at odds with workers' attitudes, beliefs, and values, its chances of successful implementation are diminished, and a training program designed to change workers' beliefs may be far more difficult to deliver. However, highly skilled delivery of a sophisticated training curriculum may still be successful.

Skill development of workers has different challenges. As members of a professional work force, most workers would presumably be interested in opportunities to upgrade skills to better serve their clients—at least as long as the new skills are supported in the work setting and the worker bears no significant costs for learning them. Obviously, workers may not want to participate in training if they are not compensated for their time or are required to pay for transportation to the training site. Workers may also be reluctant to participate in training if it causes them to fall further behind in their work. Finally, psychic costs can occur when workers are introduced to new practice methods that have a fundamentally different orientation from their previous training or professional values.

Collins et al. (2007) distinguished between a top-down and bottom-up orientation to the role of training in policy implementation. A top-down approach may be used when legislation is both clear and noncontroversial and training activities primarily concern information. Workers then can receive the information, learn it, and carry out their duties in concert with policy intent. Bottom-up approaches may be more appropriate for many of the complex training programs needed in child welfare. Such training programs would demonstrate a realistic understanding of the context of the work, would be developed with extensive input from workers and clients to determine training needs as well as needed competencies, would use consultative models in which workers seek guidance with real cases, and would make it possible to use training activities to direct feedback upward regarding the successes and challenges of implementing new polices.

Workforce development generally, and training more specifically, is often considered separately from the overall organizational effort. But workforce development clearly fits within most models of policy implementation in the human services. As mentioned at the beginning of the chapter, the worker is the critical component of work in child welfare and youth services. In medical interventions, relatively impersonal factors such as medicines and techniques (like surgery and rehabilitation) are critical. In contrast, in social services interventions, the relationship is almost always the critical factor.

Public policy changes at the national or state level often require changes to the behavior of individuals. For example, the Fostering Connections Act requires development of a transition plan, in which workers must be trained and supported. More generally, however, increasing attention in legislation to the needs of transitioning youths has required a broader cultural shift among agencies, which must prepare to meet the needs of adolescents and transition-age youths. This requires extensive redevelopment of at least some segments of the workforce, as well as adjustments to the organizational environment.

To effectively implement policies related to youth transition, the workforce must consist of people who like, value, and can engage with adolescents (and now, young adults) and can reorient their focus from protecting children to helping young people achieve independence. This can be a tremendously difficult shift for an agency. Decades of policy and practice aimed at child protection (and earlier child rescue), reinforced by constant media scrutiny and the potential for lawsuits, have led agencies to engage in defensive practices. Principles of youth development can conflict with a child protection orientation. Allowing youths to develop life skills requires practice, and sometimes failure. These are the challenges that remain in developing an effective workforce to carry out the policy intent of existing legislation.

Conclusion

An effective workforce is critical to both policy and practice. Organizations and scholars have addressed workforce challenges in a variety of fields, including child welfare and youth work. But the connection between workforce issues and the social aims of policy and practice is often not highlighted.

Some policies can be implemented with limited workforce involvement—for example, certification for access to benefits like Medicaid or higher education funding. But many require interpersonal connection—for example, transition planning and case management. This type of work requires substantially more expertise and a more professional workforce. Job qualifications should be rigorous, and preparation for the work requires more professional education and skills training.

Workforce issues are critical for the many reasons articulated in this chapter. But simply providing more training is not the answer. Also essential are a range of practices for hiring and supporting the workers who deliver the services that help youths transition out of foster care and into adulthood. These workers are the implementers of policy decisions, and they represent policy in the interaction with youths. They include not just the frontline independent living workers, but various personnel in public and private programs, foster parents and group care staff, community-based youth workers, and supervisory and managerial staff. Workforce strategies require organizational commitment to the work. Workers, no matter how competent, will have little success delivering transition services if the public and private agencies are not operating from principles that put youths and young adults first.

CHAPTER 9

Developing Community-Based Supports

Optimal practice in child welfare is community based. Working to ensure that youths are well connected to the community before termination of the agency's responsibility requires attention at both individual and system levels. While youths are in the foster care system, they live in a setting monitored by the child welfare agency. After they leave the system, the same level of oversight does not exist. Some youths may initially transition to another type of program. But at some point, they live on their own without program assistance. At the individual level, according to federal policy, workers and youths must develop an individualized transition plan that should focus on community connections in multiple domains (housing, employment, and relationships). There is likely some variation in how detailed and focused on community connections the transition plans are. Various mechanisms can be used to develop, facilitate, and enhance these connections. Community collaborations and planning efforts are part of the systemic approach to community practice. Although some of this does occur already, more intentional and sustained efforts are needed.

The theoretical frameworks reviewed in chapters 3 and 4 have multiple implications for community practice. The development of adolescents and young adults in foster care requires attention to social settings and networks. Life course theory is explicit that individual development is embedded in social context and that social ties to others are central (Mitchell, 2003). The emerging-adulthood concept reflects the idea that changing social conditions affect the life stage of young adulthood (Arnett, 2000). A social capital perspective emphasizes the critical importance of networks and connections to success in life (Briggs, 1997).

In regard to political frameworks, youth voice, advocacy, and civic participation are core components necessary to build the strength of a youth constituency. All of these are relevant in the many community settings in which young people are engaged. Most vulnerable young people lack political engagement in community settings, which puts them at a disadvantage and at grave risk of exclusion from political decision making that maintains (and exacerbates) their marginal status. It is within communities that youths can begin their engagement. These communities may initially be small (for example, a group home, youth commission, or online discussion group), providing the opportunity to build skill and develop confidence for engagement in larger, more complex settings.

This chapter and the next discuss some of the practical implications of these theoretical perspectives. This chapter provides a community orientation to work with transitioning youths. It describes theories of community practice with a focus on the social-support aspect of community (through social networks and opportunities). The next chapter discusses community-based programs focused on transitioning youths. A focus on community in regard to youths leaving care suggests several areas for community-based practice. These include organizing communities to be supportive places for young adults leaving foster care (and young adults more generally), connecting (or reconnecting) transitioning youths with an appropriate local physical community, making sure they have a variety of social connections, and empowering them to create a shared community of youths presently and formerly in foster care.

Importance of Community

Communities provide the needed link between individuals and their larger social and political environments. Without the interceding layer of the community, individuals can be overwhelmed by the larger environment—unable to fully understand social forces and to find a role for themselves—resulting in a sense of isolation. Communities are relational; they typically provide a web of interconnectedness among individuals, families, peers, and organizations. Like families, communities are essential to human development. They provide guidance and feedback regarding norms of behavior. Because family ties can be fragile for youths in foster care, the relational power of community may take on an amplified role for them.

Extensive sociological and social work research has examined concepts of community. Warren (1978) defined community as the "combination of social units and systems that perform the major social functions" (p. 9) to meet people's needs at the local level. According to Warren, communities perform five critical functions: (1) production, distribution, and consumption of material necessities; (2) socialization to the norms, traditions, and values of those within the community; (3) social control through laws and rules to enforce the prevailing norms; (4) opportunities to meet people's social needs through activities, interests, and groupings; and (5) mutual support to care for the variety of members' human needs.

Individual resilience can be linked with aspects of the community experience. Taylor (1997) distinguished between "enabling niches," where people are supported in becoming knowledgeable and competent and are able to build solid relationships both within and outside of the community, and "entrapping niches," where individuals become stigmatized and isolated. The foster care experience has the potential to become an entrapping niche if the experience isolates the young person from networks and from full participation in the community. Allowing youths to extend time in care after age 18, or return to care after leaving at 18, may shift foster care to an enabling niche if the experience is perceived as supportive and helpful. Whether or not a youth in foster care has a choice (about staying in care, transition planning, and accessing services) is critical to whether foster care is viewed as entrapping or enabling.

Some consider community practice to be the core of all social work; while most often associated with community organizing, social action, and planning, it is foundational to all types of social work practice (Hardcastle, 2011). Community practice can be central to clinical or interpersonal practice that is situated within the community and addresses the individual's interaction with larger systems. It is also part of policy practice. Communities, if sufficiently empowered, can be a major influence in developing social policies. Communities are also key to policy implementation, which occurs at the ground level within communities. Communities that agree with policy goals can facilitate implementation, and communities that disagree can thwart it.

Scholars of community practice have articulated a range of models to encapsulate the wide variety of work that occurs under this label. For example, Weil and Gamble (1995) identified an eight-component model: (1) neighborhood and community organizing, (2) organizing functional communities, (3) community social and economic development, (4) social planning, (5) program development and community liaison, (6) political and social action, (7) coalition building and maintenance, and (8) social movements. Rothman's (2007) model articulated three foci: (1) social planning and policy, (2) community capacity development, and (3) social advocacy. Within these categories, he articulates several specific modes of intervention. Boehm and Cnaan (2012) identified several additional models and offered some critiques, primarily that existing community practice models do not address the unique and changing needs of various communities. They noted that many community practice models have a top-down orientation rather than a community-generated orientation. Clearly, there is a wide range of strategies for approaching community work, and efforts need to be flexible to choose mechanisms that are appropriate for each community, its context, and its goals.

Regardless of a practitioner's specific orientation to community practice, some values are inherent to all modalities. Empowerment is integral to community practice. Weil and Gamble (1995) identified the purpose of community practice as "empowerment-based interventions to strengthen participation in democratic processes, assist groups and communities in advocating for their basic needs and organizing for social justice, and improve the effectiveness and responsiveness of human services systems" (p. 57). Youth empowerment is achieved through youth participation and partnerships. Achieving meaningful community and social change requires that adults treat young people as partners in the community development process and that adults and young people work together to develop a network of adult allies who have the requisite resources (Chawla & Driskell, 2006).

This book has described a range of opportunities in which youths have had a real voice (for example, serving on advisory boards and as trainers). Here, rather than focusing on specific practices, I emphasize the context that is needed to foster such youth-led initiatives. The organizational setting is important. Youth empowerment approaches need to be supported by agency contexts that are designed for empowerment. Successful implementation of empowerment-based programs requires participatory management and the creation of an organizational culture that is based on working in partnership with others (Gutiérrez, GlenMaye, & DeLois, 1995). In these settings, social workers are better able to share power with clients.

Many scholars emphasize the importance of senior managers to empowerment in organizations. Hardina (2005) described 10 actions associated with empowerment-oriented strategies in organizations: (1) creating formal structures to support the participation of clients in organizational decision making, (2) creating partnerships with clients to design and evaluate programs, (3) developing policies and procedures to deliver culturally appropriate services, (4) developing decision-making practices that minimize power differentials among workers and between clients and workers, (5) promoting team-building among workers, (6) promoting psychological empowerment of workers, (7) creating a leadership structure committed to empowering workers and clients, (8) increasing workers' job satisfaction, (9) encouraging workers to advocate for improvements in services and policies, and (10) increasing the political power of the organization and its clients. Organizations must also be effectively connected with each other in the community to facilitate the development of an empowered community.

Unfortunately, public child welfare systems lack many of these attributes. Workforce studies frequently find that workers in child welfare systems do not feel empowered in their work, and this is related to job turnover. In addition, workers in these environments have difficulty extending empowerment-oriented approaches to clients. Child welfare systems as large governmental bureaucracies have often been criticized for being disconnected from communities, and many efforts have been undertaken to more fully engage with communities. Rycraft and Dettlaff (2009) described an "artificial fence" between child welfare and the community and noted that child welfare agencies have traditionally functioned in isolation. Child welfare agencies have viewed themselves as the sole providers of child protection services, largely because of the many federal and state laws and policies that direct the functioning of agencies. Successful collaborations do exist, but many collaborations are small, isolated, and not reported in the literature (Rycraft & Detlaff, 2009).

Conducting a study on efforts to address racial disproportionality in the child welfare system, Rycraft and Dettlaff (2009) identified four primary factors as barriers to engagement of the child welfare agency and the community: (1) the community perception of the child welfare agency as unhelpful, (2) a lack of outreach to the community by the agency, (3) caseworkers' lack of familiarity with community resources, and (4) lack of collaboration between the child welfare agency and community agencies. Formal contracting processes and informal collaborations aim to enhance a community orientation in the work. When the relationship is sustained and a level of trust has been achieved, these connections may take on a partnership orientation.

The transition out of foster care requires explicit attention to the community, and for some youths, especially those coming from residential settings, specific types of programming are needed to facilitate a successful move to living in the community. There is a partially recognized necessity that the service systems should parallel normative family life and developmental processes whenever possible. A continuum approach to leaving care aims for independence to occur in stages rather than as an abrupt transition from congregate care. One program model is described in Box 9.1.

Types of Communities

Communities take many forms, particularly in modern society. Shriver (2011) said community is complex and difficult to define, and described some of the traditional perspectives on community: community as place (a geographic location), function (social activities needed for living such as work, education, and enforcement of norms), mediator or link (the place where the individual and society meet), way of relating (an affective focus relating to identity or feelings of membership), and social system (a more comprehensive, holistic view). Shriver also identified some newer approaches to thinking about community

---

Box 9.1: Practice Highlight—Stepping Out

The Stepping Out program in Massachusetts was initially developed by a private agency but has since been adopted by the state child welfare agency. Congregate care providers are required to incorporate a Stepping Out component in their residential services for transitioning youth (personal communication with D. Ferrier, executive director of Rediscovery and Youth Harbors, Justice Resource Institute, Boston, April 3, 2015). Stepping Out offers a tiered approach to independence. After leaving foster care, youth live in a community setting with some supports. It offers a

new community-based transitional support service designed to help youth with a successful transition to living in the community. It continues to provide support after that youth leaves a pre-independent or independent living program. It allows for the continuation of the case management function from residential care into the transitional period. Additionally, Stepping Out provides follow-up regarding connections to community supports and linkage to education and vocational activities. (Commonwealth of Massachusetts, Executive Office of Health and Human Services, 2014)

---

that include key concepts such as community building, community renewal, community assets and strengths, social capital, and civil society.

Fellin (2001) described communities as "social units with one or more of the following three dimensions: (1) a functional spatial unit meeting sustenance needs; (2) a unit of patterned interaction; (3) a symbolic unit of collective identification" (p. 1). Thus, communities can be based on geographical location, shared identity or interests, or personal networks. These are the categories I use later to discuss youths leaving care. Communities are interrelated subsystems that perform important functions for their members. The subsystems are not organized or coordinated by a centralized authority; although interrelated, they are defined by their own internal norms and operations. People have multiple connections to several communities (Hardcastle, 2011).

Locality-Based Communities

Youths may live in one place before entering foster care, another while in care, and yet another after leaving care. They may also move multiple times during each of these three stages, either within the same community or to a different one. Although researchers and practitioners are aware that this happens, there is little understanding of the details of these movements.

Child welfare systems are required to consider the location of foster placements, particularly regarding proximity to family to facilitate visitation. Berrick (2006) acknowledged both the strengths and weaknesses of placing children in their neighborhoods of origin. The benefits are that it may minimize academic disruption, encourage cultural continuity, and encourage parents to visit their children in care (which is related to the likelihood of reunification). The potential negative effect is that it can expose them to distressed neighborhoods, which may have negative effects on academic performance, physical and mental health, and behavior. Huang and Ryan (2014) investigated where youth were placed in foster care and whether specific neighborhood characteristics were associated with delinquency. The results indicated that foster care placements cluster in neighborhoods of high concentrated disadvantage, low ethnic heterogeneity, low collective efficacy, prevalent disorder, and violent culture.

The nature of the community settings into which youths transition usually receive little attention. Particularly if youths are left without program supports, given their limited education and job skills, their ability to afford a safe, clean apartment is limited. Therefore, in addition to their individual inability to meet their needs, they may also be living in communities that have serious economic stressors. There are very limited data on this, however.

One intriguing approach to the study of community for foster care alumni was conducted by Batsche and Reader (2012), who used Geographic Information Systems data to conduct spatial analysis of the housing options available to youths transitioning from care. The geographic focus was one county in Florida. The authors evaluated rental properties on the basis of three inclusion criteria (affordability, proximity to public transportation, and proximity to grocery stores), three exclusion criteria (high crime, prostitution, and sexual predator residence), and three suitability criteria (proximity to health care, mental health care, and youth-serving organizations). They found that only 27 of the 145 assisted rental properties in the county met the criteria for safe and effective housing. Even fewer were appropriate when transportation to postsecondary education and child-development services (for parenting youths) were included. The authors contrasted this number to the average of 125 youths who age out of foster care in the county each year, clearly demonstrating the challenges of finding housing that is both suitable and affordable. These data, while focused on one county, portray a challenge often articulated by those working in the field. Not only the housing setting for transitioning youths, but also the community setting requires attention. Additional studies of this type are needed to understand the community environments of youths transitioning out of foster care.

There is also very little research available on youths' ability to engage with community resources and use positive supports when they are available. Youths' challenges with attachment to individuals is well established, but there is little related information about their ability to attach to community settings. Interventions are not always explicit in helping youths understand community resources and address barriers to access. Most independent living training is related to the more practical aspects of transition (for example, getting a driver's license and opening a bank account). Other facets to be addressed might include: Do they feel comfortable walking into a local library to obtain information on community resources? Are they at ease walking into a church or other religious setting? Do they know how to pursue volunteer opportunities that may aid their civic engagement? These simple steps that many individuals take for granted may be enormously challenging for youths moving from foster care to life on their own.

Nonplace Shared Identities and Interests

Shriver (2011) defined *nonplace community* as "a community in which attachment to a specific place or geographic territory is absent and is not considered essential for community to exist" (p. 465). People can be part of several nonplace communities at the same time. These include identity-based communities (for example, religious groups, professional communities). "Nonplace perspectives on community can help us maintain a sense of community and can give us reassurance and security even when we are separated from other community members or when we move from one geographic location to another" (p. 466). Youths currently and formerly in foster care often express this shared sense of identity.

Nonplace communities can include virtual communities. A virtual community is "an aggregation of individuals that interact around a shared interest" and is at least partially supported by technology; it might be either member-initiated or sponsored by an organization and could be either social or professional in orientation (Porter, 2004, cited in Shriver, 2011). Virtual communities may be particularly important for transitioning youths. As for all youths, communication via technology is highly normative and can be more comfortable (and therefore used more) than face-to-face communication. As a result of maltreatment histories and their effects on attachment, transitioning youths may be more comfortable with these types of communications. There are risks with social media and other technologies of communication that may add to the vulnerability of young people, and some protection is needed for all youths. But a clear benefit for youths currently and formerly in foster care is that online profiles allow them to claim their identity and define who they are on the basis of their own criteria of interests and connections rather than on a label related to their time in care (Fitch, 2012).

Two major communities of youths in foster care with an online presence are Foster Club (https://www.fosterclub.com) and Foster Care Alumni (http://www.fostercarealumni.org/). Foster Club's mission is to "lead the efforts of young people in and from foster care to become connected, educated, inspired and represented so they can realize their personal potential and contribute to a better life for their peers" (https://www.fosterclub.com/article/about-us/mission). "Connected" refers to both a peer support network and people in the community. "Represented" means having their voices heard in policy and other arenas. The FosterClub.com Web site is a primary community tool for young people, providing information, message boards, and discussion of foster care topics. As a Web site, it can be accessed at any time (a characteristic not shared by most place-based communities).

The mission of Foster Care Alumni of America (http://www.fostercare-alumni.org/mission/) includes both connecting the alumni community to each other as sources of support and information and transforming policy and practice to improve opportunities for those currently in and those who have been in foster care. Foster care alumni have expertise regarding life in foster care. This perspective is critical to improving policy.

Other resources for online connecting also exist for youths in foster care and other youth populations. Individuals can decide to join or not join, and can seek online communities that best meet their needs at a specific time. These opportunities for connection are not (and are not meant to be) a substitute for in-person communities. Multiple communities are needed by all. They have an important place in allowing young people from foster care to find a shared community.

Personal Communities

A critical role of personal communities is to provide social support. The literature on social support is extensive; it is central to numerous positive domains of health, mental health, and well-being for all individuals and families and is, consequently, a focus of study for researchers from a variety of disciplines. Social support is clearly important, but questions remain regarding how to deliver social support through policy and programs (as opposed to naturally occurring social support). Networks are critical but can vary in multiple ways.

Early work on the social support of youths leaving care presupposed that these young people lacked support, but research has uncovered that many, although not all, have networks of support (Collins, Spencer, & Ward, 2010; Hiles, Moss, Wright, & Dallos, 2013; Perry, 2006). Various aspects of these personal support networks have been examined, including their size, type of relationships, and functions needed and provided.

Hiles et al. (2013) conducted a review of the international literature on social support for youths leaving care, which included 47 empirical studies, and identified five themes: (1) the influence of past experiences on social support in the present; (2) the range of potential supportive relationships during the transition from care; (3) relationships with birth families; (4) the crucial role of practical support; and (5) the youths' perspective on their experience of leaving care. Hiles et al. (2013) reported some evidence that earlier negative experiences with relationships, trust, and attachment continued to cause difficulty establishing and using support networks, but also some evidence (albeit less common) that young people with a history of more stable placements in foster care and a gradual transition to independence had more successful transition experiences. Several past negative experiences (loss and violations of trust) and the stress of new identities caused challenges that led young people to struggle to ask for support. Consequently, it is imperative that those offering support demonstrate their understanding of the young person's experiences. Reliability and consistency were identified as essential elements of social support. Instrumental support (helping with practical tasks related to accommodation, employment, or education) was particularly valued (Hiles et al., 2013). Cushing et al. (2014) suggested that further research and conceptualization of social support for these youths needs to move beyond more traditional measures in terms of type of support (for example, instrumental and emotional) to include a sense of attachment, trust, care, and belonging. They argued that the relationships are valuable in themselves.

The range of sources of social support was highlighted by Hiles et al. (2013). Collins, Spencer, and Ward (2010) reported on a study of youths who had aged out; the youths reported contact with birth families (especially siblings and mothers), outreach workers, and mentors. In regard to youths in foster care, one study found that multiple social networks (such as biological family, peers, and foster care) appear to be important in reducing psychological distress among young people (Perry, 2006). Relationships with foster parents and professional staff have also been found helpful for youths (Lemon, Hines, & Merdinger, 2005). Collins et al. (2012) noted that most study participants mentioned adults encountered through the child welfare system (such as a program staff member, therapist, or foster mother). Many of these relationship had lasted three or more years, and their key characteristics in the eyes of the transitioning youths were acceptance, encouragement, reliability, and ability to provide assistance when needed. Although these qualities commonly define a good relationship, they might be felt more acutely because of challenges in past relationships.

The role of adult mentors in providing support to youths in foster care is getting significant attention. This includes those mentors who are already in the youth's environment, often referred to as natural mentors, and those who may be introduced to the youth through a mentoring program. Studies have found that youths in foster care who have at least one positive and significant naturally occurring mentoring relationship tend to fare better in the transition to adulthood (Ahrens et al., 2008; Greeson, Usher, & Grinstein-Weiss, 2010; Osterling & Hines, 2006). Natural mentoring relationships have been associated with fewer arrests, less depression and stress, and more satisfaction with life (Munson & McMillen, 2009). Mentoring programs are discussed in the next chapter.

Specific types of support may be helpful in achieving specific outcomes. For example, Hass et al. (2014) found that support is important for youths throughout their educational careers. In a qualitative study with 19 youths in foster care enrolled in higher education, they found that social support such as the school reaching out to youths, care, empathy, and advocacy from educators helped youths to stay motivated and engaged in learning. Instrumental support such as career advice, scholarships, and college access also strongly benefited youths. Finally, they found that youths need safe havens or refuges from stresses in their lives. School is one place where safety can be discovered and new competencies can be developed.

While individuals are usually the identified source of support, organizations might also serve this role, at least to some extent. Focused on the importance of social capital, community-based associations are central to Putnam's thesis (2000) regarding the role of community networks in American life. Either institutions or individuals may initiate these relationships; however, individuals may use this type of capital to gain access to instrumental and emotional support. Furthermore, these institutions are more likely to facilitate social leverage (Ward, 2009). One advantage of organizational support is the usually greater stability compared with individuals who may move away, become ill, or otherwise be unable to maintain a relationship (Collins, Spencer, and Ward 2010).

Youth Development Opportunities

Positive youth development is not solely about relationships and social support, which are good things in their own right, but also about appropriate opportunities. "Positive youth development occurs when opportunities are made available to youths in meaningful ways and when relationships support young people to develop their own unique capacities and abilities" (Sanders & Mumford, 2014, p. 161). Positive youth development counters historical and still predominant approaches that focus on the problems young people have and that view youth "as a period fraught with hazards, and many young people... as potential problems that must be straightened out before they can do serious harm to themselves or others" (Damon, 2004, p. 14). Damon further articulated the interaction of youth and community that is inherent in the positive youth development approach, which sees the child as a full partner in the community–child relations, bearing a full share of rights and responsibilities" (p. 19). Programming within a positive youth development paradigm casts a wide net but is characterized as asset-based, collaborative, community-oriented, competence-building, offering connectedness and cultural membership, holistic, long-range, normative, promotive, and universal (Collins et al., 2004).

Although primarily associated with community-based intervention, positive youth development has a place in public child welfare. Some experts have expressed the need for public child welfare to shift toward practice approaches more oriented to positive youth development to effectively serve young people (Seita, 2000). This is aspirational; characteristics of bureaucracy make it difficult to accomplish. But the attraction of the concept continues to ignite efforts to change systems and organizations. Recently, "positive youth justice" has been proposed, using a positive youth development framework with the juvenile justice population (Butts, Bazemore, & Meroe, 2010).

Youth development fits well with efforts toward normalcy for youths in foster care (as identified in recent legislation). Exposure to the wide variety of normative activities for young people is assumed to have numerous developmental benefits that reduce the stigma of foster care involvement and potentially lead to both connections and personal development. This may also be related to the eventual better outcomes that are concerning to policymakers. As one expert practitioner working with transitioning youths stated,

> *If our foster youth are to be expected to compete with their peers in postsecondary education and the job market in order to sustain self-sufficiency, the normative milestones of adolescence are critical. They need to be in the school play, to play on sports teams, babysit for their neighbors, volunteer at their church. And they need an adult that is telling them, "good job"—otherwise, how do they know what a good job is? Their systems of care (child welfare, education, health-care providers) need to encourage and promote these opportunities and engage caregivers not just to allow them but to be a part of them.* (personal communication with M. Banks, adolescent program supervisor, Department of Children and Families, Boston, March 11, 2015)

In program implementation it may be challenging to fully articulate "normalcy" for youths in foster care, but a youth development perspective is quite helpful in this regard. As more organizations move further in this direction, one example that works in collaboration with the state child welfare agency to provide normal, community-based activities, is described in Box 9.2.

> **Box 9.2:** Practice Highlight—Rise Above Foundation
>
> The Rise Above Foundation offers Massachusetts children in foster care enriching activities, opportunities, and experiences. It was founded in 2009 to promote comfort, a sense of normalcy, and self-esteem among youth in foster care by providing funds for expenses such as prom attendance, soccer registration, and clarinet lessons. Applications are accepted online. Children and youths are eligible if they are in the physical care and custody of the Massachusetts Department of Children and Families (DCF). Also eligible are young adults 18 years and older who were in the care of DCF as minors and who have voluntarily signed up to continue in care post-18, or who have returned to care after age 18.
>
> Cofounder Wade Sulzman said that Rise Above allows young people
>
> > *the opportunity to have a childhood, the opportunity to feel the same as other classmates. Hopefully we're opening the door so they can participate. Foster youth are always being told "no." Rise Above allows us to say "yes" to a childhood for kids in foster care.* (personal communication with W. Sulzman, cofounder and president, Rise Above Foundation, Boston, April 9, 2015)

Finally, similar to the earlier discussion about the role of organizations in facilitating both worker and youth empowerment, youth development also requires organizational and community commitment in order to be successful. Rauner (2000) identified characteristics of a caring organization as (1) modeling care at every level of the organization (youths, families of youths, and staff); (2) devoting institutional resources to support staff in their personal growth, balance of work and family lives, and empowerment; (3) understanding the value of interpersonal relationships and devoting organizational time and energy to maintaining them; (4) valuing attentiveness and being willing to prioritize staff training that demonstrates that they are listening to the youths they serve; (5) ensuring consistency between its stated mission and actions; (6) formally concerning itself with the entirety of a young person's life and requiring that staff know what is happening in the multiple contexts of the youth's life; (7) providing opportunities for youths to contribute ideas regarding organizational policies and practices; (8) institutionalizing youth participation in agency hiring procedures and staff evaluations; (9) integrating programs with other systems such as neighborhoods, community resource organizations, and other programs within the organization; and (10) making the development of other community members and professionals a programmatic priority. In this way, caring context at the organizational and community level translate to caring supports for individual young people. This multilevel approach provides the necessary scaffolding within the community to support young people in a variety of circumstances.

Conclusion

Community orientation requires further enhancement during the transition process. Community is a central concept in social work, and it is particularly important to youths aging out of care, but it has been largely missing in that context. This might be because the core concept in child welfare is family, and therefore, community is given a lesser role. Reorientation requires focusing on the communities from which youths come, are currently a part of, and go to upon leaving care. This includes, at a minimum, their geographic location, their feelings of likeness to others, their nonplace communities, and the range of social supports in multiple domains. These foci offer numerous opportunities for policy and programming.

Community practices must be cognizant of the vulnerabilities of this population (for example, limited family support and history of trauma) to reduce potential vulnerabilities in community settings. While the focus of this chapter has been the positive effects of community, threats can exist as well. Hence, guidance in engaging in various communities is part of the work that is needed. Some youths and young adults in foster care may easily engage in a variety of community supports, but some are likely to have more difficulty.

Personal relationships are important for young people, and multiple good relationships are important for connections. Similarly, building multiple communities is also necessary. One critical community is the one shared with other youths in foster care; when successful, it can provide invaluable support and the potential to move toward social action to change systems. Youths can make choices about the communities in which they want to engage. Being able to navigate various community settings is a skill that will serve young people well as they move forward through their lives.

CHAPTER 10

Programs and Evaluation

Within federal Chafee guidelines, state and county child welfare systems have substantial discretion in designing programs. Thus, states and localities are highly variable in their approach to assisting youths in the transition from foster care. Individual states determine through a planning process the services that they will offer consistent with identified needs and available resources. The amount of federal funding is not extensive, so states must make choices about the use of program funding.

In addition to federal Chafee funding, other funding sources can be tapped as well. Some other federal sources might serve vulnerable youths, of whom youths formerly in foster care are one category. State, local, public, or private funding may exist that allows state and local programs to devise their own interventions. There can be great innovation and commitment. But there is also minimal standardization and limited use of existing knowledge to develop and implement programming. Evaluation is not consistently part of the process. As a result, there is no compelling body of research that could be used to identify programs that should be replicated.

Common areas of programming include training in life skills, budgeting and financial management, health and nutrition, and educational and employment services (help obtaining a high school diploma, enrolling in postsecondary education, and getting and keeping a job). Other components might focus on prevention of substance abuse, teenage pregnancy, or other problems. Mentoring and other interventions to promote positive interactions with adults are becoming more prominent. Creative new strategies are also being developed.

This chapter reviews some of the core programming areas targeted to youths transitioning from care. There are numerous program types (and multiple variations within types), and this chapter can only provide a summary of the core issues, key evaluation evidence, and potential innovations. It is organized into three areas of program focus: independent living and life skills, concrete supports (housing, education, and employment), and relationship-based strategies (permanency and mentoring). It also reviews the practice of evaluation and some challenges to conducting it and using its evidence to inform program decisions.

Independent Living and Life
Skills Preparation

Consistent with the Independent Living Initiatives of 1986, the earliest efforts to support youths leaving care focused on independent living skills, so evaluation of this program area is the most fully developed. Although many additional program models have been developed, living skills remain a core component and in some places may be the only intervention. Independent living programs typically include training in independent living skills, personal development, and educational and vocational support.

Before passage of the FCIA, a report by the U.S. General Accounting Office (1999) concluded that the effectiveness of these programs was unknown. The report identified several limitations of existing programs: Few vocational apprenticeships were available, training in living skills was not experiential, transitional housing services were limited, and ongoing support after leaving foster care was variable in terms of eligibility criteria and amount of support. Questions regarding the effectiveness of these services remain. Yet independent living programs and services have proliferated and are widespread. In the early 2000s, there were at least 87 such programs in 32 states and the District of Columbia (HHS, ACF, 2008); they now number in the hundreds (Mathematica Policy Research, 2011).

Most early evaluations were based on specific agency programs and thus were small-scale, exploratory, nonrandom, retrospective, and without comparison groups. Many of these studies reported some modest improvements in measured outcomes, but the lack of strong research designs made it difficult to draw conclusions. In one early study that used comparison groups, Scannapieco, Schagrin, and Scannapieco (1995) compared case records of an independent living group ($n = 44$) at exit from care with a comparison group ($n = 46$) and found differences in graduation and employment rates and self-sufficiency. Lindsey and Ahmed (1999) conducted a mail survey of an independent living group ($n = 44$) and a comparison group ($n = 32$) one to three years after leaving care and found differences between them in living independently, paying housing expenses, and educational attainment.

More recently, Lemon et al. (2005) compared two groups of youths in foster care (those who had received independent living services and those who had not) and found that although the independent living group may have been more at risk than the comparison group, they were achieving comparable success in terms of educational attainment, which might be attributed to their participation in independent living program services and their greater connection to caseworkers and counselors. Pecora et al. (2006) found that placement stability while in care and extensive independent living services (as well as provision of concrete resources) contributed to better educational and employment outcomes for youths transitioning to adulthood.

One national study of independent living (Cook, 1994), although lacking a comparison group, used regression models to examine the effect of independent living skills training and found that youths receiving skills training in five key areas (money management, credit management, consumer skills, education, and employment) had significantly better outcomes in living independently than those receiving no training in these areas. The study concluded, "For the best results, services needed to be targeted toward the outcomes that they were intended to improve, and they needed to be provided in combination" (p. 227). This is an important lesson for the variety of interventions designed for youths. Too often, programs are not specific in regard to their theory of change (how the planned intervention is expected to lead to specific outcomes). Programs are often ill defined, broad based, and lacking in clarity about their specific interventions, theories of intervention, and planned impacts.

Numerous independent living skills programs either are not evaluated or their evaluations are not reported in the research literature. A variety of resources are available for providing life skills training to youths, including training curricula, workbooks, videos, games, and exercises. There is wide variation in the quality of the materials, their content, and their targets. It is also problematic that there is no common methodology for the delivery of life skills. Naccarato and DeLorenzo (2008) reviewed 19 studies of independent living services and made three recommendations for improving practice: Work to recruit and engage youths to attend programs consistently, create a standardized curriculum for use across states, and put in place mechanisms to ensure that youths' needs and skills are matched to the interventions offered.

Donkoh, Underhill, and Montgomery (2006) conducted a review, published by the Cochrane Collaboration, of randomized and quasi-randomized controlled trials to evaluate the effectiveness of independent living programs for young people leaving foster care. Outcomes measured included educational attainment, employment, health, housing, and other relevant life skills. The study team identified 2,196 citations and examined 54 papers but found no study that met the methodological criteria. Summarizing the results of these studies, the researchers concluded that, generally, participants in independent living programs had better outcomes; however, the weak study methodology makes it difficult to draw any reliable implications for policy and practice. Adverse effects were rarely observed.

Since this review, more methodologically rigorous randomized designs have been used to evaluate some Chafee-funded programs through the Multi-Site

Evaluation of Foster Youth Programs, which selected four independent living programs on the basis of factors such as program size, intensity, and excess demand for services. Programs participating in the evaluation included an employment services program in Kern County, California; a one-on-one intensive, individualized life skills program in Massachusetts; and a tutoring and mentoring program and a classroom-based life skills training program, both in Los Angeles County, California. Each of the four sites was evaluated separately (Courtney et al., 2008) (Chapin Hall, 2015, http://www.chapinhall.org/research/ report/multi-site-evaluation-foster-youth-programs). The overall conclusion was that there was little evidence of effectiveness in any of the four programs. One of these programs and its evaluation are described in more detail below.

The Los Angeles classroom-based life skills training program had a five-week curriculum consisting of 10 three-hour classes held twice a week in 19 community colleges throughout Los Angeles County (HHS, ACF, 2008). The program was based on seven competency areas: education, employment, daily living skills, survival skills, choices and consequences, interpersonal and social skills, and computer and Internet skills. Instructors had some flexibility in designing their classes. An outreach component consisted of recruitment, short-term case management, and documentation of services. For the evaluation, 234 youths were assigned to the treatment group, and 248 youths were assigned to a control group. Concrete measures of the transition to adulthood were examined: completion of a high school diploma or GED, current employment status, earnings and net worth, economic hardship and receipt of financial assistance, residential stability and homelessness, delinquency, and pregnancy. The evaluation found few impacts on any outcome assessed. A large percentage of youths in foster care reported receiving help acquiring various kinds of life skills from sources other than the program. This raised questions as to whether classroom-based life skills training adds much to what youths in foster care are already obtaining from other sources (HHS, ACF, 2008).

Although several studies have demonstrated some modest impacts of independent living services, more rigorous evaluations found little evidence of this. This is sobering, considering that independent living skills training has been a foundational effort to assist youths with transitioning from care. The services do not appear able to alter outcomes in a meaningful way. Perhaps this is because the services do not provide enough assistance to address the serious level of need. Or perhaps they focus too narrowly on skill development to the neglect of other critical components of transition. Avery (2010) noted that independent living programs "have proven inadequate to prepare youth for independence in any meaningful way. Too many youth leave care unconnected to committed adults in their lives who could buffer the challenges they face and serve as safe havens in times of need" (p. 399).

Another potential explanation is that although the programs that were evaluated were not effective, other independent living skills programs could be, particularly when coupled with other program components. The many independent living programs that exist must clarify their program model, be willing to test it with appropriate evaluation designs, and report the findings in the research literature to build a knowledge base.

Concrete Supports

Housing

Housing supports remain highly variable; there are limited federal or state policy supports that provide housing for this population (Collins & Curtis, 2011). Most of the initiatives occur in localities and are developed through concentrated efforts by public and private entities. Housing interventions vary in whether they focus on emergency, transitional, or permanent housing; what accompanying supportive services they provide; and whether they target the aging-out population or other adolescent and young adult populations with housing needs. Other sources (for example, Casey Family Programs, 2005; National Center for Housing and Child Welfare, 2013) provide additional information about the range of housing options and specific localized programs.

A recent report (Dworsky, Dillman, Dion, Coffee-Borden, & Rosenau, 2012) identified 58 housing programs for youths formerly in foster care, which they divided into three types: single sites (either a single multi-unit building or group of buildings), sites dispersed throughout a community and usually rented from a private landlord, and host homes (private homes headed by a foster family or other single adult who receives a monthly subsidy). Programs generally provide one of the following: a subsidized unit in a building owned and managed by the program, monthly rental assistance in the form of a voucher, or a stipend for living expenses. Most serve young people between the ages of 18 and 21 (although some extend the age range beyond 21). The geographic distribution of profiled programs was heavily skewed toward states on the east and west coasts and in the Southwest and upper Midwest. Most programs are small, most require young people to pay at least a minimal amount of rent or contribute to a personal savings account, many provide a range of supportive services in addition to case management, most programs require participants to be employed or in school, and many also require young people to participate in life skills training or attend community meetings.

The effects of the programs have not been rigorously evaluated; of the 58 programs, researchers found evidence of or references to an evaluation for only six, and the quality and quantity of evaluation information varied substantially (Dworsky et al., 2012).

Higher Education

There appear to be a lot of programmatic supports for higher education, through the federal ETV program as well as state programs, private organizations, and the colleges themselves. Casey Family Programs (2015) listed several programs, of which two are described in the following paragraphs.

At Western Michigan University, the Center for Fostering Success aims to improve college graduation and career achievement rates among youths and young adults aging out of the foster care system. The Center for Fostering Success (http://wmich.edu/fosteringsuccess) was officially approved in 2012. It offers the Seita Scholars Program, which supports up to 160 students annually with tuition payment, campus coaching support, leadership opportunities, career mentors, and other strategies. The Center also works with colleges and universities across Michigan to conduct research to inform best practice to help youths move from foster care through education and into a career. At least part of the impetus for these efforts is related to the class-action lawsuit in Michigan (*Dwayne v. Snyder*).

At the University of Massachusetts–Boston, the U-ACCESS program (http://www.umb.edu/life_on_campus/uaccess) serves "to empower and support students who are experiencing complex personal and social issues that may derail their academic success." Emancipated youths formerly in foster care are one of the key constituencies, but other disadvantaged student populations can also use the services. U-ACCESS offers case management, information and resources referral, and a food pantry. The food pantry is available to any UMass Boston students who are experiencing hunger and struggling to buy food. The office collaborates with on-campus units and programs as well as off-campus community service providers and state agencies in the greater Boston area.

U-ACCESS also aims to provide leadership on issues of housing instability and food insecurity. In a survey it conducted of the college student population, nearly 5 percent of respondents reported being homeless since starting college and about 5 percent of respondents could not (or did not know whether they could) continue sleeping in their current place for two weeks. Nearly 25 percent said that food insecurity or housing instability negatively affected their class performance. U-ACCESS held a conference in 2014, which it hopes to make an annual event, designed to increase knowledge about homelessness, emancipation from foster care, and food insecurity.

Employment

Most employment programs do not specifically target youths transitioning out of foster care but rather larger categories of disadvantaged youths. Youth employment programs, including those offered under the FCIA, are designed to support youths in their transition from school to work, and from adolescence to adulthood, by connecting them to employment opportunities at a formative age. Proponents of youth employment programs have suggested that youths benefit from these programs because they contain a key element for future success on the job market, namely, work experience. However, the data on public youth employment programs are not encouraging.

Edelstein and Lowenstein (2014) reviewed employment programs for youths transitioning from care, including Department of Labor programs (YouthBuild, Job Corps, and the Summer Youth Employment Program) and programs funded by the Workforce Innovation and Opportunity Act, the National Guard Youth Challenge program, and Youth Corps. Details of the characteristics of youths served, the duration of the programs, and program elements are provided in the report. The authors also reviewed evaluation findings based on randomized controlled trials of these employment and training programs; only the National Guard Youth Challenge evaluation has shown long-term positive effects (Edelstein & Lowenstein, 2014).

Another, newer approach to employment is the use of social enterprise models, which offer employment training in supportive work environments, within a socially conscious business model:

> *The location at the crossroads of market, government, and civil society provides a margin of extra support from the public and philanthropic funding streams that allow nonprofit business ventures to absorb the social costs of employing workers with a range of disadvantages while competing in the market place.* (Cooney & Shanks, 2010, p. 41)

One social enterprise focused on youths leaving care is described in Box 10.1.

Box 10.1: Practice Highlight—More Than Words

More Than Words is an online and retail bookstore with two locations in Massachusetts: Waltham and Boston. Youths who work at More Than Words come from the foster care system or are court involved, homeless, or out of school. While supporting career readiness, the program does not focus on résumé preparation and job search.

(continued)

The program model identifies both a "business" job and a "you" job. The "business" job involves all the functions of running the bookstore. Youth facilitate peer-led trainings and weekly team meetings, track and forecast business finances, manage sales, guide tours, plan and host monthly events, manage marketing and promotions, and engage in various other work-related activities such as customer service. The "you" job focuses on the youth's own development in regard to more traditional independent living skills. It focuses on transition planning to achieve essential personal milestones (such as obtaining an identification card and opening a bank account) and taking steps toward education, employment, and housing goals. Opportunities are provided for youths to participate in experiential workshops, mock interviews, education coaching, and regular meetings with transition managers. After completing the core social enterprise program, youths transition into the graduate program, which provides an additional 24 months of follow-up support and regular assessments to ensure that they are achieving measurable positive outcomes in education, employment, and self-efficacy.

Jodi Rosenbaum, founder and chief executive officer, said that youths entering the bookstore immediately get a "sense of mattering." There is a professional feel to the environment. Young people apply for a job and, if hired, are held to standards of performance—there are real consequences for not showing up for scheduled shifts, for example. Young people from foster care have a long history of services being provided for them. At More Than Words, they are provided a chance, but they need to do it for themselves—with coaching, mentoring, and training support from program staff. Seeing youths reach their goals can shift how others view them as well.

The challenge to the model is finding the appropriate balance between supporting young people's growth and running a business. It needs to be a real business, not a job training program or employment workshop, or the youths will see through it for what it is. And yet, to help vulnerable young people transition to successful adulthood, it must also engage them at their current stage of development. Because of this dual challenge, it is unlikely that a social enterprise of this nature will generate surplus revenue to cover other program costs (personal communication with J. Rosenbaum, founder and CEO, More Than Words, Boston, April 3, 2015).

Web site: https://www.mtwyouth.org

Asset Building

Asset building policies allow people to invest in their own future (Ackerman & Alsott, 1999) and can take many forms. The general model is to encourage savings (often through matching an individual's contributions) for planned purchases that can further facilitate accumulation of assets and, consequently, a move toward greater self-sufficiency.

Youths in foster care have often missed out on opportunities to learn about saving and investing (typically provided by parents), and this may put them at a disadvantage. The Jim Casey Youth Opportunity Passport™ (which has several sites) trains youths between 14 and 24 in financial literacy. Upon completion of the training, they receive a personal bank account and an individual development account (IDA) containing $100. They may withdraw money from the IDA for approved assets; the program matches savings on a 1:1 basis up to $1,000 per year (Peters, Sherraden, & Kuchinksi, 2012). IDAs have been designed to support education, home ownership, or a business start-up. The Opportunity Passport IDAs can be used for assets such as books, computers, software, housing costs including security deposits, vehicles, microenterprise costs, health care expenses, and investments (Peters et al., 2012). Peters et al. (2012), in a study examining this program at four sites and involving interviews with eight staff members and 38 youth participants, found wide variation in the degree to which young people were successful in saving and purchasing assets; saving money remains difficult for these young people given their typically precarious financial situation.

Relationship–Based Strategies

Wisely, if belatedly, there has been increased attention to the relationship element of youths' lives and interventions developed to address it. Some relationship-based strategies focus on permanency, others on relationships more generally, and others on mentoring.

Knowing that many youths return to live with family members after leaving foster care, one strategy is to work to make these connections while youths are still in care. Avery (2010) stated, "Reestablishing these family connection[s] for teens before they exit out of foster care, no matter what age they are, is the strongest and most positive youth development program the child welfare system can offer" (p. 400). Avery reported on a promising practice model, Permanent Parents for Teens, which aimed to find permanent adoptive parents for teenagers who were freed for adoption or to find committed permanent parents who would morally adopt teenagers who were not freed for adoption but were in danger of discharge from foster care to homelessness. Almost 50 percent of the teenagers referred to the program were permanently placed into homes by the end of it. Most of the teenagers had been living in institutional settings; the average age was 15.7; they had long foster care histories; and many had multiple and severe special needs, including emotional, behavioral, learning, psychiatric, developmental, and medical and other physical needs. As a promising practice model, further development and evaluation is needed to cull important lessons for replication and to establish a base of knowledge.

In addition to permanent relationships, other types of relationships may also be useful for youths. Nesmith and Christophersen (2014) reported an evaluation of an agency-based program aimed at increasing supportive relationships for youths in foster care. The model, Creating Ongoing Relationships Effectively, focused on three areas: building supportive relationships, youth empowerment, and trauma-informed practice. As part of a private agency's work in youth transition, a 12- to 15-week program emphasized relationship development skills and targeted both foster parents and youths. Eighty-eight adolescents participated in the evaluation, 58 in the program and 30 in a comparison group that received traditional services. The evaluation demonstrated some limited but promising improvements in relationship building and ability to find someone to turn to.

Other interventions are specific to mentoring. Early attention to mentoring for adolescents in foster care was provided by Mech, Pryde, and Rycraft (1995), writing at a time when permanency for adolescents was not at the forefront; the options of adoption and family reunification were not believed to be realistic, and, consequently, independent living and development of support systems; the primary focus for adolescents. These authors cited Freedman (1993) for a mentoring formula that included a one-to-one relationship between a pair of unrelated individuals; an age difference in which the mentor is the older and more experienced person; and a relationship that is developmental; with a focus on enhancing the character and competence of the youths receiving mentoring.

Mech et al. (1995) collected information from 29 mentor programs in 15 states to examine the trends in mentor programs for adolescents in foster care. They identified five types of mentorships on the basis of their focus: life skills, cultural empowerment (matching youths from minority cultural or ethnic groups with adults from the same group), business (matching adolescents with mentors from the business community and focused on job placement), parenting (matching teenage mothers and pregnant teenagers with experienced mothers), and mentoring through a group home model focused on preparing for independent living. Mentorships focused on life skills were the majority (80 percent). They concluded that mentoring was receiving considerable support in child welfare, and although it was not a panacea for youths transitioning out of foster care, "the process of connecting foster wards with a cross-section of community citizens can do much to offset a tendency to become overly dependent on experts and professionals, for answers to societal problems" (Mech et al., 1995, pp. 326–327) The authors also raised some of the issues we still grapple with: Can good mentoring be engineered rather than evolving naturally? What are the challenges to connecting across social differences? What are the particular challenges to developing relationships with youths who have been harmed in the past?

In the years since these early studies, much more attention has been given to determining the potential of this type of programming. Given the evidence that natural mentoring relationships can have a protective influence on youth resilience, there has been widespread excitement about mentoring programs that might build solid, growth-producing relationships. Research on formal mentoring has, however, lagged behind the enthusiastic development of programs.

Although mentoring relationships may provide an important corrective experience in the form of a stable and consistent adult presence (Rhodes et al. 1999), facilitating such experiences for youths in foster care poses particular challenges. Not all mentoring relationships are successful. Because of their often challenging life circumstances and difficult past, there can be particular difficulties in developing a strong relationship between youth and mentor. An unsuccessful mentoring relationship could cause additional harm; a disappointing relationship could be detrimental to the well-being of any young person (Spencer et al., 2010). Thus, mentoring programs for youths in foster care must be approached with great care. They cannot be relied on to make up for a lack of real resources and opportunities in youths' lives.

Spencer (personal communication with R. Spencer, associate professor, Boston University, March 10, 2015) stated that mentoring provides something that we all need and can't have enough of. Youths involved in child welfare systems have systemic forces working against them in their effort to develop natural support networks, such as disruption in family ties and movement to new foster homes and schools. Mentors are important, but so are the full range of supports (good schools, access to higher education, and good jobs). If program planners identify the relationship between the adult and the youth to be the "tool of intervention," then "we have to get the relationship right"—we have to know how to do this and do it well. We are still building the knowledge base needed to construct and support effective mentoring relationships that can be sustained. Mentoring programs for youths in foster care and those who have transitioned from care must be highly intentional and supported by strong administrative practices. One such program is described in Box 10.2.

Box 10.2: Practice Highlight—Silver Lining Mentoring

The Silver Lining Mentoring (SLM) mission is to offer mentoring that "empowers youth in foster care to flourish through committed mentoring relationships and the development of essential life skills." (Silver Lining Mentoring, 2015)

The program offers one-to-one mentoring for youths age 7 and older. There is no upper age limit; the relationship can continue well into adulthood, and volunteers are committed to staying with the youth. The program offers intensive training, screening, and support for mentors; clinically trained master's-level staff support mentors and youth. SLM relationships last an average of 26 months, which is three times the national average. This allows stronger relationships and greater potential to affect critical outcomes.

The Leaders program, focused on youths in foster care age 14 and older who are preparing to age out of foster care, provides individualized life skills training, monthly life skills workshops, paid internships, and a peer network. A savings incentive program is also a component of the Leaders Program. "Learn and Earn" is for those 16 and older in the Leaders program. As they complete different experiential activities in the life skills curriculum, youths can earn money and save it to invest in an independent living asset (for example, vocational training course). SLM matches youths' savings toward asset accumulation.

Web site: http://silverliningmentoring.org/

Evaluation

Ethical intervention with vulnerable populations requires evaluation. Human services programs cannot be offered without a commitment to establishing an evidence base. Collins-Camargo (2014) noted a key hazard inherent in child welfare evaluation: the pressure to implement promising programs before evaluation evidence is available. Many who work in child welfare, including with youths transitioning from care, are looking for better ways to help their clients, and in many cases, program administrators are under pressure to demonstrate success. For both reasons, programs that seem promising or are consistent with core beliefs about a problem may be implemented without thoroughly weighing the evidence. Collins-Camargo (2014) warned, "It is critical to take the time needed to pilot programs and measure both short- and long-term results. The cost of implementing new programs is too great to not use evidence in decision making" (p. 670).

Program evaluation must take three interrelated elements into consideration: methodology, conceptualization, and context.

Methodology

Evaluation must balance the need to establish an evidence base (which often requires the use of randomized research designs) and the realities of agency-based and community-based practices. The appropriate type of evaluation design depends on the state of knowledge in a field and the planned use of the findings. In the early days of independent living programming and related services, small-scale evaluations were appropriate. The more recent randomized designs have contributed substantially by forcing us to look closely at our interventions, develop improved theories of change, and add or modify additional components. Increasingly, cost analyses must also be conducted.

Evaluation studies look very different if they are undertaken within an agency or conducted by funded university researchers in partnership with an agency. External resources, particularly federal grants, allow studies that are larger in scope, have a stronger theoretical basis, and require more rigor. The purpose of an external study is primarily to contribute to a knowledge base. Studies conducted within an agency tend to be smaller, less rigorous, and primarily used for program decision making. Agency capacity to conduct research and evaluation varies widely. Some settings with in-house evaluation units and designated staff can conduct more complex studies.

All evaluations can contribute to the knowledge base in different ways. Small, agency-based evaluations are needed because this is where the bulk of the work of delivering services takes place. These evaluations can have a level of rigor appropriate to the research question and the agency-based context; they do not all require a randomized design. If all the various types of independent living skills programs had been evaluated and reported over the years, we might have a much better understanding of promising options to pursue for further testing. These small studies might also uncover important components of interventions that work or specific contextual factors that are needed in order for outcomes to occur. For example, small, agency-based evaluations may identify characteristics of outreach workers who are particularly effective in assisting youths.

Conceptualization

Good conceptualization should be required regardless of other considerations of evaluation (such as auspices, funding, and rigor). Conceptualization of program design and the logic of the link between intervention and intended outcome is a critical and often overlooked task. To some extent, this part of the evaluation is more important than its methodological tasks. Programs can partner with local universities to obtain methodological skills, but the conceptualization and design of the intervention is the primary responsibility of the programs' director and staff.

Logic models have a recognized role as tools in program development and evaluation (for example, Wholey, 1987). Although there are different kinds of models, for purposes of program evaluation and performance measurement, the preference is for those that provide a one-page diagram linking the identified program components to inputs, outputs, and targeted outcomes (Lynch-Cerullo & Cooney, 2011).

Program models represent the underlying logic of the links between program goals, program components, and specific activities, and how these fit together to produce anticipated outcomes (Chen & Rossi, 1983; Hernandez, 2000). Yin (1994) identified the importance of the logic model as "its requirement of an explicit conceptualization of the chain of events, sufficiently detailed that operational measures can be envisaged for each step in the chain. This conceptualization actually reflects the 'theory' of the intervention" (p. 253). Numerous resources now exist for creating logic models. One prominent tool is offered by the W. K. Kellogg Foundation (2004).

The finalized logic model can provide guidance regarding data collection and use of data for program improvement. The process of developing the model can be an equally critical factor. This process, which is often extensive and time-consuming, allows various stakeholders to engage in articulating the program theory. This can provide more clarity and allow program staff (especially those delivering the service) to fully understand why the program is being delivered (Lynch-Cerullo & Cooney, 2011; Patton, 2008). Kaplan and Garret (2005) examined the use of logic models in three community-based initiatives to evaluate their benefits and challenges for program development and conceptualization. Communities that articulated underlying program assumptions found this to be the most useful part of the process, although very few sites completed this task.

Conceptualization is essential for all projects, regardless of scale. Without it, numerous rival hypotheses can be offered to explain observed effects. Sometimes the link is direct and easy to articulate; for example, provision of housing and housing supports will reduce homelessness during the time of the intervention.

Cook's (1994) national study of independent living skills programs provided important information about the observed links between specific services and outcomes. This challenges us to add specificity to our programs regarding the manner in which they are linked to outcomes. For example, a general mentoring program may have little opportunity to influence educational outcomes unless there is a specific, articulated, and robust component of the intervention that is aimed at attainment of educational goals.

Context

Public child welfare settings are highly complex environments and generally have difficulty implementing randomized research designs. Among agency administrators, most evaluation activity is centered on outcomes needed for performance measurement to respond to federal and state monitoring. Collins-Camargo (2014) identified some of the challenges as scrutiny and external demands from the courts, media, and other systems, which affects agencies' ability to participate in research projects and respond to findings; the differing missions, perspectives, and priorities of universities and public and private child welfare agencies; the hesitancy of agencies to open their practices to observation and assessment, as well as the added workload of data collection in an already overburdened system; the limitations of agency-based management information systems; and the fact that researchers' primary focus on rigorous design may not be well suited to all child welfare environments.

Lawrence et al. (2013) identified three aspects of the child welfare system that should be taken into consideration when planning an evaluation: Child welfare organizations are unique systems that operate within larger contexts, they have a direct influence on workers and practice with families, and the goals of evaluation often go beyond assessing outcomes for one program and aim to improve child welfare practice in general. Context is particularly important, because changes in both internal and external sociopolitical environments have great impact on programs, policies, practices, and evaluation. The authors suggested that child welfare evaluations use participatory methods as well as mixed methods, and recognize organizational context such as climate and work environment in the conduct of the evaluation.

Conclusion

Similar to the growth of policy development in this area, there has been an expanding range of programming models to assist youths transitioning out of foster care. Table 10.1 gives some examples of the various programs currently existing across the United States. Although there are numerous good intentions, a solid evidence base has not been attained. Interventions occur on a small scale within individual programs. Many are never reported in the research literature, so that potentially good programs are not shared, replicated, and tested. The basis on which programs are developed may be unclear, related more to staff ideas or available funding sources than to an articulated program theory or conceptual model. Promising programs may be terminated or changed depending on many factors not related to specific findings. These characteristics of program development are not unique to transition-age youths but can be found in a wide variety of social service interventions.

Although numerous independent living skills programs have been offered, research suggests that this intervention has limited impact. Recognizing that

Table 10.1 Selected Programs for Youths Leaving Foster Care

Program	Description
Foster Care to Success http://www.fc2success.org/	Scholarships and grant assistance, care packages for students, academic and personal mentoring **Locations:** Multiple states and the District of Columbia
Opportunity Passport http://www.jimcaseyyouth.org/savings-and-asset-building	Financial literacy training and individual development accounts **Locations:** Connecticut, Florida, Georgia, Hawaii, Indiana, Iowa, Maine, Michigan, Nebraska, Rhode Island, Tennessee
Youth Villages YVLife Set http://www.youthvillages.org/what-we-do/yvlifeset.aspx#sthash.GYAz8nTk.dpbs	Intensive case management **Locations:** Florida, Georgia, Massachusetts, Mississippi, North Carolina, Oregon, Tennessee
Alabama Reach http://reach.ua.edu/	Empowering youth currently and formerly in foster care, orphans, emancipated minors, wards of the state, and homeless youths to pursue higher education **Location:** University of Alabama
Child Welfare Academy http://www.uaa.alaska.edu/childwelfareacademy/etv.cfm	Postsecondary education support, intensive case management, and help navigating the college system; administration of Education and Training Voucher funds **Location:** University of Alaska, Anchorage
Arizona Friends of Foster Children Foundation http://www.affcf.org/post-secondary-scholarships/	Postsecondary scholarships for youths formerly in foster care **Location:** Can be used at any postsecondary institution
Jewish Family & Children's Service, Youth in Transition program http://www.jfcsaz.org/site/c.aj IQK6NLfJ0E/b.6318953/k.11 06/Youth_In_Transition.htm	Transition services related to independent living, career planning, and relationships needs **Location:** Phoenix area
Guardian Scholars http://www.guardianscholars.ucla.edu/ (available at several California universities)	Support to youth formerly in foster care attending university through services including mentoring and referral to campus resources, housing, student groups, enrichment workshops, and connections to scholarships **Location:** California
Just in Time http://jitfosteryouth.org/	Basic needs, financial skills, career building, college readiness, and help furnishing apartments **Location:** San Diego

(continued)

Program	Description
Larkin Extended Aftercare for Supported Emancipation http://www.larkinstreetyouth.org/programs/housing/lease/	Homelessness prevention, counseling, employment training, referrals, and case management **Location:** San Francisco
Orangewood Children's Foundation http://www.orangewoodfoundation.org/	Mentoring and peer mentoring; drop-in resource center; financial, educational, and emergency assistance; scholarships and grants; transitional housing; affordable housing and supportive services for transition to independence **Location:** Santa Ana, Orange County, California
United Friends of the Children http://www.unitedfriends.org/	College readiness and educational guidance, life skills training, transitional housing, career services, advocacy, and mental health counseling **Location:** Los Angeles
Bridging the Gap http://unitedwaydenver.org/what-is-bridging-the-gap	Housing assistance, independent living coaching, financial literacy training, community connections, Youth Voice video project, educational and employment support services, and advocacy **Location:** Denver
West End Neighborhood House http://www.westendnh.org/youth-families/services-for-foster-care-youth/	Case management, financial and other education and training, medication management, job placement assistance, mental health services, life skills instruction, mentoring, and employment on an urban farm and farmers market **Location:** Wilmington, Delaware
Casa Valentina http://www.casavalentina.org/	Affordable housing and wrap-around services for youth pursuing a GED, diploma, or vocational or certificate program **Location:** Miami
TransitionZ http://www.chriskids.org/strong-community/transitionz-program	Supervised apartment living, transitional housing, emergency shelter, and other housing services; support for educational goal attainment; transitional housing and support services for those youths with a mental health diagnosis; service learning and volunteer opportunities; education and coaching on health and wellness, parenting, life skills, financial literacy, communication and social skills, and identifying and using community resources; counseling and therapy; transportation **Location:** Atlanta

(continued)

Program	Description
Hawaii Foster Youth Coalition http://www.kukuicenter.org/ hawaii-foster-youth-coalition/	Training in leadership, independent living skills, financial literacy, healthy relationships, computer skills, and conflict resolution; job training and preparation for higher education through workshops and mentoring; legislative advocacy; training for social workers and foster parents
	Locations: Hawaii (multiple sites)
BeREAL http://www.bereal neworleans.org/	Transition coaches and mentors to provide support in various ways: developing an education and career plan; academic incentives and scholarships; weekly book club; recreational and birthday outings; housing support; a safe place to talk with trusted people about fears, hopes, concerns, and dreams
	Location: New Orleans
Maine Youth Transition Collaborative http://maine-ytc.org/	Statewide collaborative focused on economic success, youth leadership, and community engagement
	Location: Maine
Hope Forward http://www.hope-forward.org/	Job training **Location:** Baltimore

independent living skills alone are unlikely to have a large impact on most outcomes, we have seen increasing development in program areas related to concrete support and development of relationships and social support. In regard to concrete supports, there appears to be significant movement in the arena of supports for higher education. Less attention has been paid to housing and employment, two critical areas that require more consideration.

There is often an issue of scale when discussing programs. Many programs remain small, and if promising, effort should focus on program expansion, in part to facilitate the collection of better evaluation data. A related issue is that little institutionalized support exists for many programs. Hence, during budget-cutting efforts, programs that are not entitlements and that have comparatively short histories are most likely to be threatened.

In all program areas, greater attention to evaluation is needed. This requires a program specification process, use of program theory, and ongoing agency-based evaluation and feedback mechanisms for program improvement. Because many agencies do not have the in-house capacity for program evaluation, partnerships with universities offer a partial solution if the differing goals of agencies and universities can be reconciled in a way that benefits knowledge development for use in program planning.

CHAPTER 11

Conclusion

This book has used theoretical frameworks, research and evaluation findings, policy analyses, and practice examples to illuminate a macro perspective on services for youths aging out of foster care, focusing on larger systems issues that are particularly relevant to this issue. These primary macro systems—of policy, community, and organizations—intersect in many ways. Policy provides the framework in which the work takes place and is implemented within organizational and community settings. Youths, too, are part of the policy process, and their role can (and should) be enhanced in some of the ways identified in this book. Policy should not be viewed in a top-down fashion, but as a bottom-up or collaborative effort carried out through policy networks.

This final chapter further integrates the content of the earlier chapters and proposes some next steps for developing policy, programs, and practices to support vulnerable youths' transition to adulthood. The work that has been done over the last few decades demonstrates a high level of sustained commitment by many individuals and organizations to providing more and better supports for young people leaving care. Numerous strategies have been proposed and implemented (but not always evaluated) in an effort to help youths with this transition. There is always a challenge in keeping the efforts focused. Numerous other social problems, social challenges, and crises await our attention and have equal merit. But progress requires concentrated attention to the development of more supportive, institutionalized responses.

A variety of sociological and political theories have been discussed that might be (and in a few cases, have been) applied to leaving care. These theoretical perspectives can enhance a primarily psychological approach that focuses on the individual youth and his or her challenges related to building skills and attachments. Individually oriented approaches are key to addressing the concerns of youths, but enhanced attention to systems, institutions, and structures is also needed. This more macro-oriented approach is consistent with the social work commitment to social justice and use of ecological models to accurately assess, and effectively intervene, in change processes.

This book focused on a small number of sociological and political frameworks that appear to have particular applications for transitioning youths—most notably the importance of community networks and youth participation in decision making. Other perspectives from sociology and political science may also offer road maps for analysis and intervention—particularly those that focus on organizations and institutions, because they may be able to help with entrenched processes and procedures that do not effectively serve youths leaving care but are difficult to change.

Other social sciences offer compelling theories and methods that may shed new light on the search for critical solutions. Anthropology, for example, would enhance our understanding of cultural perspectives of youths and young adults and the transition experience. Artifacts (such as those displayed in the Foster Care Museum) may provide a rich and unique perspective. Stories can have a profound influence on policymakers' perspectives; often they have far more impact than data. Geography, with its emphasis on natural and built environments and use of spatial analysis, may be particularly useful in understanding the community experiences of youths currently and formerly in foster care.

Data have demonstrated that youths aging out of foster care have consistently poor outcomes in a number of domains, across studies, and in comparison to youths who have not been in foster care. Yet these outcome data must be used cautiously to avoid stigmatizing the youths. Youths who were in the foster system who achieve success in adult domains cannot be viewed as unusual. Like all young people, they have a variety of strengths and weaknesses.

The generally poor outcomes also should not be viewed solely through the lens of the aging-out experience. Although youths need support during this transition, serious deficits are also related to the challenges that brought them into care (such as abuse, trauma, and poverty) and experiences that occur while in care (separation from family and community, frequent moves, disrupted education, and lack of participation in decisions that affect them). It is also necessary to recognize disparities based on race and social class that affect life experiences and treatment by systems. A broader understanding of the reasons for poor outcomes should be taken into account when developing interventions that are systemic, broad-based, comprehensive, and long-standing. It helps explain why narrowly constructed and time-limited interventions, such as life skills training, are unlikely to have a sustained impact.

Policies and policy frameworks that are relevant to this social problem are now fairly well known. Important policy-related considerations include understanding the sources of the policies, the values on which they are based, and how they have developed over time. Theoretical perspectives related to framing problems and populations as well as institutional perspectives related to path dependence and other constraining factors help explain how policies are designed and how subsequent policy choices reinforce original approaches. Theories related to the social construction of populations targeted by policy tell a fairly clear story regarding the risks of dependency characterization. This offers clear impetus to youths and their advocates to claim their rights to better treatment in the policy process.

Policies affecting youths leaving care are nested within the child welfare system, and this constrains approaches to interventions in several ways. Child welfare systems not only have their own challenges, related to stigma for example, but also were established and developed to address other problems (child rescue). They are not geared for adolescents and young adults and are ill prepared to meet their needs. Yet there is no appropriate young-adult-oriented system that could effectively meet the developmental needs of these youths. In fact, the larger society lacks effective methods to serve young adults. Policies and the resulting institutions and instruments must be constructed along normative lines related to education, employment, and health. There is a lot of work to do in this area.

Implementation frameworks shed light on the multiple and complex systems engaged in helping youths transition from care. Federal, state, and local governments, private agencies, community partners, individual workers, and the youths themselves all play a part in turning legislation into practice. Communications and interactions of various types—formal guidance and directives, contracted relationships, community partnerships and coalitions, and training programs—through top-down, bottom-up, and lateral devices—provide assistance to youths in transition.

The bulk of the work happens within communities and programs. Community-based models of practice hold great promise, yet they are challenged by the longstanding models of child welfare practice that have not been fully adapted to community levels. More fully connecting work by large state agencies with community providers would benefit child welfare practice in general and support for youths transitioning out of foster care in particular. A stronger understanding of youths' relationships to multiple communities is also needed to be more planful in helping them develop much-needed community connections. Technology can have a central role in sustaining these connections.

Concepts such as "collaboration" and "empowerment" require more critical attention. Although they are highly valued and commonly used in discussion of community approaches, they are not always well articulated regarding specific purposes and strategies. As we have seen in examples from the literature, these concepts are ubiquitous but not always clear. A fuller understanding of the purposes of collaboration; the benefits and limitations to each party; and most importantly, the impact on outcomes would be of benefit. Despite the clear value of empowerment to social work practice, the means of expanding power to marginalized groups are not well understood, and the impact on practice is uneven. Most youths leaving care lack substantial power to influence conditions in their environment. Efforts such as those described in this book can be effective, but they need to be expanded to gain important, sustained, and positive attention to the needs and rights of youths.

Global Perspective

Adding a global lens to our understanding of youths leaving care is also important. Much can be learned by using an international comparative approach that illuminates the role of social context in influencing policy development and practice strategies. Variations in culture, politics, history, economics, and other elements drive differences in policy and practice in different countries.

In the industrialized western countries, there is now substantial focus on the circumstances of youths leaving foster care. Originally confined to few countries (Australia, the United Kingdom, and the United States), interest in this issue is expanding globally in both research and practice. Nearly all countries have some type of care system; therefore, the issue of what happens to young people when they age out is likely to be universal. But young people's specific experiences, needs, opportunities, and risks—as well as the strengths and limitations of care systems—are likely to be influenced by context. As in the United States, core interventions often include transition planning, life skills training, housing support, access to education and employment, and family reunification. The relevance and form of these approaches depend on factors within the national and cultural context and other aspects of the social ecology (Pinkerton, 2011). For example, job skills needed for career success vary across different countries. In addition, the nature of professional social work within a country may influence the types of interventions. Thus, a comparative analysis can identify some of the factors unique to the U.S. social context and may point to creative approaches used elsewhere that might be adapted here.

In the contemporary world, attention to perspectives other than those from the United States is required for good practice. Increasing globalization provides numerous opportunities for shared learning among social work researchers and practitioners. Moreover, the global context for social work and social policy will require sustained efforts to compare and understand different structures, concepts, and methods for approaching work with transitioning youths.

Additional Conclusions

Youths aging out of care have become the focus of policy and practice and are no longer completely neglected as they were before the Independent Living Initiative in 1986. Other critical legislation (most notably FCIA and the Fostering Connections Act) has brought more resources, expanded intervention strategies, and established new practice requirements (for example, youth participation in transition planning). In addition, there has been federal funding for training for social workers and other constituencies, evaluating transition programs, and developing a national database. These developments are all to the good and serve to establish this as a policy domain.

As an outgrowth of child welfare policies, support for youths aging out of foster care remains substantially connected to the existing child welfare system. This has both positive and negative implications. On the positive side, it provides infrastructure for some core intervention activities (for example, training) and continuity through the transition to adulthood. But it also requires substantial modification to effectively meet the needs of transitioning youths and young adults. The child protection model is inappropriate, and rather stifling, for young people approaching 18 and older. Extending time in care without also changing our philosophical approach and practice response will likely matter little. Ward (2009) found that experiences among youths who left foster care and returned to it after age 18 were different and more positive than their experiences in care before age 18. Their personal agency in choosing to engage with the department put an entirely different frame on their experience.

Thus, to serve young adults transitioning out of care, the child welfare system needs core adaptations—a workforce that understands and wants to work with this population, attention to the developmental needs of this population (related to flexibility, choice, and appropriate risk taking), promotion of suitable ties to the community (people, opportunities, and infrastructure such as transportation), and ongoing efforts to organize young people to effect system change and engage in the policy process.

The larger landscape of policy and practice is also changing in ways that will affect prospects for youths aging out of care. This includes the broader changes in social welfare provision, decline in consensus about the importance of addressing human suffering, acrimonious and polarized debate about government involvement in addressing need, stalemate at the federal level leading to increasing disparities at state levels, unacknowledged and unresolved issues related to racism, and widening inequality. Even potentially effective interventions may not work if they are overwhelmed by these forces. To counter these forces, advocacy and large-scale solutions are needed that provide substantial resources in a comprehensive manner to address poverty and inequality. Supportive policies for youths leaving care will have a much more difficult time accomplishing their goals if the broader social welfare environment is not supportive of young adults.

State-level disparities will likely increase in the near term, resulting in unequal opportunities for young people to successfully age out of care. Some states have committed to building fairly extensive supports. Other states, because of resource and political constraints, are less likely to do so. These differing levels of support will allow us to further compare across states in terms of impact on outcomes. Future research should also examine outcomes after youths leave care at the more advanced ages of 20 or 21. We then may be able to determine the extent to which longer stays in foster care contribute to better outcomes as well as the best mix of interventions between ages 8 and 21.

Next Steps in Reform

Cohen (2005) noted that, historically, "proposed strategies for reforming child welfare included new legislation, new policies and programs, more research, more resources, more litigation, and redesigning the child welfare workforce" (p. 654). The same conclusion could be made regarding youths leaving care. Current knowledge, policy, and practice are the result of concerted efforts by a wide range of actors: youths themselves, their allies and advocates, professional social workers in various settings and roles, members of other professions working with youths, legal professionals, policymakers (legislators and public managers), researchers, and many others.

Cohen (2005) identified four traditions of systems reform: social reform, policy analysis, social learning, and social mobilization. Social reform is large in scale and often driven by major national legislation. Policy analysis seeks the most effective solutions (given constraints) and may draw on program evaluations. The social learning tradition is observed in the organizational and multiorganizational systems that are engaged in the world of practice (for example, reorganizing and transforming service delivery, possibly through privatization). In terms of social mobilization, within child welfare, class action litigation is used to force social change on behalf of the disempowered. Policy analysis and social learning tend toward incremental approaches; social reform and social mobilization are more likely to attempt change on a grander scale. These four traditions use differing paradigms of knowledge building, change strategies, and tools. Cohen suggested that meaningful child welfare system change is stymied, in part, because of the siloed nature of these different efforts and the lack of joint efforts across the various traditions.

Conclusion

This is an important caution in thinking about next steps in improving support for youths transitioning from care. This book has described a number of strategies from these four traditions. Using these categories, I recap some of them in the following sections.

Social Reform

Federal legislation has had a definite impact on services for transitioning youths. It has led to the development of independent living skills programming; broadened programming and provided additional assistance through the Chafee program; extended key resources such as financial aid for higher education and health insurance through Medicaid; placed greater emphasis on planning and preparation for independence; allowed for the extension of foster care; and most recently, encouraged efforts to provide youths with more normal developmental experiences.

These legislative successes are important and can provide many youths transitioning out of foster care with needed additional supports. But multiple limitations remain. Legislation has not focused primarily on creating permanency for adolescents and young adults, it does not offer enough resources to serve all youths in a comprehensive manner, and there remains substantial interstate inequity. Youths in some localities can tap a wide range of supports for an extended period of time, while those in other localities remain largely on their own in their transition experience. Policies relevant to youths aging out remain incremental in nature. A more uniform strategy with guaranteed access for needed supports will be an important next step.

Further large-scale social reform strategies are needed in the related areas of social welfare policy, family policy, and child welfare policy. More comprehensive assistance in these areas would serve transitioning youths in important ways. Optimally, these policies would strengthen families so that youths never need to transition from foster care to independent living. Policies for the range of young adults are also necessary in multiple areas, but primarily employment and higher education. Universalistic approaches are needed for the population of young adults, a group that is typically denied policy attention, with enhanced targeting of the more vulnerable young adults, such as those exiting state systems.

Policy Analysis

Traditions of policy analysis emphasize the construction of models and the use of evidence to identify solutions to specific problems. Numerous academic, government, and research organizations have been engaged in efforts to assemble evidence to determine what is working (and not working) in efforts to help youths leaving care. All activities to develop an evidence base and to use the evidence to put forward solutions have contributed.

There are apparent weaknesses to our approaches to policy, programming, and practice. We know that a singular focus on life skills development is inadequate; that when we do teach life skills, experiential practice is critical; and that relationships are foundational to assisting youths—reconnection with family, trusting relationships with social workers and other professionals, authentic mentoring relationships within programs and with natural mentors in the community. But we know very little about how to promote these connections in a deliberate intervention.

Research in the tradition of policy analysis is ongoing, and evidence continues to accumulate. Despite all we have learned in the last two decades, there is much more we do not know. The contributions of the Midwest Study and the Foster Care Alumni Study to understanding young adult outcomes and potential reasons for those outcomes have been substantial. Yet even these rigorous studies only cover two small regions of the United States The NYTD will help somewhat to give a national picture, but it, too, will be limited because of known limitations in administrative data (for example, variation among jurisdiction in data systems). Rich qualitative studies also are required to add depth to our understanding of the experiences of youths leaving care. Much more research needs to be done to inform policy development.

One concern is the lack of institutionalized infrastructure to produce this evidence. In comparison to policy domains such as health, income support, employment, and education, the search for solutions to the concerns of the child welfare population has far fewer institutionalized supports. As a system only serving vulnerable and marginalized populations, the child welfare system lacks this same level of support.

Social Learning

Organizations and their collaborative networks are the key players in the social learning tradition. They are engaged in practice and act to improve procedures through various changes in service delivery structures and processes that are rooted in experience. A key attribute of this type of approach is that it tends to evolve through local experimentation rather than top-down mandates; examples include community partnerships, privatization, and shared decision making in organizations (Cohen, 2005).

Organizations, both bureaucracies and community based, play a key role, particularly in regard to policy implementation and programming. In many organic ways, the service delivery system and its various actors make incremental changes in an effort to improve practices. The feedback that organizations provide to inform policy making is crucial to a realistic understanding of the potential of policy approaches. Organizations, as we have seen, can also function as social innovators (in areas of youth-led initiatives, social entrepreneurship, and promoting normalcy, for example). When that happens, policies then need to catch up to the ideas generated in the field. This bodes well for the production of new knowledge that can grapple with potential real-world solutions and eventually test them for possible replication.

Social Mobilization

Although class-action lawsuits have been used as a strategy to force systems change for youths, of perhaps more importance is the mobilization of youth constituencies to work on their own behalf. Earlier chapters documented both theoretical perspectives and practice approaches aimed at organizing youths in foster care to have greater impact in the policy arena. There seems to be some momentum in these efforts. Because these youths are young adults and, for the most part, have transitioned out of foster care, they may have greater strength than youths under age 18 who are still in care. Communication technologies make it easier for youth to connect with each other and to contribute to decision making. This may also contribute to more effective links with other groups advancing the concerns of young adults.

Working across Traditions

As Cohen (2005) observed, the four reform traditions described earlier often work separately. This is a risk also in advancing reform efforts related to youths leaving care. As a result of its more recent emergence and early stage of development, however, the system that governs the process of leaving care is not as firmly institutionalized as other child welfare systems. For this reason, greater work across traditions might be possible to advance reform efforts on multiple fronts.

Social work is in a unique position to lead in this way. The position of social workers in program development and service delivery gives them a central role in policy implementation. Social work education that reinforces multilevel understanding, community-based intervention, and engagement in policy practice offers a unique perspective. The best of social work combines research evidence with professional practice in multiple environments and a robust articulation of moral commitment to a more equitable society. Sustained attention in practice, policy, and research is needed to increase the likelihood that more youths leaving care will achieve the same levels of well-being as other young adults and be able to maintain this well-being through their life course.

References

Ackerman, B. A., & Alstott, A. (1999). *The stakeholder society*. New Haven, CT: Yale University Press.

Administration for Children and Families. (2012). *About NYTD*. Retrieved from www.acf.hhs.gov/programs/cb/resource/about-nytd?page=all

Adoption and Safe Families Act, P.L. 105-89, 42 U.S.C. §1305, 111 Stat. 2115 (1997).

Adoption Assistance and Child Welfare Act, P.L. 96-272, 42 U.S.C. §1305, 94 Stat. 500 (1980).

Adu-Gyamfi, J. (2013). Can children and young people be empowered in participatory initiatives? Perspectives from young people's participation in policy formulation and implementation in Ghana. *Children and Youth Services Review, 35*, 1766–1772.

Ahrens, K., DuBois, D. L., Garrison, M., Spencer, R., Richardson, L. P., & Lozano, P. (2011). Qualitative exploration of relationships with important non-parental adults in the lives of youth in foster care. *Children and Youth Services Review, 33*, 1012–1023.

Ahrens, K., DuBois, D. L., Richardson, L., Fan, M., & Lozano, P. (2008). Youth in foster care with adult mentors during adolescence have improved adult outcomes. *Pediatrics, 121*, e246–e252.

Alwin, D. F. (2012). Integrating varieties of life course concepts. *Journal of Gerontology, 67B*(2), 206–220.

Alwon, F., & Reitz, A. (2000). *The workforce crisis in child welfare*. Washington, DC: Child Welfare League of America.

American heritage dictionary of the English language. (1980). Boston: Houghton Mifflin.

Amodeo, M., Bratiotis, C., & Collins, M. E. (2009). Examining perceptions of the impact of child and family services reviews on training: Reports from state training administrators. *Administration in Social Work, 33*(4), 423–438.

Amodeo, M., & Collins, M. E. (2007). Applying positive youth development principles in practice with youth with problem behaviors. *Families in Society, 88*(1), 75–85.

Amodeo, M., Collins, M. E., & Clay, C. M. (2009). Toward best practice and innovation in independent living training: Experiences from the multi-site evaluation of federally-funded projects. *Children and Youth Services Review, 31*, 185–192.

Anderson-Nathe, B. (2008). So what? Now what? Implications for youth work practice. *Child & Youth Services, 30*(1–2), 123–138.

Anglin, J. P. (2002). Risk, well-being, and paramountcy in child protection: The need for transformation. *Child & Youth Care Forum, 31*(4), 233–255.

Aquilino, W. S. (1991). Family structure and home-leaving: A further specification of the relationship. *Journal of Marriage and Family, 53*, 999–1010.

Aries, P. (1962). *Centuries of childhood: A social history of family life.* New York: Random House.

Armstrong, M. I., Coy, L., McNeish, R., Menendez, P., & Policella, D. (2013). *A national review of child welfare pre-service curriculum development methods and training materials.* Tampa: University of South Florida.

Arnett, J. (2000). Emerging adulthood: A theory of development from the late teens through the twenties. *American Psychologist, 55*, 469–480.

Arnett, J. (2004). *Emerging adulthood: The winding road from late teens through the twenties.* New York: Oxford University Press.

Association for Child and Youth Care Practice. (2010). *Competencies for professional child and youth work practitioners.* College Station, TX: CYC Certification Board.

Avery, R. J. (2010). An examination of theory and promising practice for achieving permanency for teens before they age out of care. *Children and Youth Services Review, 32*, 399–408.

Bachrach, P., & Baratz, M. (1962). The two faces of power. *American Political Science Review, 56*, 947–952.

Bardach, E. (1977). *The implementation game: What happens after a bill becomes a law.* Cambridge, MA: MIT Press.

Bardach, E. (2005). *A practical guide for policy analysis: The eightfold path to more effective problem solving.* Washington, DC: Congressional Quarterly Press.

Barth, R. P. (1990). On their own: The experiences of youth after foster care. *Child and Adolescent Social Work, 7*, 419–440.

Barth, R. P. (1997). Effects of age and race on the odds of adoption versus remaining in long term out-of-home care. *Child Welfare 76*(2), 285–308.

Barth, R. P., Landsverk, J., Chamberlain, P., Reid, J. B., Rolls, J. A., Hurlburt, M. S., et al. (2005). Parent training programs in child welfare services: Planning for a more evidence-based approach to serving biological parents. *Research on Social Work Practice, 15*(5), 353–371.

Bass, S., Shields, M. K., & Behrman, R. E. (2004). Children, families, and foster care: Analysis and recommendations. *Future of Children, 14*, 1, 4–29.

Batsche, C. J., & Reader, S. (2012). Using GIS to enhance programs serving emancipated youth leaving foster care. *Evaluation and Program Planning, 35*, 25–33.

Baumgartner, F. R., & Jones, B. D. (1993). *Agendas and instability in American politics*. Chicago: University of Chicago Press.

Belfield, C., & Levin, H. M. (Eds.) (2007). *The price we pay: Economic and social consequences of inadequate education*. Washington, DC: Brookings Institution Press.

Bengtson, V. L., & Allen, K. R. (1993). The life course perspective applied to families over time. In P. G. Boss, W. J. Doherty, R. LaRossa, W. R. Schumm, & S. K. Steinmetz (Eds.), *Sourcebook of family theories and methods: A contextual approach* (pp. 469–504). New York: Springer.

Berrick, J. D. (2006). Neighborhood-based foster care: A critical examination of location-based placement criteria. *Social Service Review, 80*, 569–583.

Berry, J. M., & Wilcox, C. (2009). *The interest group society* (5th ed.). New York: Pearson Longman.

Berzin, S. C., & De Marco, A. C. (2010). Understanding the impact of poverty on critical events in emerging adulthood. *Youth & Society, 42*, 278–300.

Best J. (1987). Rhetoric in claims-making: Constructing the missing children problem. *Social Problems, 34*, 101–121.

Best, J. (1995). *Images of issues: Typifying contemporary social problems*. New York: Aldine de Gruyter.

Birkland, T. A. (2011). *An introduction to the policy process: Theories, concepts, and models of public policy making*. New York: Routledge.

Blome, W. W., & Steib, S. D. (2014). The organizational structure of child welfare: Staff are working hard, but it is hardly working. *Children and Youth Services Review, 44*, 181–188.

Boehm, A., & Cnaan, R. A. (2012). Towards a practice-based model for community practice: Linking theory and practice. *Journal of Sociology & Social Welfare, 29*(1), 141–168.

Bork, R. H. (2012). *From at-risk to disconnected: Federal youth policy from 1973–2008* (Doctoral dissertation, Columbia University). (UMI No. 3505118)

Bourdieu, P. (1984). *Distinction: A social critique of the judgment of taste*. London: Routledge.

Bowlby, J. (1983). *Attachment and loss: Volume 1*. New York: Basic Books.

Briggs, X. D. (1997). Social capital and the cities: Advice to change agents. *National Civic Review, 86*(2), 111–117.

Britner, P. A., & Kraimer-Rickaby, L. (2005). Abused and neglected youth. In D. L. DuBois & M. J. Karcher (Eds.), *Handbook of youth mentoring* (pp. 482–492). Thousand Oaks, CA: Sage Publications.

Bullock, R., Courtney, M. E., Parker, R., Sinclair, I., & Thoburn, J. (2006). Can the corporate state parent? *Children and Youth Services Review, 28*, 1344–1358.

Burt, M., Aron, L. Y., & Lee, E. (2001). *Helping America's homeless: Emergency shelter or affordable housing.* Washington, DC: Urban Institute Press.

Butts, J. A., Bazemore, G., & Meroe, A. S. (2010). *Positive youth justice: Framing justice interventions using the concepts of positive youth development.* Washington, DC: Coalition for Juvenile Justice.

Byrne, T., Metraux, S., Kim, M., Culhane, D. P., Moreno, M., Toros, H., & Stevens, M. (2014). Public assistance receipt among older youth exiting foster care. *Children and Youth Services Review, 44,* 307–316.

California Fostering Connections to Success Act, Cal. AB. 12 (2010–2011). Chapter 559 (Cal. Stat. 2010).

Carman, J. G. (2009). Nonprofits, funders and evaluation: Accountability in action. *American Review of Public Administration, 39,* 374–390.

Casey Family Programs. (2005). *It's my life: Housing.* Seattle: Author.

Casey Family Programs. (2015). *Improving higher education outcomes for young adults in foster care.* Retrieved from http://www.casey.org/media/Supporting Success_Resources.pdf

Center for Information and Research on Civic Learning and Engagement. (2011). *Understanding a diverse generation of youth civic engagement in the United States.* Medford, MA: Tufts University.

Center for the Study of Social Policy. (2012). *For the welfare of children: Lessons learned from class action litigation.* Washington, DC: Author.

Center for the Study of Social Policy. (2014a). *The Affordable Care Act and implications for youth aging out of foster care.* Retrieved from http://www.cssp.org/policy/2013/The-Affordable-Care-Act-and-Implications-for-Youth-Aging-Out-of-Foster-Care.pdf

Center for the Study of Social Policy. (2014b). Progress of the New Jersey Department of Children and Families, Monitoring Period XIV (April 1–December 31, 2013), Monitoring Report, Charlie and Nadine H. v. Christie. http://www.cssp.org/publications/child-welfare/class-action-reform/2014/Charlie-and-Nadine-H.-v.-Christie-Monitoring-Report-XIV_July-17-2014.pdf

Center for the Study of Social Policy. (2015). *Promoting well-being through the reasonable and prudent parent standard: A guide for states implementing the Preventing Sex Trafficking and Strengthening Families Act (H.R. 4980).* Washington, DC: Author.

Chawla, L., & Driskell, D. (2006). Global perspectives on children and youth as catalysts for community change. *Journal of Community Practice, 14*(1–2), 183–200.

Checkoway, B. (2011). What is youth participation? *Children and Youth Services Review, 33,* 340–345.

Checkoway, B., Allison, T., & Montoya, C. (2005). Youth participation in public policy at the municipal level. *Children and Youth Services Review, 27,* 1149–1162.

References

Checkoway, B., & Richards-Schuster, K. (2003). Youth participation in community evaluation research. *American Journal of Evaluation, 24*, 21–33.

Chen, H. T., & Rossi, P. H. (1983). Evaluating with sense: The theory-driven approach. *Evaluation Review, 7*, 283–302.

Child Abuse Prevention and Treatment Act, P.L. 93-247, 42 U.S.C. § 5101 (1974).

Christens, B. D., & Dolan, T. (2011). Interweaving youth development, community development, and social change through youth organizing. *Youth & Society, 43*, 528–548.

Clay, C. M., Amodeo, M., & Collins, M. E. (2010). Youth as partners in curriculum development and training delivery: Roles, challenges, benefits and recommendations. *Families in Society, 91*(2), 135–141.

Cobb, R., & Elder, C. (1983). *Participation in American politics: The dynamics of agenda building.* Baltimore: Johns Hopkins University Press.

Cohen, B. J. (2005). Reforming the child welfare system: Competing paradigms of change. *Children and Youth Services Review, 27*, 653–666.

Coleman, J. S. (1988). Social capital in the creation of human capital. *American Journal of Sociology, 94*, S95–S120.

Collins, M. E. (2001). Transition to adulthood for vulnerable youth: A review of research and implications for policy. *Social Service Review, 75*, 271–291.

Collins, M. E. (2004). Enhancing services to youths leaving foster care: Analysis of recent legislation and its potential impact. *Children and Youth Services Review, 26*, 1051–1065.

Collins, M. E., Amodeo, M., & Clay, C. M. (2004). *Integrating a youth development perspective into transition planning: A curriculum for child welfare outreach workers.* Boston: Boston University School of Social Work.

Collins, M. E., Amodeo, M., & Clay, C. M. (2007). Training as a factor in policy implementation: Lessons from a national evaluation of child welfare training. *Children and Youth Services Review, 29*, 1487–1502.

Collins, M. E., & Clay, C. (2009). Influencing policy for youth transitioning from care: Defining problems, crafting solutions, and assessing politics. *Children and Youth Services Review, 31*, 743–751.

Collins, M. E., & Curtis, M. (2011). Conceptualizing housing careers for vulnerable youths: Implications for policy. *American Journal of Orthopsychiatry, 81*, 390–400.

Collins, M. E., Kim, S. H., & Amodeo, M. (2010). Empirical studies of child welfare training effectiveness: Methods and outcomes. *Child & Adolescent Social Work Journal, 27*, 41–62.

Collins, M. E., Lemon, C., & Street, E. (2000). A consumer view of Teen Living Programs: Teens' satisfaction with program components and service delivery. *Families in Society, 81*(3), 284–293.

Collins, M. E., Paris, R., & Ward, R. (2008). The permanence of family ties: Implications for youth transitioning from foster care. *American Journal of Orthopsychiatry, 78*, 54–62.

Collins, M. E., & Pinkerton, J. (2008). The policy context of leaving care services: A case study of Northern Ireland. *Children and Youth Services Review, 30*, 1279–1288.

Collins, M. E., Schwartz, I. M., & Epstein, I. (2001). Risk factors for adult imprisonment in a sample of youth released from residential child care. *Children and Youth Services Review, 23*(3), 203–226.

Collins, M. E., Spencer, R., & Ward, R. (2010). Supporting youth in the transition from foster care: Formal and informal connections. *Child Welfare, 89*(1), 125–143.

Collins-Camargo, C. (2014). Research and evaluation. In G. P. Mallon & P. M. Hess (Eds.), *Child welfare for the 21st century: A handbook of practices, policies and programs* (2nd ed, pp. 660–679). New York: Columbia University Press.

Collins-Camargo, C., McBeath, B., & Ensign, K. (2011). Privatization and performance-based contracting in child welfare: Recent trends and implications for social service administrators. *Administration in Social Work, 35*, 494–516.

Commission on Youth at Risk. (2010). *Charting a better future for transitioning foster youth.* Washington, DC: American Bar Association.

Commonwealth of Massachusetts, Executive Office of Health and Human Services. (2014, July). *Caring together overview: CBHA level of care meetings.* Retrieved from https://www.masspartnership.com/pdf/Caring%20 Together%20Overview%207.2014.pdf

Connor, B. v. Patrick. (2011). U.S. District Court for the District of Massachusetts Case 3:10-cv-30073. Retrieved from http://www.childrensrights.org/ wp-content/uploads//2010/04/2010-04-15_ma_complaint_as_filed.pdf

Consolidated Omnibus Budget Reconciliation Act of 1985, P.L. 99-272, 100 Stat. 82 (1986).

Cook, R. (1994). Are we helping foster care youth prepare for their future? *Children and Youth Services Review, 16*, 213–229.

Cooney, K., & Shanks, T.R.W. (2010). New approaches to old problems: Market-based strategies for poverty alleviation. *Social Service Review, 84*, 29–55.

Copeland, V. C., & Wexler, S. (1995). Policy implementation in social welfare: A framework for analysis. *Journal of Sociology and Social Welfare, 22*, 51–68.

Côté, J. E. (2000). *Arrested adulthood: The changing nature of maturity and identity.* New York: New York University Press.

Courtney, M., Dworsky, A., Brown, A., Cary, C., Love, K., & Vorhies, V. (2011). *Midwest evaluation of the adult functioning of former foster youth: Outcomes at age 26.* Chicago: Chapin Hall at the University of Chicago.

Courtney, M., Dworsky, A., Lee, J., & Raap, M. (2009). *Midwest evaluation of the adult functioning of former foster youth: Outcomes at age 23 and 24.* Chicago: Chapin Hall at the University of Chicago.

Courtney, M., Dworsky, A., & Napolitano, L. (2013). *Providing foster care for young adults: Early implementation of California's Fostering Connections Act.* Chicago: Chapin Hall at the University of Chicago.

Courtney, M. E., Dworsky, A., & Pollack, H. (2007). *When should the state cease parenting? Evidence from the Midwest study* (Chapin Hall Center for Children Issue Brief No. 115). Chicago: Chapin Hall.

Courtney, M. E., Dworsky, A., Ruth, G., Keller, T., Havlicek, J., & Bost, N. (2005). *Midwest evaluation of the adult functioning of former foster youth: Outcomes at age 19.* Chicago: Chapin Hall Center for Children.

Courtney, M. E., & Heuring, D. H. (2005). The transition to adulthood for youth "aging out" of the foster care system. In D. W. Osgood, E. M. Foster, C. Flanagan, & G. R. Ruth (Eds.), *On your own without a net: The transition to adulthood for vulnerable populations* (pp. 27–67). Chicago: University of Chicago Press.

Courtney, M. E., Zinn, A., Zielewski, E. H., Bess, R. J., Malm, K. E., Stagner, M.W., & Pergamit, M. (2008). *Multi-site evaluation of foster youth programs.* Retrieved from http://www.chapinhall.org/research/report/multi-site-evaluation-foster-youth-programs

Culhane, D., Metraux, S., & Moreno, M. (2011). *Young adult outcomes of youth exiting dependent or delinquent care in Los Angeles County.* Retrieved from http://fosteryouthalliance.org/wpcontent/uploads/2011/11/Young_Adult_Outcomes_Youth_Exiting_Fact_Sheet.pdf

Curry, D., Caplan, P., & Knuppel, J. (1994). Transfer of training and adult learning (TOTAL). *Journal of Continuing Social Work Education, 6*(1), 8–14.

Curry, D., Eckles, F., Stuart, C., & Qaqish, B. (2009). National child and youth care practitioner professional certification: Promoting competent care for children and youth. *Child Welfare, 89*(2), 57–77.

Cushing, G., Samuels, G. M., & Kerman, B. (2014). Profiles of relational permanence at 22: Variability in parental supports and outcomes among young adults with foster care histories. *Children and Youth Services Review, 39,* 73–83.

Cusick, G. R., & Courtney, M. E. (2007). Offending during late adolescence: How do youth aging out of care compare with their peers? Chicago: Chapin Hall Center for Children.

Dahl, R. A. (1958). A critique of the ruling elite model. *American Political Science Review, 52,* 463–469.

Daining, C., & DePanfilis, D. (2007). Resilience of youth in transition from out-of-home care to adulthood. *Children and Youth Services Review, 29,* 1158–1178.

Damon, W. (2004). What is positive youth development? *Annals of the American Academy of Political and Social Science, 59*(1), 13–24.

Day, A., Riebschleger, J., Dworsky, A., Damashek, A., & Fogarty, K. (2012). Maximizing educational opportunities for youth aging out of foster care by engaging youth voices in a partnership for social change. *Children and Youth Services Review, 34*, 1007–1014.

DeBellis, M. (2001). Developmental traumatology: The psychobiological development of maltreated children and its implications for research, treatment, and policy. *Development and Psychopathology, 13*, 539–564.

DiMaggio, P. J., & Powell, W. W. (1983). The Iron Cage revisited: Institutional isomorphism and collective rationality in organizational fields. *American Sociological Review, 48*, 147–160.

Donkoh, C., Underhill K., & Montgomery, P. (2006). *Independent living programmes for improving outcomes for young people leaving the care system.* Retrieved from http://www.cochrane.org/CD005558/BEHAV_independent-living-programmes-for-improving-outcomes-for-young-people-leaving-the-care-system doi: 10.1002/14651858.CD005558.pub2

Dupuis, J., & Mann-Feder, V. (2013). Moving towards emancipatory practice: Conditions for meaningful youth empowerment in child welfare. *International Journal of Child, Youth & Family Studies, 3*, 371–380.

Dworsky, A., Dillman, K., Dion, M. R., Coffee-Borden, B., & Rosenau, M. (2012). *Housing for youth aging out of foster care: A review of the literature and program typology.* Washington, DC: Mathematica Policy Research.

Dworsky, A., White, C., O'Brien, K., Pecora, P., Courtney, M., Kessler, R., et al. (2010). Racial and ethnic differences in the outcomes of former foster youth. *Children and Youth Services Review, 32*, 902–912.

Edelstein, S., & Lowenstein, C. (2014). *Supporting youth transitioning out of foster care. Issue brief 3: Employment programs* (OPRE Report No. 2014–70). Washington, DC: U.S. Department of Health and Human Services, Administration for Children and Families, Office of Planning, Research and Evaluation.

Elder, G. H., Jr. (1998). The life course as developmental theory. *Child Development, 69*(1), 1–12.

Ellett, A., & Leighninger, L. (2007). What happened? *Journal of Public Child Welfare, 1*(1), 3–34.

Elmore, R. F. (1980). Backward mapping: Implementation research and policy decisions. *Political Science Quarterly, 94*(4), 610–616.

Erikson, E. (1968). *Youth: Identity and crisis.* New York: W. W. Norton.

Faller, K. C., Grabarek, M., & Ortega, R. M. (2010). Commitment to child welfare work: What predicts leaving and staying? *Children and Youth Services Review, 32*, 840–846.

References

Fanshel, D., & Shinn, E. B. (1978). *Children in foster care: A longitudinal investigation*. New York: Columbia University Press.

Faulkner, K. M. (2009). Presentation and representation: Youth participation in ongoing public decision-making projects. *Childhood, 16*(1), 89–104.

Fellin, P. (2001). *The community and the social worker*. Itasca, IL: F. E. Peacock.

Festinger, T. (1983). *No one ever asked us: A postscript to foster care*. New York: Columbia University Press.

File, T. (2013). *Young-adult voting: An analysis of presidential elections, 1964–2012* (Current Population Survey Report No. P20-572). Washington, DC: U.S. Census Bureau.

Fingerman, K., Miller, L., Birditt, K., & Zaritt, S. (2009). Giving to the good and the needy: Parental support of grown children. *Journal of Marriage and Family, 71*, 1220–1233.

Finkelstein, M., Wamsley, M., Currie, D., & Miranda, D. (2004). *Youth who chronically AWOL from foster care: Why they run, where they go, and what can be done*. New York: Vera Institute of Justice, NYC Administration for Children's Services.

Fitch, D. (2012). Youth in foster care and social media: A framework for developing privacy guidelines. *Journal of Technology in Human Services, 30*, 94–108.

Flanagan, C., & Levine, P. (2010). Civic engagement and the transition to adulthood. *Future of Children, 20*(1), 159–179.

Foster Care Independence Act, P.L. 106-169, 42 U.S.C. §1305, 113 Stat. 1822 (1999).

Foster Youth Museum. (2015). *About*. Retrieved from http://fosteryouthmuseum.org/about/

FosteringConnections.org Project. (2013). *Perspectives on fostering connections: A series of white papers on the Fostering Connections and Increasing Adoptions Act of 2008*. Retrieved from http://www.fostercareandeducation.org/Materials/Database.aspx?EntryId=1874&Command=Core_Download

Fostering Connections to Success and Increasing Adoptions Act of 2008, P.L. 110-351, 122 Stat. 3949 (October 7, 2008).

Frederick, T. J., Chwalek, M., Hughes, J., Karabanow, J., & Kidd, S. (2014). How stable is stable? Defining and measuring housing stability. *Journal of Community Psychology, 42*, 964–979.

Freedman, M. (1993). *The kindness of strangers*. San Francisco: Jossey-Bass.

Funders' Collaborative on Youth Organizing. (2009). *What is youth organizing?* Retrieved from http://www.fcyo.org/aboutyouthorganizing

Furlong, A., Woodman, D., & Wyn, J. (2011). Changing times, changing perspectives: Reconciling "transition" and "cultural" perspective on youth and young adulthood. *Journal of Sociology, 47*, 355–370.

Furstenberg, F. F., Jr., & Hughes, M. E. (1995). Social capital and successful development among at-risk youth. *Journal of Marriage and Family, 57*, 580–592.

Gainsborough, J. F. (2010). *Scandalous politics: Child welfare policy in the states.* Washington, DC: Georgetown University Press.

Garbarino, J. (1982). *Children and families in the social environment.* Hawthorne, NY: Aldine.

Garlington, S. B. (2015). *The role of religion in social welfare provision and policy: Congregations in a U.S. city.* Boston: Boston University Graduate School of Arts and Sciences.

Gaventa, J. (1980). *Power and powerlessness: Quiescence and rebellion in an Appalachian valley.* Urbana: University of Illinois Press.

Geenen, S., & Powers, L. E. (2007). "Tomorrow is another problem": The experiences of youth in foster care during their transition into adulthood. *Children and Youth Services Review, 29*, 1085–1101.

General Assembly of the United Nations. (1989). *Convention on the Rights of the Child.* Retrieved from http://www.un.org

Germain, C. B., & Gitterman, A. (1996). *The life model of social work practice: Advances in theory and practice.* New York: Columbia University Press.

Gleeson, J. P., Smith, J. H., & Dubois, A. C. (1993). Developing child welfare practitioners: Avoiding the single-solution seduction. *Administration in Social Work, 17*(3), 21–37.

Glisson, C., & Hemmelgarn, A. (1998). The effects of organizational climate and interorganizational coordination on the quality and outcomes of children's service systems. *Child Abuse & Neglect, 22*, 401–421.

Goggin, M. L., Bowman, A., Lester, J., & O'Toole, L. (1990). *Implementation theory and practice: Toward a third generation.* Glenview, IL: Scott Foresman.

Goldscheider F., & Goldscheider, C. (1993). Whose nest? A two-generation view of leaving home during the 1980s. *Journal of Marriage and Family, 55*, 851–862.

Goldscheider, F., & Goldscheider, C. (1999). *The changing transition to adulthood: Leaving and returning home.* Thousand Oaks, CA: Sage Publications.

Gormley, W. T., Jr. (2012). *Voices for children: Rhetoric and public policy.* Washington, DC: Brookings Institution Press.

Granovetter, M. (1973). The strength of weak ties. *American Journal of Sociology, 78*, 1360–1380.

Grason, H., & Guyer, B. (1995). Rethinking the organization of children's programs: Lessons from the elderly. *Milbank Quarterly, 73*, 565–597.

Greeson, J.K.P., Usher, L., & Grinstein-Weiss, M. (2010). One adult who is crazy about you: Can natural mentoring relationships increase assets among young adults with and without foster care experience? *Children and Youth Services Review, 32*, 565–577.

186

References

Gutiérrez, L., GlenMaye, L., & DeLois, K. (1995). The organizational context of empowerment practice: Implications for social work administration. *Social Work, 40,* 249–258.

Hacker, J. S. (2008). *The great risk shift: The new economic insecurity and the decline of the American dream.* New York: Oxford University Press.

Hahn, H., Isaacs, J., Edelstein, S., Steele, E., & Steuerle, C. E. (2014). *Kids' share 2014: Report on federal expenditures on children through 2013.* Washington, DC: Urban Institute.

Hall, G. S. (1904). *Adolescence.* New York: Appleton.

Han, L., Hsu, V., & Ishikawa, D. (2009). *Aging out: Improving outcomes for older foster care youth.* Los Angeles: UCLA School of Public Affairs, Public Policy Department.

Hardcastle, D. A. (2011). *Community practice: Theories and skills for social workers* (3rd ed.). New York: Oxford University Press.

Hardina, D. (2005). Ten characteristics of empowerment-oriented social service organizations. *Administration in Social Work, 29*(3), 23–42.

Hart, R. (1992). *Children's participation: From tokenism to citizenship.* Florence, Italy: UNICEF International Child Development Centre.

Hass, M., Allen, Q., & Amoah, M. (2014). Turning points and resilience of academically successful foster youth. *Children and Youth Services Review, 44,* 387–392.

Havlicek, J. (2011). Lives in motion: A review of former foster youth in the context of their experiences in the child welfare system. *Children and Youth Services Review, 33,* 1090–1100.

Hawkins, R. L. (2005). From self-sufficiency to personal and family sustainability: A new paradigm for social policy. *Journal of Sociology and Social Welfare, 4,* 77–92.

Hegar, R. L., & Hunzeker, J. M. (1988). Moving toward empowerment-based practice in public child welfare. *Social Work, 33,* 499–502.

Henig, A. (2009). Employment aid for youth aging out of foster care: Extending one-stop career centers to include a division for foster care youth. *Family Court Review, 47,* 570–585.

Hernandez, M. (2000). Using logic models and program theory to build outcome accountability. *Education and Treatment of Children, 23,* 24–40.

Hess, P., Kanak, S., & Atkins, J. (2009). *Building a model and framework for child welfare supervision.* Retrieved from http://muskie.usm.maine.edu/helpkids/rcpdfs/BuildingAModelandFrameworkforCWSupervision.pdf

Higher Education Opportunity Act, P.L. 110-315, 20 U.S.C. § 1001 (2008).

Hiles, D., Moss, D., Wright, J., & Dallos, R. (2013). Young people's experience of social support during the process of leaving care: A review of the literature. *Children and Youth Services Review, 35,* 2059–2071.

Hill, M., & Hupe, P. (2002). *Implementing public policy*. London: Sage Publications.

Hines, A. M., Lemon, K., Wyatt, P., & Merdinger, J. (2004). Factors related to the disproportionate involvement of children of color in the child welfare system: A review and emerging themes. *Children and Youth Services Review, 26*, 507–527.

Hines, A. M., Merdinger, J., & Wyatt, P. (2005). Former foster youth attending college: Resilience and the transition to young adulthood. *American Journal of Orthopsychiatry, 75*, 381–394.

Hirschman, A. O. (1970). *Exit, voice, and loyalty: Responses to decline in firms, organizations, and states*. Cambridge, MA: Harvard University Press.

Hoffman, S. D., & Maynard, R. A. (2008). *Kids having kids: Economic costs & social consequences of teen pregnancy* (2nd ed.). Washington, DC: Urban Institute Press.

Holland, J., Reynolds, T., & Weller, S. (2007). Transitions, networks and communities: The significance of social capital in the lives of children and young people. *Journal of Youth Studies, 10*(1), 97–116.

Holloway, S., & Valentine, G. (2000). Spatiality and the new social studies of childhood. *Sociology, 34*, 763–783.

Howlett, M., & Ramesh, M. (2002). The policy effects of internationalization: A subsystem adjustment analysis of policy change. *Journal of Comparative Policy Analysis: Research and Practice, 4*, 31–50.

Huang, H., & Ryan, J. P. (2014). The location of placement and juvenile delinquency: Do neighborhoods matter in child welfare? *Children and Youth Services Review, 44*, 33–45.

Hudson, R. B., & Gonyea, J. G. (2012). Baby boomers and the shifting political construction of old age. *Gerontologist, 52*, 272–282.

Hyde, J., & Kammerer, N. (2009). Adolescents' perspectives on placement moves and congregate settings: Complex and cumulative instabilities in out-of-home care. *Children and Youth Services Review, 31*, 265–273.

Hynes, B. O., & Hayes, N. (2011). Who benefits from early childcare subsidy design in Ireland? *Journal of Poverty and Social Justice, 19*(3), 277–288.

Indian Child Welfare Act of 1978, P.L. 95-608, 92 Stat. 3069 (November 8, 1978).

Jansson, B. (2015). *The reluctant welfare state* (8th ed.). Belmont, CA: Wadsworth.

Jim Casey Youth Opportunities Initiative. (n.d.). *Foster care to 21: Doing it right* (Issue Brief No. 1). Retrieved from http://www.jimcaseyyouth.org/sites/default/files/documents/Issue%20Brief%20-%20FC%20to%2021.pdf

Jimenez, J. (2006). The history of child protection in the African American community: Implications for current child welfare policies. *Children and Youth Services Review, 28*, 888–905.

Jonson-Reid, M. (2004). Child welfare services and delinquency: The need to know more. *Child Welfare, 83*(2), 157–173.

References

Jonson-Reid, M., Drake, B., & Kohl, P. L. (2009). Is the overrepresentation of the poor in child welfare caseloads due to bias or need? *Children and Youth Services Review, 31*, 422–427.

Kahne, J., & Middaugh, E. (2008). *Democracy for some: The civic opportunity gap in high school* (Center for Information and Research on Civic Learning and Engagement Working Paper). Retrieved from http://www.civicyouth.org/PopUps/WorkingPapers/WP59Kahne.pdf

Kaplan, S. A., & Garrett, K. E. (2005). The use of logic models by community-based initiatives. *Evaluation and Program Planning, 28*, 167–172.

Kay, A. (2005). A critique of the use of path dependency in policy studies. *Public Administration, 83*, 553–571.

Keller, T. E., Cusick, G. R., & Courtney, M. E. (2007). Approaching the transition to adulthood: Distinctive profiles of adolescents aging out of the child welfare system. *Social Service Review, 81*, 453–484.

King, L., & Rukh-Kamaa, A. (2013). Youth transitioning out of foster care: An evaluation of a Supplemental Security Income policy change. *Social Security Bulletin, 73*(3), 53–57.

Kingdon, J. (2003). *Agendas, alternatives and public policies* (2nd ed.). Boston: Little, Brown.

Kirby, P., Lanyon, C., Cronin, K., & Sinclair, R. (2003). *Building a culture of participation: Involving children and young people in policy, service planning, delivery and evaluation*. Nottingham, England: Department for Education and Skills.

Klindera, K., & Menderweld, J. (2001). *Youth involvement in prevention programming*. Retrieved from http://www.advocatesforyouth.org/publications/publications-a-z/532-youth-involvement-in-prevention-programming

Lawrence, C., Strolin-Goltzman, J., Caringi, J., Claiborne, N., McCarthy, M., Butts, E., & O'Connell, K. (2013). Designing evaluations in child welfare organizations: An approach for administrators. *Administration in Social Work, 37*, 3–13.

Leashore, B. (1985). Demystifying legal guardianship: An unexplored option for dependent children. *Journal of Family Law, 23*, 391–400.

Leber, C., & LeCroy, C. W. (2012). Public perception of the foster care system: A national study. *Children and Youth Services Review, 34*, 1633–1638.

Lee, J. S. (2014). An institutional framework for the study of the transition to adulthood. *Youth & Society, 46*, 706–730.

Lemon, K., Hines, A. M., & Merdinger, J. (2005). From foster care to young adulthood: The role of independent living programs in supporting successful transitions. *Children and Youth Services Review, 27*, 251–270.

Levenson, M. (2015, March 31). Strains grow for DCF workers. *Boston Globe*. Retrieved from http://www.bostonglobe.com/metro/2015/03/31/dcf/vi7CKCiGrlOHQRrAwb0NGJ/story.html#

Liebmann, T., & Madden, E. (2010). Hear my voice—Perspectives of current and former foster youth. *Family Court Review, 48,* 255–261.

Lin, N. (1999). Building a network theory of social capital. *Connections, 22*(1), 28–51.

Lindsey, E. W., & Ahmed, F. U. (1999). The North Carolina Independent Living Program: A comparison of outcomes for participants and nonparticipants. *Children and Youth Services Review, 21,* 389–412.

Lipsky, M. (1980). *Street-level bureaucracy: Dilemmas of the individual in public services.* New York: Russell Sage Foundation.

Longoria, R. A. (2005). Is inter-organizational collaboration always a good thing? *Journal of Sociology and Social Welfare, 32*(3), 123–138.

Lukes, S. (2005). *Power: A radical view* (2nd ed.). London: Macmillan.

Lynch-Cerullo, K., & Cooney, K. (2011). Moving from outputs to outcomes: A review of the evolution of performance measurement in the human service nonprofit sector. *Administration in Social Work, 35,* 364–388.

MacRae, D., Jr., & Whittington, D. (1997). *Expert advice for policy choice: Analysis and discourse.* Washington, DC: Georgetown University Press.

Mallon, G. P. (1998). After care, then where? Outcomes of an independent living program. *Child Welfare, 77,* 61–78.

Mallon, G. P., & Hess, P. M. (2014). Introduction. In G. P. Mallon & P. M. Hess (Eds.), *Child welfare for the 21st century: A handbook of practices, policies and programs* (2nd ed., pp. 1–10). New York: Columbia University Press.

Maloney, W. A., Jordan, G., & McLaughlin, A. M. (1994). Interest groups and public policy: The insider/outsider model revisited. *Journal of Public Policy, 14*(1), 17–38.

Mares, A. S., & Jordan, M. (2012). Federal aftercare programs for transition-aged youth. *Children and Youth Services Review, 34,* 1509–1518.

Masten, A. S. (2001). Ordinary magic: Resilience processes in development. *American Psychologist, 56,* 227–238.

Mathematica Policy Research. (2011). *Synthesis of research and resources to support at-risk youth* (OPRE Report 2011–22). Washington, DC: U.S. Department of Health and Human Services, Administration for Children and Families, Office of Planning, Research and Evaluation.

Mattingly, M. A., Stuart, C., & VanderVen, K. (2002). North American certification project (NACP) competencies for professional child and youth work practitioners. *Journal of Child and Youth Care Work, 17,* 16–49.

McGowan, B. G. (2014). Historical evolution of child welfare services. In G. P. Mallon & P. M. Hess (Eds.), *Child welfare for the 21st century: A handbook of practices, policies and programs* (2nd ed., pp. 11–43). New York: Columbia University Press.

References

McMahon, R. C., & Fields, S. A. (2015). Criminal conduct subgroups of "aging out" foster youth. *Children and Youth Services Review, 48*, 14–19.

McRoy, R. (2014). Disproportionate representation of children and youth. In G. P. Mallon & P. M. Hess (Eds.), *Child welfare for the 21st century: A handbook of practices, policies and programs* (2nd ed., pp. 680–693). New York: Columbia University Press.

Mech, E. V., Pryde, J. A., & Rycraft, J. R. (1995). Mentors for adolescents in foster care. *Child and Adolescent Social Work Journal, 12*, 317–328.

Mennen, F., & O'Keefe, M. (2005). Informed decisions in child welfare: The use of attachment theory. *Children and Youth Services Review, 27*, 577–593.

Meyer, J., & Rowan, B. (1983). Institutionalized organizations: Formal structure as myth and ceremony. In W. Meyer, B. Rowan, & T. E. Deal (Eds.), *Organizational environments ritual and rationality* (pp. 21–44). Thousand Oaks, CA: Sage Publications.

Mezey, S. (2000). *Pitiful plaintiffs: Child welfare litigation and the federal courts*. Pittsburgh: University of Pittsburgh Press.

Mills, C. W. (1956). *The power elite*. New York: Oxford University Press.

Milner, J., & Hornsby, W. (2004). Training of child welfare staff and providers: Findings from the child and family service review. *Protecting Children, 19*(3), 4–14.

Minow, M., & Weissbourd, R. (1993). Social movements for children. *Daedulus, 122*(1), 1–29.

Mitchell, B. (2003). Life course theory. In J. J. Ponzetti (Ed.), *International encyclopedia of marriage and family* (2nd ed., pp. 1051–1055). New York: Macmillan.

Mitchell, L., Thomas, M. L., & Parker, B. (2014). The children and family services reviews. In G. P. Mallon & P. M. Hess (Eds.), *Child welfare for the 21st century: A handbook of practices, policies and programs* (2nd ed., pp. 567–582). New York: Columbia University Press.

Morrison, T. (1997). Learning, training, and change in child protection work: Toward reflective organizations. *Social Work Education, 16*(2), 20–43.

Morse, J. M., Markowitz, N., Zanghi, M., & Burns, P. (2003). *Partnering with youth: Involving youth in child welfare training and curriculum development*. Portland: Edmund S. Muskie School of Public Services, Institute for Public Sector Innovation, University of Southern Maine.

Multiethnic Placement Act, P.L. 103-382, 108 Stat. 4056 (1994).

Munson, M. R., & McMillen, J. C. (2009). Natural mentoring and psychosocial outcomes among older youth transitioning from foster care. *Children and Youth Services Review, 31*, 104–111.

Munson, S., McCarthy, M., & Dickinson, N. (2014). Child welfare workforce issues. In G. P. Mallon & P. M. Hess (Eds.), *Child welfare for the 21st century: A handbook of practices, policies and programs* (2nd ed., pp. 624–642). New York: Columbia University Press.

Naccarato, T., & DeLorenzo, E. (2008). Transitional youth services: Practice implications from a systematic review. *Child and Adolescent Social Work Journal, 25*, 287–308.

National Association of Social Workers. (2013). *NASW standards for social work practice in child welfare*. Washington, DC: NASW Press.

National Center for Housing and Child Welfare. (2013). *HUD's Family Unification Program*. Retrieved from http://www.nchcw.org/uploads/7/5/3/3/7533556/fup_overview_june_2012.pdf

National Collaborating Centre for Determinants of Health. (n.d.). *Let's talk universal and targeted approaches to health equity*. Antigonish, Canada: St. Francis Xavier University.

National Foster Care Awareness Project. (2000). *Frequently asked questions: About the Foster Care Independence Act of 1999 and the John H. Chafee Foster Care Independence Program*. Retrieved from http://www.nrcyd.ou.edu/publication-db/documents/chafee-faq1.pdf

National Resource Center for Youth Development. (2014, August 12). *State by state facts*. Retrieved from http://www.nrcyd.ou.edu/state-pages/search

National Youth in Transition Database. (2012). *Highlights from state reports to the National Youth in Transition Database, Federal Fiscal Year 2011* (Data Brief No. 1). Washington, DC: U.S. Department of Health and Human Services, Administration for Children and Families, Children's Bureau.

Nelson, B. (1984). *Making an issue of child abuse: Political agenda setting for social problems*. Chicago: University of Chicago Press.

Nesmith, A., & Christophersen, K. (2014). Smoothing the transition to adulthood: Creating ongoing supportive relationships among foster youth. *Children and Youth Services Review, 37*, 1–8.

Netting, F. E., Kettner, P. M., & McMurtry, S. L. (1993). *Social work macro practice*. White Plains, NY: Longman.

Newacheck, P. W., & Benjamin, A. E. (2004). Intergenerational equity and public spending. *Health Affairs, 23*(5), 142–146.

Nicholson-Crotty, J., & Nicholson-Crotty, S. (2004). Social construction and policy implementation: Inmate health as a public health issue. *Social Science Quarterly, 85*(2), 240–256.

Nowak, K. B. (2014). What is an ombudsman? Retrieved from http://www.ncsl.org/research/human-services/childrens-ombudsman-offices.aspx

References

Okpych, N. (2012). Policy framework supporting youth aging-out of foster care through college: Review and recommendations. *Children and Youth Services Review, 34*, 1390–1396.

Okpych, N. (2015). Receipt of independent living services among older youth in foster care: An analysis of national data from the U.S. *Children and Youth Services Review, 51*, 74–86.

Older Americans Act, 42 U.S.C. § 3001 (1965).

O'Looney, J. (1997). Marking progress toward service integration: Learning to use evaluation to overcome barriers. *Administration in Social Work, 21*(3–4), 31–65.

Omnibus Budget Reconciliation Act of 1993, P.L. 103-66, 107 Stat. 312 (1993).

Oppenheim, E., Lee, R., Lictenstein, C., Bledsoe, K. L., & Fisher, S. K. (2012). Reforming mental health services for children in foster care: The role of child welfare class action lawsuits and systems of care. *Families in Society, 93*, 286–293.

Osterling, K. L., & Hines, A. M. (2006). Mentoring adolescent foster youth: Promoting resilience during development transitions. *Child and Family Social Work, 11*, 242–253.

O'Toole, L. J. Jr. (1986). Policy recommendations for multi-actor implementation: An assessment of the field. *Journal of Public Policy, 6*, 181–210.

O'Toole, L. J. Jr. (1995). Rational choice and policy implementation: Implications for interorganizational network management. *American Review of Public Administration, 25*, 43–57.

O'Toole, L., & Meier, K. J. (2011). *Public management: Organizations, governance and performance.* New York: Cambridge University Press.

Ozawa, M., & Lee, Y. S. (2011). Generational inequity in social spending: The United States in comparative perspective. *International Social Work, 56*(2), 162–179.

Palinkas, L. A., Fuentes, D., Finno, M., Garcia, A. R., Holloway, I. W., & Chamberlain, P. (2014). Inter-organizational collaboration in the implementation of evidence-based practices among public agencies serving abused and neglected youth. *Administration and Policy in Mental Health, 41*, 74–85.

Parenti, M. (1970). Power and pluralism: A view from the bottom. *Journal of Politics, 32*, 501–530.

Park, J. M., Metraux, S., Brodbar, B., & Culhane, D. P. (2004). Public shelter admission among young adults with child welfare histories by type of service and type of exit. *Social Service Review, 78*, 284–303.

Park, J. M., Metraux, S., & Culhane, D. P. (2005). Childhood out-of-home placement and dynamics of public shelter utilization among young homeless adults. *Children and Youth Services Review, 27*, 533–546.

Patient Protection and Affordable Care Act, P.L. 111-148, 42 U.S.C. § 18001 (2010).

Patton, M. Q. (2008). *Utilization-focused evaluation* (4th ed.). Thousand Oaks, CA: Sage Publications.

Pearrow, M. M. (2008). A critical examination of an urban-based youth empowerment strategy: The Teen Empowerment program. *Journal of Community Practice, 16*, 509–525.

Pecora, P. J. (2012). Maximizing educational achievement of youth in foster care and alumni: Factors associated with success. *Children and Youth Services Review, 34*, 1121–1129.

Pecora, P. J., Kessler, R. C., O'Brien, K., White, C. R., Williams, J., Hiripi, E., et al. (2006). Educational and employment outcomes of adults formerly placed in foster care: Results from the Northwest Foster Care Alumni Study. *Children and Youth Services Review, 28*, 1459–1491.

Pelton, L. H. (1978). Child abuse and neglect: The myth of classlessness. *American Journal of Orthopsychiatry, 48*, 608–617.

Perez, B. F., & Romo, H. D. (2011). "Couch surfing" of Latino foster care alumni: Reliance on peers as social capital. *Journal of Adolescence, 34*(2), 239–248.

Pergamit, M. R., McDaniel, M., Chen, V., Howell, E., & Hawkins, A. (2012). *Providing Medicaid to youth formerly in foster care under the Chafee option: Informing implementation of the Affordable Care Act.* Washington, DC: U.S. Department of Health and Human Services.

Perry, B. L. (2006). Understanding social network disruption: The case of youth in foster care. *Social Problems 53*(3), 371–391.

Personal Responsibility and Work Opportunity Reconciliation Act, P.L. 104-193, 42 U.S.C. §1305, 110 Stat. 2105 (1996).

Peters, C., Sherraden, M., & Kuchkinski, A. M. (2012). *Enduring assets: Findings from a study on the financial lives of young people transitioning from foster care.* St. Louis: Jim Casey Youth Opportunities Initiative.

Pierce, J. J., Siddiki, S., Jones, M. D., Schumacher, K., Pattison, A., & Peterson, H. (2014). Social construction and policy design: A review of past applications. *Policy Studies Journal, 42*(1), 1–29.

Pierson, P. (2000). Increasing returns, path dependence, and the study of politics. *American Political Science Review, 94*(2), 251–267.

Pinkerton, J. (2011). Constructing a global understanding of the social ecology of leaving out of home care. *Children and Youth Service Review, 33*, 2412–2416.

Porter, E. (2004). A typology of virtual communities: A multidisciplinary foundation for future research. *Journal of Computer Mediated Communication, 10*, 1.

Portes, E. (1998). Social capital: Its origins and applications in modern sociology. *Annual Review of Sociology, 24*, 1–24.

Portz, J. (1996). Problem definitions and policy agendas: Shaping the educational agenda in Boston. *Policy Studies Journal, 24*, 371–386.

References

Pressman, J., & Wildavsky, A. (1973). *Implementation*. Berkeley: University of California Press.

Preston, S. (1984). Children and the elderly: Divergent paths for America's dependents. *Demography, 21*, 435–457.

Preventing Sex Trafficking and Strengthening Families Act, 42 U.S.C., §1305, 128 Stat. 1919 (2014).

Promoting Safe and Stable Families Amendments of 2001, P.L. 107-133, 42 U.S.C. § 629, 115 Stat. 2413 (2001).

Putnam, R. D. (2000). *Bowling alone: The collapse and revival of American community*. New York: Simon & Schuster.

Quality Improvement Center on the Privatization of Child Welfare Services. (2006). *Literature review on the privatization of child welfare services*. Louisville: University of Kentucky.

Quinn, J. (2004). Professional development in the youth development field: Issues, trends, opportunities, challenges. *New Directions for Youth Development, 104*, 13–24.

Rauner, D. M. (2000). *They still pick me up when I fall*. New York: Columbia University Press.

Reilly, T. (2003). Transition from care: Status and outcomes of youth who age out of foster care. *Child Welfare, 82*(6), 727–746.

Renne, J., & Mallon, G. P. (2014). Unpacking permanency for youth. In G. P. Mallon & P. M. Hess (Eds.), *Child welfare for the 21st century: A handbook of practices, policies and programs* (2nd ed., pp. 455–467). New York: Columbia University Press.

Rhodes, J. E., Haight, W. L., & Briggs, E. C. (1999). The influence of mentoring on the peer relationships of foster youth in relative and nonrelative care. *Journal of Research on Adolescence, 9*, 185–201.

Roberts, D. (2002). *Shattered bonds: The color of child welfare*. New York: Basic Civitas Books.

Roholt, R. V., & Rana, S. (2011). Improving community-based youth work: Evaluation of an action research approach. *Child and Youth Services, 32*, 317–335.

Romzek, B. S., & Johnston, J. M. (2005). State social services contracting: Exploring the determinants of effective contract accountability. *Public Administration Review, 65*, 436–449.

Roosevelt Campus Network. (2015, March 31). *Blueprint for the millennial America*. Retrieved from http://www.scribd.com/doc/44487427/Blueprint-for-Millennial-America

Rothman, J. (1996). The interweaving of community intervention approaches. *Journal of Community Practice, 3*(3–4), 66–99.

Rothman, J. (2007). Multi modes of intervention at the macro level. *Journal of Community Practice, 15*(4), 11–40.

Rutter, M. (1987). Psychosocial resilience and protective mechanisms. *American Journal of Orthopsychiatry, 57*, 316–331.

Ryan, J. P., Marshall, J. M., Herz, D., & Hernandez, P. (2008). Juvenile delinquency in child welfare settings: Investigating group home effects. *Children and Youth Services Review, 30*, 1088–1099.

Rycraft, J. R., & Dettlaff, A. J. (2009). Hurdling the artificial fence between child welfare and the community: Engaging community partners to address disproportionality. *Journal of Community Practice, 17*, 464–482.

Rycus, J. S., & Hughes, R. C. (1998). *Field guide to child welfare.* Washington, DC: Child Welfare League of America.

Sabatier, P., & Jenkins-Smith, H. (1999). The advocacy coalition framework: An assessment. In P. Sabatier (Ed.), *Theories of the policy process* (pp. 117–166). Boulder, CO: Westview Press.

Sabatier, P., & Mazmanian, D. (1979). The conditions of effective implementation. *Policy Analysis, 5*, 481–504.

Samuels, G., & Pryce, J. (2008). What doesn't kill you makes you stronger: Survivalist self-reliance as resilience and risk among adults aging out of foster care. *Children and Youth Services Review, 30*, 1198–1210.

Sanders, J., & Mumford, R. (2014). Youth-centred practice: Positive youth development practices and pathways to better outcomes for vulnerable youth. *Children and Youth Services Review, 46*, 160–167.

Scannapieco, M., Schagrin, J., & Scannapieco, T. (1995). Independent living programs: Do they make a difference? *Child and Adolescent Social Work Journal, 12*, 381–389.

Schattschneider, E. E. (1960). *The semi-sovereign people.* New York: Holt, Rinehart and Winston.

Scherrer, J. L. (2012). The United Nations Convention on the Rights of the Child as policy and strategy for social work action in child welfare in the United States. *Social Work, 57*, 11–22.

Schneider, A., & Ingram, H. (1993). Social construction of target populations: Implications for politics and policy. *American Political Science Review, 87*(2), 334–347.

Schoeni, R., & Ross, K. (2005). Material assistance from families during the transition to adulthood. In R. Settersten, Jr., F. Furstenberg, Jr., & R. Rumbaut (Eds.), *On the frontier of adulthood: Theory, research, and public policy* (pp. 396–416). Chicago: University of Chicago Press.

Schworn, P. (2014, June 20). State filings for custody of children soaring. *Boston Globe.* Retrieved from https://www.bostonglobe.com/metro/2014/06/19/

wake-scandal-dcf-seeks-remove-far-more-children-from-troubled-homes/ QA23yhpm6VeYLauk5rJNhI/story.html

Scott, L. D., Jr., McMillen, J. C., & Snowden, L. R. (2015). Informal and formal help seeking among older black male foster care youth and alumni. *Journal of Child and Family Studies, 24*, 264–277.

Scott, W. R., Deschenes, S., Hopkins, K., Newman, A., & McLaughlin, M. (2006). Advocacy organizations and the field of youth services: Ongoing efforts to restructure a field. *Nonprofit and Voluntary Sector Quarterly, 35*, 691–714.

Second Chance Act, 42 U.S.C. § 17501 (2008).

Seita, J. R. (2000). In our best interest: Three necessary shifts for child welfare workers and children. *Child Welfare, 79*(1), 77–92.

Settersten, R. A., Jr. (2007). Passages to adulthood: Linking demographic change and human development. *European Journal of Population, 23*, 251–272.

Settersten, R. A., Jr., & Ray, B. (2010). What's going on with young people today? The long and twisting path to adulthood. *Future of Children, 20*(1), 19–41.

Shanahan, M. (2000). Pathways to adulthood: Variability and mechanisms in life course perspective. *Annual Review of Sociology, 26*, 667–692.

Shanahan, S. (2007). Lost and found: The sociological ambivalence toward childhood. *Annual Review of Sociology, 33*, 407–428.

Shockley, C., & Thompson, A. (2012). Youth workers in college: A replicable model for professional development. *Children and Youth Services Review, 34*, 735–739.

Shriver, J. M. (2011). *Human behavior and the social environment: Shifting paradigms in essential knowledge for social work practice* (5th ed.). Boston: Allyn & Bacon.

Silva, J. M. (2012). Constructing adulthood in an age of uncertainty. *American Sociological Review, 77*, 505–522.

Silver Lining Mentoring. (2015). *What we do*. Retrieved from http://silverliningmentoring.org/what-we-do/

Simmel, C. (2012). Highlighting adolescents' involvement with the child welfare system: A review of recent trends, policy development, and related research. *Children and Youth Services Review, 34*, 1197–1207.

Skocpol, T. (1991). Targeting within universalism: Politically viable policies to combat poverty in the United States. In C. Jencks & P. Peterson (Eds.), *The urban underclass* (pp. 411–436). Washington, DC: Brookings Institution Press.

Smith, B. D., & Donovan, S.E.F. (2003). Child welfare practice in organizational and institutional context. *Social Service Review, 77*, 541–563.

Smith, W. B. (2011). *Youth leaving foster care: A developmental, relationship-based approach to practice*. New York: Oxford University Press.

Snyder, S. M., & Medeiros, R. A. (2013). Typologies of substance use and illegal behaviors. A comparison of emerging adults with histories of foster care and the general population. *Children and Youth Services Review, 35,* 753–761.

Social Security Act, Title IV-E, 42 U.S.C. §1305 (1935).

Spencer, R., Collins, M. E., Ward, R., & Smashnaya, S. (2010). Mentoring for young people leaving foster care: Promise and potential pitfalls. *Social Work, 55,* 225–234.

Steen, J. A., & Smith, S. (2012). An organizational view of privatization: Is the private foster care agency superior to the public foster care agency? *Children and Youth Services Review, 34,* 851–858.

Stein, M. (2006). Young people aging out of care: The poverty of theory. *Children and Youth Services Review, 28,* 422–434.

Stein, T. J. (2003). The Adoption and Safe Families Act: How Congress overlooks available data and ignores systemic obstacles in its pursuit of political goals. *Children and Youth Services Review, 25,* 669–682.

Stewart, C. J., Kum, H., Barth, R. P., & Duncan, D. F. (2014). Former foster youth: Employment outcomes up to age 30. *Children and Youth Services Review, 36,* 220–220.

Stott, T. (2013). Transitioning youth: Policies and outcomes. *Children and Youth Services Review, 35,* 218–227.

Swartz, T. T. (2008). Family capital and the invisible transfer of privilege: Intergenerational support and social class in early adulthood. *New Directions for Child and Adolescent Development, 2008*(119), 11–24.

Swartz, T. T., Kim, M., Uno, M., Mortimer, J., & O'Brien, K. B. (2011). Safety nets and scaffolds: Parental support in the transition to adulthood. *Journal of Marriage and Family, 73,* 414–429.

Szilagyi, M. (1998). The pediatrician and the child in foster care. *Pediatric Review, 19,* 39–50.

Tao, K. W., Ward, K. J., O'Brien, K., DiLorenzo, P., & Kelly, S. (2013). Improving permanency: Casework perspectives of older youth in another planned permanent living arrangement. *Child and Adolescent Social Work Journal, 30,* 217–235.

Taylor, J. (1993). *Poverty and niches: A systems view.* Unpublished manuscript.

Taylor, J. (1997). Niches and ecological practice: Extending the ecological perspective. In D. Saleebey (Ed.), *The strengths perspective in social work practice* (pp. 217–227). New York: Longman.

Testa, M. F., & Miller, J. (2014). Guardianship. In G. P. Mallon & P. M. Hess (Eds.), *Child welfare for the 21st century: A handbook of practices, policies and programs* (2nd ed., pp. 355–372). New York: Columbia University Press.

Thomas, M. L. (2012). One hundred years of Children's Bureau support to the child welfare workforce. *Journal of Public Child Welfare, 6,* 357–375.

References

Tisdall, E.K.M., & Davis, J. (2004). Making a difference? Bringing children's and young people's views into policy-making. *Children & Society, 18*, 131–142.

Treseder, P. (1997). *Empowering children and young people: Promoting involvement in decision making*. London: Save the Children.

Unrau, Y. A., Font, S. A., & Rawls, G. (2012). Readiness for college engagement among students who have aged out of foster care. *Children and Youth Services Review, 34*, 76–83.

Unrau, Y. A., Seita, J. R., & Putney, K. S. (2008). Former foster youth remember multiple placement moves: A journey of loss and hope. *Children and Youth Services Review, 30*, 1256–1266.

U.S. Department of Health and Human Services. (2014). *AFCARS report: Preliminary FY 2013 estimates*. Retrieved from http://www.acf.hhs.gov/sites/default/files/cb/afcarsreport21.pdf

U.S. Department of Health and Human Services, Administration for Children and Families. (2008). *Evaluation of the life skills training program: Los Angeles County*. Washington, DC: United States Department of Health and Human Services, Administration for Children and Families.

U.S. Department of Health and Human Services, Administration for Children and Families, Children's Bureau. (2011). *The AFCARS report—Preliminary FY 2010 estimates as of June 2011*. Washington, DC: U.S. Department of Health and Human Services.

U.S. Department of Health and Human Services, Administration for Children and Families, Children's Bureau. (2014). *Reports from the transition to adulthood and independent living training grants*. Retrieved from https://www.childwelfare.gov/topics/management/training/curricula/caseworkers/core/outofhomecare/transition-living/transition-living-reports/

U.S. Department of Health and Human Services, Administration for Children and Families, Family and Youth Services Bureau. (2015). *Positive youth development*. Retrieved from http://www.acf.hhs.gov/programs/fysb/positive-youth-development

U.S. General Accounting Office. (1999). *Foster care: Effectiveness of independent living services unknown* (Report No. GAO/HEHS-00-13). Washington, DC: General Accounting Office.

U.S. Government Accountability Office. (2014). *Foster care: HHS needs to improve oversight of Fostering Connections Act implementation* (Report No. GAO-14-347). Washington, DC: Author.

Van Meter, D., & Van Horn, C. (1975). The policy implementation process. *Administration and Society, 6*, 445–488.

Vance, F. (2010). A comparative analysis of competency frameworks for youth workers in the out-of-school time field. *Child & Youth Care Forum, 39*, 421–441.

Vaughn, M. G., Shook, J. J., & McMillen, J. C. (2008). Aging out of foster care and legal involvement: Toward a typology of risk. *Social Service Review, 82,* 419–446.

W. K. Kellogg Foundation. (2004). *Using logic models to bring together planning, evaluation, and action: Logic model development guide.* Battle Creek, MI: Author.

Wacquant, L.J.D. (1998). Negative social capital: State breakdown and social destitution in America's urban core. *Netherlands Journal of Housing and the Built Environment, 13*(1), 25–40.

Waldfogel, J. (1998). Rethinking the paradigm for child protection. *Future of Children, 8*(1), 104–119.

Ward, R. L. (2009). *"I took a break, but now I am back": Foster youths' perspectives on leaving and returning* (Doctoral dissertation, Boston University Graduate School of Arts and Sciences).

Warren, R. L. (1978). *The community in America* (3rd ed.). Chicago: Rand McNally.

Weil, M. O., & Gamble, D. N. (1995). Community practice models. In R. L. Edwards (Ed.-in-Chief), *Encyclopedia of social work* (19th ed., Vol. 1, pp. 577–594). Washington, DC: NASW Press.

Werner, E. E., & Smith, R. S. (1982). *Vulnerable but invincible: A longitudinal study of resilient children and youth.* New York: McGraw-Hill.

Werner, E. E., & Smith, R. S. (2001). *Journeys from childhood to midlife: Risk, resilience and recovery.* Ithaca, NY: Cornell University Press.

Wertheimer, R. (2002). *Youth who "age out" of foster care: Troubled lives, troubling prospects.* Washington, DC: Children Trends.

White, K. R., & Wu, Q. (2014). Application of the life course perspective in child welfare research. *Children and Youth Services Review, 46,* 146–154.

Wholey, J. S. (1987). Evaluability assessment: Developing program theory. In L. Bickman (Ed.), *Using program theory in evaluation: New directions for program evaluation* (pp. 77–92). San Francisco: Jossey-Bass.

Workforce Innovation and Opportunity Act, 29 U.S.C. § 3101 (2014).

Yin, R. K. (1994). *Case study research: Design and methods.* Newbury Park, CA: Sage Publications.

Youth Communication (A. Desetta, Ed.). (1996). *The heart knows something different: Teenage voices from the foster care system.* New York: Persea Books.

Zelizer, V. A. (1985). *Pricing the priceless child: The changing social value of children.* New York: Basic Books.

Zullo, R. (2006). Is social service contracting coercive, competitive, or collaborative? Evidence from the case allocation patterns of child protection services. *Administration in Social Work, 30*(3), 25–42.

Index

Index

Index

Index

Index